FireSigns

Design Thinking, Design Theory

Ken Friedman and Erik Stolterman, editors

FireSigns

A Semiotic Theory for Graphic Design

Steven Skaggs

The MIT Press
Cambridge, Massachusetts
London, England

This book was set in Stone Sans and Stone Serif by Toppan Best-set Premedia Limited. Printed and bound in the United States of America.

Library of Congress Cataloging-in-Publication Data

Names: Skaggs, Steven, author.
Title: FireSigns : a semiotic theory for graphic design / Steven Skaggs.
Description: Cambridge, MA : The MIT Press, 2017. | Series: Design thinking, design theory |
    Includes bibliographical references and index.
Identifiers: LCCN 2016020054 | ISBN 9780262035439 (hardcover : alk. paper)
Subjects: LCSH: Semiotics and art. | Graphic arts.
Classification: LCC N72.S46 S59 2017 | DDC 740—dc23 LC record available
    at https://lccn.loc.gov/2016020054

10 9 8 7 6 5 4 3 2 1

Contents

Epilogue   231

Series Foreword

As professions go, design is relatively young. The practice of design predates professions. In fact, the practice of design—making things to serve a useful goal, making tools—predates the human race. Making tools is one of the attributes that made us human in the first place.

Design, in the most generic sense of the word, began over 2.5 million years ago when *Homo habilis* manufactured the first tools. Human beings were designing well before we began to walk upright. Four hundred thousand years ago, we began to manufacture spears. By forty thousand years ago, we had moved up to specialized tools.

Urban design and architecture came along ten thousand years ago in Mesopotamia. Interior architecture and furniture design probably emerged with them. It was another five thousand years before graphic design and typography got their start in Sumeria with the development of cuneiform. After that, things picked up speed.

All goods and services are designed. The urge to design—to consider a situation, imagine a better situation, and act to create that improved situation—goes back to our prehuman ancestors. Making tools helped us to become what we are—design helped to make us human.

Today, the word "design" means many things. The common factor linking them is service, and designers are engaged in a service profession in which the results of their work meet human needs.

Design is first of all a process. The word "design" entered the English language in the 1500s as a verb, with the first written citation of the verb dated to the year 1548. *Merriam-Webster's Collegiate Dictionary* defines the verb "design" as "to conceive and plan out in the mind; to have as a specific purpose; to devise for a specific function or end." Related to these is the act of drawing, with an emphasis on the nature of the drawing as a plan or map, as well as "to draw plans for; to create, fashion, execute or construct according to plan."

Half a century later, the word began to be used as a noun, with the first cited use of the noun "design" occurring in 1588. *Merriam-Webster's* defines the noun as "a particular purpose held in view by an individual or group; deliberate, purposive planning; a mental project or scheme in which means to an end are laid down." Here, too, purpose and planning toward desired outcomes are central. Among these are "a preliminary sketch or outline showing the main features of something to be executed; an underlying scheme that governs functioning, developing or unfolding; a plan or protocol for carrying out or accomplishing something; the arrangement of elements or details in a product or work of art." Today, we design large, complex process, systems, and services, and we design organizations and structures to produce them. Design has changed considerably since our remote ancestors made the first stone tools.

At a highly abstract level, Herbert Simon's definition covers nearly all imaginable instances of design. To design, Simon writes, is to "[devise] courses of action aimed at changing existing situations into preferred ones" (Simon, *The Sciences of the Artificial*, 2nd ed., MIT Press, 1982, p. 129). Design, properly defined, is the entire process across the full range of domains required for any given outcome.

But the design process is always more than a general, abstract way of working. Design takes concrete form in the work of the service professions that meet human needs, a broad range of making and planning disciplines. These include industrial design, graphic design, textile design, furniture design, information design, process design, product design, interaction design, transportation design, educational design, systems design, urban design, design leadership, and design management, as well as architecture, engineering, information technology, and computer science.

These fields focus on different subjects and objects. They have distinct traditions, methods, and vocabularies, used and put into practice by distinct and often dissimilar professional groups. Although the traditions dividing these groups are distinct, common boundaries sometimes form a border. Where this happens, they serve as meeting points where common concerns build bridges. Today, ten challenges uniting the design professions form such a set of common concerns.

Three performance challenges, four substantive challenges, and three contextual challenges bind the design disciplines and professions together as a common field. The performance challenges arise because all design professions:

1. act on the physical world;

2. address human needs; and

3. generate the built environment.

In the past, these common attributes were not sufficient to transcend the boundaries of tradition. Today, objective changes in the larger world give rise to four substantive challenges that are driving convergence in design practice and research. These substantive challenges are:

1. increasingly ambiguous boundaries between artifacts, structure, and process;
2. increasingly large-scale social, economic, and industrial frames;
3. an increasingly complex environment of needs, requirements, and constraints; and
4. information content that often exceeds the value of physical substance.

These challenges require new frameworks of theory and research to address contemporary problem areas while solving specific cases and problems. In professional design practice, we often find that solving design problems requires interdisciplinary teams with a transdisciplinary focus. Fifty years ago, a sole practitioner and an assistant or two might have solved most design problems; today, we need groups of people with skills across several disciplines, and the additional skills that enable professionals to work with, listen to, and learn from each other as they solve problems.

Three contextual challenges define the nature of many design problems today. While many design problems function at a simpler level, these issues affect many of the major design problems that challenge us, and these challenges also affect simple design problems linked to complex social, mechanical, or technical systems. These issues are:

1. a complex environment in which many projects or products cross the boundaries of several organizations, stakeholder, producer, and user groups;
2. projects or products that must meet the expectations of many organizations, stakeholders, producers, and users; and
3. demands at every level of production, distribution, reception, and control.

These ten challenges require a qualitatively different approach to professional design practice than was the case in earlier times. Past environments were simpler. They made simpler demands. Individual experience and personal development were sufficient for depth and substance in professional practice. While experience and development are still necessary, they are no longer sufficient. Most of today's design challenges require analytic and synthetic planning skills that cannot be developed through practice alone.

Professional design practice today involves advanced knowledge. This knowledge is not solely a higher level of professional practice. It is also a qualitatively different form of professional practice that emerges in response to the demands of the information society and the knowledge economy to which it gives rise.

In a recent essay ("Why Design Education Must Change," *Core77*, November 26, 2010), Donald Norman challenges the premises and practices of the design profession. In the past, designers operated in the belief that talent and a willingness to jump into problems with both feet gives them an edge in solving problems. Norman writes:

In the early days of industrial design, the work was primarily focused upon physical products. Today, however, designers work on organizational structure and social problems, on interaction, service, and experience design. Many problems involve complex social and political issues. As a result, designers have become applied behavioral scientists, but they are woefully undereducated for the task. Designers often fail to understand the complexity of the issues and the depth of knowledge already known. They claim that fresh eyes can produce novel solutions, but then they wonder why these solutions are seldom implemented, or if implemented, why they fail. Fresh eyes can indeed produce insightful results, but the eyes must also be educated and knowledgeable. Designers often lack the requisite understanding. Design schools do not train students about these complex issues, about the interlocking complexities of human and social behavior, about the behavioral sciences, technology, and business. There is little or no training in science, the scientific method, and experimental design.

This is not industrial design in the sense of designing products, but industry-related design, design as thought and action for solving problems and imagining new futures. This new MIT Press series of books emphasizes strategic design to create value through innovative products and services, and it emphasizes design as service through rigorous creativity, critical inquiry, and an ethics of respectful design. This rests on a sense of understanding, empathy, and appreciation for people, for nature, and for the world we shape through design. Our goal as editors is to develop a series of vital conversations that help designers and researchers to serve business, industry, and the public sector for positive social and economic outcomes.

We will present books that bring a new sense of inquiry to the design, helping to shape a more reflective and stable design discipline able to support a stronger profession grounded in empirical research, generative concepts, and the solid theory that gives rise to what W. Edwards Deming described as profound knowledge (Deming, *The New Economics for Industry, Government, Education*, MIT, Center for Advanced Engineering Study, 1993). For Deming, a physicist, engineer, and designer, profound knowledge comprised systems thinking and the understanding of processes embedded in systems; an understanding of variation and the tools we need to understand variation; a theory of knowledge; and a foundation in human psychology. This is the beginning of "deep design"—the union of deep practice with robust intellectual inquiry.

A series on design thinking and theory faces the same challenges that we face as a profession. On one level, design is a general human process that we use to understand and to shape our world. Nevertheless, we cannot address this process or the world in its general, abstract form. Rather, we meet the challenges of design in specific challenges, addressing problems or ideas in a situated context. The challenges we face as designers today are as diverse as the problems clients bring us. We are involved in design for economic anchors, economic continuity, and economic growth. We design for urban needs and rural needs, for social development and creative communities. We are involved with environmental sustainability and economic policy, agriculture, competitive crafts for export, competitive products and brands for micro-enterprises, developing new products for bottom-of-pyramid markets, and redeveloping old products for mature or wealthy markets. Within the framework of design, we are also challenged to design for extreme situations, for biotech, nanotech, and new materials, and design for social business, as well as conceptual challenges for worlds that do not yet exist such as the world beyond the Kurzweil singularity—and for new visions of the world that does exist.

The Design Thinking, Design Theory series from the MIT Press will explore these issues and more—meeting them, examining them, and helping designers to address them.

Join us in this journey.

Ken Friedman   Erik Stolterman

Editors, Design Thinking, Design Theory Series

Preface

A sign of fire: smoke over a tree line, a charred smell in the air, a glow over the meadow at night far from the city. But there is also this: a petroglyph scratched into a rock in New Mexico, a graphic emblem on a grill starter, a warning label on a fuel truck. Or metaphorically further: a web site that excites you, a poster that enflames the imagination, an advertisement that really makes you want to buy that dress, a book whose typography and composition so ennoble its contents that you display it in your entryway. This kind of fire sign is a piece of graphic communication that stirs heat in your soul. That's the kind of fire sign this book is about: something in a visual display that ignites memory, intellect, engagement. How does that happen?

For the past twenty-five years, I have spent my professional life among two communities: graphic designers and semioticians. The community of designers manipulates visual things in order to influence people. The community of semioticians studies how things are able to influence people. You'd think they'd see a lot of each other, yet there's almost no overlap between the two communities. The intelligence of the first community is a visual/emotional intelligence while that of the second is a verbal/logical intelligence. *FireSigns* is a rope bridge across that chasm. Rickety, temporary, needing more development, but a start.

FireSigns is written to bring semiotic ideas to the designer in a way the designer can make useful. I want the information here to feel as if it is native to the graphic designer, something that we've known all along, because in many ways we *have* known it. *FireSigns* provides a network of explicit concepts and terminology to a practice that has made implicit use of semiotics without knowing it, or knowing how to talk about it.

FireSigns is also written for the semiotician. It is not written in the semiotician's native tongue, nor does it use the usual scholarly discursive practice. Notes are kept to a minimum, mostly in the first chapters. I make no attempt to defend every idea I introduce, nor follow every logical trail that leads to and from the idea. In this way, *FireSigns* is less scholarly monograph than extended essay on the theme of the semiotics of seeing—a piece of jazz in which certain semiotic themes are picked up by different instruments, the themes traded among them, exchanged, investigated, new directions suggested. I hope, then, that the semiotician will forgive what might be taken, from a scholarly point of view, as glibness; but even if unforgiving, the semiotician must discover here that the graphic design studio provides an ideal laboratory for semiotic concepts, one that is worth greater investigation.

FireSigns is divided into four parts. While, for some, it may prove tempting to leap past the abstractions of the first and second parts and go straight to the conceptual tools offered in part III or the deeper investigations of typography offered in part IV, please understand that each successive section builds upon concepts laid out previously, so that the book's practical devices grow from and depend upon the abstract fundamentals laid out in parts I and II. Along the way, nomenclature reminders are available via the glossary provided in the back of the book.

Part I provides a brief overview of the metaphysics of visual perception and the notion of visual entities. It does this from the standpoints of the philosopher and the scientist studying perception. The first chapter looks at externalist and internalist models of visual perception, then the second chapter introduces the visual entity (visent), a notion that embraces aspects that are both external and internal to experience.

Part II changes the perspective, looking at visual experience as a product of the action of signs and following the visual entity as it performs the role of a sign. The third chapter introduces Peircean notions of the sign and the triadic relation, the next chapter translates Peirce's ten sign classes into a fundamental "periodic table" model for the visual sign, while chapter 5 looks at the role of specificity and the implications of denotation and connotation.

Part III introduces three new conceptual tools—semantic profiles, the functional matrix, and the visual gamut—each developed from the concepts that were introduced in part II. These conceptual tools provide suggestive backdrops for the analysis of works of graphic design, allowing visual "personality types" to emerge along with a growing understanding of the range of possibilities for visual elements.

Finally, in part IV, specific analysis of typography is considered as a way of showing how the conceptual tools can be used to go deeper into a design topic. The last chapter discusses issues surrounding style and genre and how these can be understood in light of the ideas put forward elsewhere in the book.

It is my hope that *FireSigns* can provide a foundation for a comprehensive semiotic theory for design, a first step to be followed by other researchers. The ideas presented here are meant to be debated and built upon—or perhaps rejected—but most of all to start a conversation which might further the development of design—and semiotics as well.

Steven Skaggs

Louisville

June 2016

Acknowledgments

I want to express my gratitude to the editorial offices of the MIT Press, in particular Douglas Sery, Susan Buckley, and Matthew Abbate, and to the University of Louisville Foundation for Research which aided parts of the present project with grant support over the years. I particularly want to thank those individuals who have provided many fine hours of discussion around these topics for over a decade and whose ideas have often contributed to and improved my own thinking. Among them are the two people who were required by life circumstances to spend a great deal of time around me as I thrashed through the tribulations of authorship: my colleague in the graphic design program, Leslie Friesen, and my wife Laurie Doctor. Finally, I want to especially thank Carl Hausman, with whom I enjoyed lunch every Tuesday for some fourteen years, and the insight, criticisms, suggestions, provocations, and support he has provided, all of which had no small influence on the body of thought that became *FireSigns*.

Introduction

Graphic design is sometimes referred to as "a young discipline." The story goes that W. A. Dwiggins coined the term "graphic design" in 1922 as a way of naming the various tasks he found himself commissioned to carry out: type design, illustration, advertising layouts, and general planning of print productions. After the Second World War, wedging its way past "advertising design" and elbowing aside "commercial art," graphic design entered the university curriculum. Inclusion in the ivory tower suggested a "higher calling"[1] and intimated the possession of some deeper, more serious body of knowledge. This was to be a new paradigm: design in the academy, an old art now freshly rooted in the emerging sciences of communication.

From where we stand today, looking back over seventy years of graphic design's comfortable residence in university settings, it is worth asking: has anything, other than the tools we use, really changed at the heart of our discipline? Outside the obvious adoption of technological innovations, in what ways has our profession deepened in its understanding of itself, broadened in its awareness and application of its societal role, and developed in its methodology? Other university disciplines have seen major fundamental transformations in thought—transformations that go deeper than responses to technology. Has graphic design seen a similar transformation? I would suggest three areas in which a clear shift between traditional "commercial art" practice and current "graphic design" practice seems to have occurred. But in each of them, that perceived shift is illusory.

Shift no. 1: a consolidation of trades

There can be no question that a social shift in workplace practices happened in the early 1900s. Dwiggins alluded to how, from the time of Gutenberg, the printing trades had relied on a collection of distinct crafts—the punch-cutter, typesetter, illustrator, compositor, lettering artist, printer. The mastery of these trades was passed from master to apprentice in an oral and hands-on tradition. Dwiggins realized that he was now personally taking the reins of all of these horses.

David Jury supports the view of a fairly abrupt sea change between the 1880s and the 1910s. In his invaluable book *Graphic Design before Graphic Designers*, Jury recounts how these trades were at first consolidated and later executively managed by a particular planner who later became known as a graphic designer.[2] So there really is no dispute that a new specialist in visual communication planning emerged.

The question is where, in this process, we find new fundamental knowledge about visual communication itself. Certainly there is a new awareness, a fresh self-consciousness, an awakening here, the increasing awareness in the last century, by industry, of the importance of carefully managed, coordinated visual programs; but the subject itself has not moved. A consolidation of trades neither creates new knowledge nor suggests a means to develop it. One finds synergistic efficiencies, management improvements, but this is not a shift in the objective of the work; it is a shift in perspective, an improvement in procedure.

Shift no. 2: ideology replaces style

When we speak of graphic design, in contrast to the printing or commercial arts, we often wish to connote a wholly different *sensibility*, a way of approaching a design problem with a broader awareness of cultural and historical norms rather than working from within an inherited style. This sensibility flows from an acknowledgment of a particular Eurocentric stylistic history, a history the graphic designer actively exploits in his or her work. We assume that the graphic designer is consciously aware of this history, while the commercial artist is not. If so, then this way of thinking may well serve as a distinction between the old commercial vernacular and the art of graphic design proper. How can one identify this "change of thinking"? Through awareness of modernism as an ideology.

This ideological history traces its way back through the Swiss International Style to the Bauhaus, the school that introduced the functionalist minimalism of modernism and provided a philosophy with which to undergird the grid and rationalistic design practice. The repudiation of ornament—a desire to sweep away the historical trappings of western visual culture and start fresh—led to this minimalist aesthetic. The philosophy that was the source of this art movement grew from two traumas, industrialism and the Great War. Its formal attributes were begun as a social reaction situated at a particular place and in response to the pressures of a specific time.

The grid is therefore historically entangled; when we teach the grid, we are teaching a reaction against Victoriana and everything Victoriana represents—a reaction by Europeans living in the 1920s. It is minimalism as efficiency, unburdened with the suffocating overt suffusion of style[3] which, after all, had previously reflected the aristocratic attitudes that fueled the nationalism that led to disaster in 1914. Better to abandon style, keep things cool and clean, spare and direct. Such was the ideological foundation of modernism, principles that were expressed not in the philosopher's arguments or the scientists' empirical experiments but in the single-page artist's manifesto.

So just as in the consolidation of trades, we again have a growing awareness of difference in the commercial arts, a kind of self-consciousness, this time over a break between the stylistic impulses of the past and a new attitude based on a particular worldview or ideology. It could be argued that this ideology represents a foundation for a distinctly different and new discipline—that design was about this new way of thinking: ideology had replaced style.

But as will be shown later in this book, style is simply a function of habitual use. With the spread of modernism, grids and Helvetica type quickly developed their own stylistic overtones. The corporate world's embrace of the modernist aesthetic meant that modernism had now, in fact, become corporate style. What had seemed to hold the promise of something that could transcend style had, by the middle of the century, itself become simply another style (indeed a genre). This apparent fundamental shift in design turned out to be simply a style refresher. Style proved a difficult thing to do away with. The proletarian farmer, anxious to drive a stake through Style's vampire heart, emerged from the crypt as vampire. Today, it is difficult to see the use of modernist tropes as anything other than the donning of a particular stylistic wardrobe.

Shift no. 3: semiology and deconstruction

By the 1960s, graphic design was being taught in most major universities. At just that time, and in just those places (universities), there arose something that offered an opportunity to escape the tyranny of the style-reaction-style-reaction cycle, something that could explain the relationship of style to culture. That something was poststructuralist semiology and the method found within it: deconstruction. The application of semiology to graphic design represents the only influential attempt to date from within the academy to seriously redraw fundamental principles of the discipline.

In my view, the attempts to shake up the graphic design world during this time (late 1970s through the 1980s), made largely by a few graduate programs, represents a gutsy attempt to find another path, to call attention to, and call into question, the traditional rudimentary principles of the discipline. These traditions were wholly jettisoned by the "decon" grad school designers of the time, a strategy that served the purpose of causing us to question what we had assumed were fundamental truths about design.

Now, I don't know how many of these designers had actually read Jacques Derrida,[4] but the takeaway was a broad overview that goes something like this: something should be done to weaken the act of control by the sender on the receiver, an act that puts the author's (sender's) message in a privileged position. The sender's message, cloaked in rationality, always seemed natural, and that very naturalization made its authority unquestioned. If this authority is not countered, then the receiver of the message is politically in a vulnerable position relative to the sender. The answer to this power imbalance lies in making the communication event itself both conspicuous and tenuous. The message would be made something to be looked at, not simply read, and in doing so the information would be actively gathered by a reader already made suspicious of the intentions and power of the author. This tipping of power from author to reader was an extension of Roland Barthes's "death of the author."[5] The death of the author meant work for the reader, to be sure, but it also meant that the reader had equal power in the sender/receiver equation.

These were all laudable goals, and the experiments conducted in the 1970s were exciting. Pages of typography were overprinted with illustrative material, widely letterspaced lowercase letters proliferated (a practice Frederic Goudy had once warned against as the sign of a character who would steal sheep), and the reader was definitely aware of the designer's hand over the author's word.

But how far could this take us? The problem was that semiological poststructuralism is inherently a *linguistic* enterprise. Graphic designers were taking concepts that developed around language and applying them, as best they could make them fit, to visual works. As Ellen Lupton put it in the mid-1990s, the word deconstruction "has served to label graphic design featuring chopped up, layered, and fragmented forms imbued with ambiguous futuristic overtones," where "it has become the tag for yet another period style."[6] In their chopping, texturing, overlaying, and disorienting techniques, designers simply metaphorically illustrated some of deconstruction's principles. Given that deconstruction arose from a framework of structuralism which is rooted in linguistics, how could it have been otherwise? There is no direct connection, other than by analogy, to the visual universe, because the linear basis of linguistics is so dissimilar to the global, holistic, and deeply recursive compass of the visual. Indeed, for all its decentering, what we call "decon" in graphic design turns linguistic deconstruction on its head: in design, it is a method that makes *overt* and *explicit*—in the signifier—the non-neutrality of graphic forms and design process, while for

Derrida, Foucault et al., deconstruction is a method for uncovering the *covert* prejudicial slant that is *im*plicit in signifers that appear to be neutral. While true deconstructionism subverts the authority of the media producer and empowers the receiver, design decon pretends sympathy with the receiver while actually placing on a pedestal the *author-as-designer*. Instead of becoming a method for understanding and manipulating style (while remaining stylistically neutral), deconstruction techniques became yet another style.

Each of these strategies tried to distinguish graphic design from the commercial printing trades that had come before, but only the second and third focused on the actual content of the visual communication event. Deconstruction, like modernism before it, attempted to formulate a "new" graphic design by disrupting certain older visual habits. It failed in its larger purpose because any shift in specific visual ploys can only, in the end, become another visual habitual style. The vampire lives.

What is needed to overcome the incessant vampirism is a tool set that stands outside any particular family of appearances. Whatever it will be, it cannot be a particular visual device, look, compositional technique, or formal attribute. It must be a ghost, something that is itself bodiless, yet something with the force to drive embodiment.

Design is (yet) a folk practice

I have suggested three ways that graphic design attempted a departure from the commercial art practices that had preceded it, ways that led to fresh stylistic developments but that, on closer examination, failed to generate a real advance in the fundamental knowledge of our discipline.

Perhaps this supports the counterthesis: that graphic design is *not* a young discipline but an ancient one, that, despite being a part of the academy, graphic design is simply the continued practice of commercial art. On this thesis, graphic design is not really an academic discipline at all in the sense of a profession that has its roots in a theoretical base of prescribed, but advancing, knowledge. Could it be that graphic design is, and has always been, a folk practice?

By folk practice, I don't mean ineffective. I mean (a) a practice whose tenets are passed down orally and through repetitive imitation, like the telling of a story; (b) a practice that has heroes, saints, gods, or "stars," publicized through legends, myths, or rituals, the work of such saints being imitated by others to show both the veneration of the saint and that the imitator aspires to the values of the saint; (c) a practice typified by the belief in magic—the inability to explain how something works.

Folkism 1: oral and repetitive tradition

Commercial art's oral tradition used to be passed on through the master/apprentice mechanism, in which a young acolyte would apprentice at the workshop of a master for a period of time and learn the ways of the trade *orally and through repetitive imitation* until conforming adequately to the master's standards and ways of doing things. Today, graphic designers take studio courses in universities, but the process is largely the same: repetition and gradual development of skills as overseen by the faculty until graduation. Nowhere is a fundamental theory developed. Standards of the field are disseminated in lectures and demos through a kind of story-based conformism.

Folkism 2: the imitation of heroes

Where does this conformism come from, and what steers its changes through time? Not theory, not first principles, but precisely the *imitation of heroes*. Stories are told of the leading lights of the profession. Through "war stories" (the term itself recalls the *Iliad*) we tell of the overcoming of creative and client obstacles to achieve the difficult task, providing constant exposure to the "design gods," expecting our students to become *better*, by which we usually mean more proficient *imitators* of those gods.

Folkism 3: magic

More than anything, what identifies graphic design as a folk practice is its reliance on the power of magic. There is no question that what we do as graphic designers is in some way magical. After all, isn't it magical and astonishing that we are able with a few lines of ink on a page or a few pixels on a screen to influence people's thoughts and behaviors? We leave these little visual traces and stuff gets sold, stays organized, stock markets and money respond, great thoughts of philosophers and statesmen are passed along, the words of people long dead are still able to prod us into action, the deeds of our ancestors are remembered.

That it works is not the part that is magical, though. It's magic because we don't have the slightest clue *why or how* it all works. If our students were like four-year-olds, asking "why?" after every successive explanation, most of us who do or teach graphic design would have no answer after the third "why." Perhaps that's not something to be concerned about—magic is exciting and fun. Maybe it is all right for design to remain in a folk magic state, a potion prescribed by alchemists. We might not know exactly how, but we know in our hearts that graphic design works. We feel the goodness of it in our guts. Our faith in graphic design magic is strong.

Visual Vikings paddling forth

Here's a magic story: In the middle ages, the Vikings navigated all over—even over open water to Vinland—with the assistance of a sunstone. A sunstone was a magic crystal rock that could be held in the air and would always indicate the direction of the sun, even when the sun was behind overcast clouds. When a sunstone was recently discovered amid the wreckage of an ancient sailing vessel at the bottom of the English Channel, one of the researchers explained why it was so well adapted to the ninth century: "You don't have to understand how it works—using it is basically easy."[7]

Figure 0.1

And so it is for us in graphic design. Graphic designers are visual Vikings clutching sunstones. Sailing out of the graphic harbor, we are shown how other people trim their sails and how they hold pieces of crystal in the air to navigate. We imitate these practices, formulating compositional systems and manipulating graphic elements on screen and paper. What we can't do is explain, *in even the scantest detail*, how any of this works.

Now as it happens, sunstone is a particular variety of calcite that has a molecular property known as birefringence, so that light entering the top surface is refracted in two directions, creating a double image—unless the light's angle is exactly aligned with the crystal's molecules, in which case the image comes into single focus. The Vikings knew nothing of the physics of this process—they only knew that when the image was a single in-focus image, in that direction lay the sun—yet they were able to navigate the seas quite well using their magical sunstone. By understanding the physics behind the sunstone's magic, engineers are able to make use of birefringence in any number of applications, from LCDs to the detection of gout. Absent in the long list of current uses of birefringence? Navigation. We have found more reliable and precise means of navigating. Today we consult a GPS, not a sunstone.

If graphic designers could understand what happens in visual communication, then new applications of graphic design might arise, better explanations of graphic design solutions might be attained, and graphic design as a practice might better adapt to a new world in which the ability to design visual communications is in everyone's hand, just as the ability to navigate is in everyone's smartphone.

What we need is a theoretical basis for graphic design.

The way forward

Some years ago, I published an article in the *Journal of the American Institute of Graphic Arts*[8] in which I listed six qualities a theory for design would need to possess to be helpful to practicing designers. These six tasks are the work that any good theory of design must perform, and they define the difference between design theory and design magic.

A good and useful graphic design theory would:

1. Give us explanations (of how visual communication signifies what to whom),
2. Relate to the real world (to real-life situations and audiences),
3. Give us words (provide terminology—clear, consistent, and precise),
4. Give us a model (a paradigm for making critical judgments),

5. Give us tools (for conceptualization and presentations),

6. Be a testing lab (be verifiable through practice).

I think those six requirements still stand. We need a theory that not only helps us navigate the ship, but helps us to understand how the navigation works. Unless we foster a theoretical basis for our profession, we will be locked into the stylistic cycle, remain corseted in hero imitation, and be unable to answer students (or clients) who ask more than three "why" questions.

There have been important forerunners in this push toward theory that I argue will be truly transformative of our discipline: Hanno Ehses, Ellen Lupton, Johanna Drucker, David Crow, Richard Buchanan, Martin Krampen, Thomas Ockerse, to name a few, and there are many others. These men and women have worked to bring ideas to the field. Some of these ideas will be picked up and folded into the story that unfolds in this book. Following in their footsteps, my hope is that a new generation of designers will not be satisfied with a folk practice approach to our field. I hope that a new generation of intrepid designer-scholars will come forward to make the next advance in graphic design theory. The magic of expression and visual communication will always be there, just as it is in a great piece of music written by someone who understands music theory. Emotions have no need of rationality; but an understanding of how and why the emotions are engaged, how and why information is transferred—and founding an understanding of these things on the basis of something deeper than taste or stylistic imitation—such an understanding does not displace but *adds to* the magic.

This book is an effort to provide such a basis for graphic design theory. It is not meant to supplant the contributions of the theorists mentioned above, most of whom work from a rhetorical, cultural studies, or human factors perspective, but rather to add to those a particular semiotic perspective. The theory is constructed on the pragmatist semiotics of Charles Sanders Peirce. I do not pretend that this book covers the field of semiotics in an inclusive or definitive manner, or that the conceptual tools introduced here represent all the conceptual tools available from a semiotic perspective. Rather, I hope *FireSigns* will prove to be the opening of a conversation, to be joined by many others who share an interest in understanding the magic of graphic design, who can expand areas they feel require elaboration and correct what they feel needs to be adjusted. Most of all, it provides a working model for moving design away from folk practice and toward conceiving of design as a still magical—but understood—process of visual sign exchange.

Part I The View from Outside Sign Action

1 Visual Perception Models

A ladder of theories

Graphic design is in many ways a blend of several disciplines. In some ways it is engineering, in other ways it is art, in others psychology. As a result, a theory of graphic design must really draw from the theoretical foundations of many fields: a ladder of theories (figure 1.1). The first rung is occupied by the studies of the physiology and psychology of visual perception. The second rung is semiotics, the study of signs and signifying actions. The third is the study of visual rhetoric, devices of persuasion. The fourth is occupied by demographics, anthropology, sociology, and other "human factors"—fields that concentrate on the behaviors and preferences of groups of people in various situations, times, and places.

The first rung—the science of visual perception—is well developed and continues to expand, providing insights into how the process of vision functions. Rhetoric is beginning to be well integrated into many of our better academic graphic design programs—certainly at the graduate level, and increasingly in undergraduate programs. Meanwhile, a wide variety of data collection tools that comprise the human factors sector is already in wide use in marketing and design practice, especially for large-scale projects. This book is primarily devoted to the development of that second rung of the theory ladder, semiotics, in order to show how semiotics can contribute to design process and problem solving and how it affords insights about the process of graphic design. But it is important to be aware that these various rungs of the ladder are held together by the ladder rails—that is, the various disciplines connect, and there is, or at least there should be, an interchange and exchange of ideas between them.

So, just as at the end of the book we will hand off theory to the rhetoricians, at the beginning we actually need to start on the rung beneath semiotics: the psychology and metaphysics of visual perception. This first chapter offers a necessarily brief sketch of the science of visual perception, a summary of issues that one hopes will encourage the

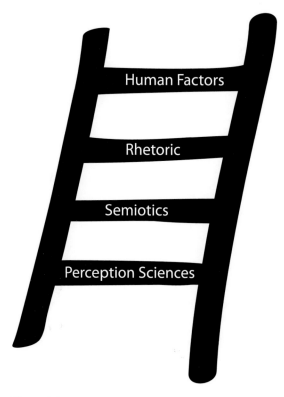

Figure 1.1
A ladder of theories. Graphic design draws from many fields, including the perception sciences (physiology and psychology of perception), semiotics, rhetorical methods, and human factors. Rhetoric (the devices of persuasive or effective communication) can be thought of as an outgrowth of semiotics. Human factors include ethnographic, demographic, and other studies of groups of individuals.

reader to seek more depth than can be given here. This is the rung where one asks, "What is it to see something?"

The scene and the seen
As I hike into the country fields near my house, I notice all kinds of things, and each provokes a variety of meanings and thoughts. That tree is an ash, and is likely to decline and die before the autumn's first frost, due to the ravages of the emerald ash borer beetle which is making its devastating way through this region. The stream below the bluff is running high, not surprising given the rain we had two days ago. There is the shadow of a large soaring bird, perhaps a buzzard but possibly a hawk.

What I am a part of, the environment itself, which includes my physical body moving through it (the one I am accustomed to calling "me"), is "the scene." The scene is the surround, the context, what the psychologists sometimes call the "environmental stimulus"—everything in the surrounding world, the undifferentiated and undiscriminated stage set for seeing. The scene is what there is *to be seen*, including the ephemeral fleeting condition of shadows and sunlight, all of which, considered now as an amalgamated whole, is about to make seeing possible.

Now, as I open my eyes upon the scene, in the very act of seeing, the scene is fractured, framed, divided in a particular way. From the totality of the scene there is now one discriminated thing, a single, seen figure of attention. As opposed to the holistic scene, "the seen" always implies such differentiation, the construction and resolution of swarming energy into an object of sight. What is now the seen is a visual entity, individuated through the sense of sight, and separated from others by differences and transformations in the light energy, variations we call edges, color, shape, motion parallax. Visual entities have what might be called a sense of "thisness" which artists refer to as "figure," and upon their being seen, all the rest of the scene—all that "other"—becomes what artists refer to as "ground."

What happens between the scene and the seen is a process called perception. Perception leads to a tentative conclusion, known as a cognition: my determination of what there is before me, furnishing my visible world, such furnishings as may only now, after perception, be given a name: "tree," "rock," "cloud." That cognition is the seen as I know it (though my "knowing" could be quite mistaken). It is my interpretation of what is there before me. The physiological, neural, and cortical machinations that are the perceptual process are not felt by me—indeed, I am not consciously aware that they occur at all. Only through optical illusions, vertigo, and some forms of hallucinations do we sometimes have a sense of the process of this stitching together of our visual reality. Even then, it is often only later reflection, or the cognitive dissonance of something not "making sense"—perhaps a vision of a lake in a desert where there could not possibly be water flowing, though it looks for all the world like water—that clues us to the artifice of the process as a constructed whole.

To me as the seer, it is the visually discriminated entity, the visual object, that is the focus of my attention and interest. Studies of visual perception attempt to understand this still mysterious process, that from a hubbub of energies we manage to see something.

But we don't only just see stuff: all the feelings, remembrances, associated thoughts, implications, or specific denotations that happen in me upon seeing something need to be accounted for too. A visually perceived thing has significance, it also *means* something. This is the connection, and the distinction, between theories of visual perception and theories of semiotics. Visual perception tries to understand how we see, semiotics tries to understand how we mean. If graphic design is the creating and ordering of visual entities in order to affect the seer in particular ways, then understanding both how we see and how meanings emerge is critical for an understanding of graphic design itself.

Back from my walk, I sit at my desk, pull out a piece of scratch paper, some red ink and a pen, scratch a few squiggly lines, then slide the paper into the top desk drawer. What I've just done is an act of graphic design. It's a simple and seemingly trivial move, yet the mystery of it has kept some of us working and teaching in the graphic design field for many years. What's so amazing about doodling on a piece of paper? Well, let's begin with some basic questions: What color is the doodle—is that color a feature of the doodle or is it in your head? Is the squiggle meaningful to you? Meaningful to anyone else? How is it meaningful? Could it be more meaningful? Could it have the power to hurt someone's feelings? To have someone fall in love with you? Could it sell a boat, ruin a marriage, ensure a bequest, save a soul? Is it possible that the marks in that desk drawer hold the secrets to the laws of space and time? Actually, if the marks in question were the ones made by Albert Einstein that he placed in his desk drawer at the patent office in Bern, Switzerland, in 1905, the answer to that last question would be yes.

The metaphysics of perception

So what happens when we see? This is the basic question that studies in perceptual psychology attempt to answer, a question so perplexing that it has flummoxed people for thousands of years and still continues its flummoxing. In a thorough review of the literature in 2007, Jessie Peissig and Michael Tarr conclude, "Despite this progress, the field is still faced with the challenge of developing a comprehensive theory that integrates this ever-increasing body of results and explains how we perceive and recognize objects."[1] The fundamental philosophical problem goes back to the earliest moments of philosophy, to metaphysics, the branch of philosophy that asks the most fundamental questions about being and existence. Does eyesight represent things the way they truly are?

In *De rerum natura*, the Roman poet Lucretius considered sight to be the result of a substance flowing from an object to the eye.[2] Even after it was appreciated that the eye functioned as a light receptor with a retina packed with cells for that purpose, basic questions persisted. Does what is seen require a mind to see it, or is it independent of mind? In a famous conversation, Albert Einstein and the Bengali writer and philosopher Rabindranath Tagore debated the universality of the "truth" of observed objects.[3] (Figure 1.2 suggests their positions.)

Einstein: The problem begins whether Truth is independent of our consciousness.

Tagore: What we call truth lies in the rational harmony between the subjective and objective aspects of reality, both of which belong to the super-personal man.

E: Even in our everyday life we feel compelled to ascribe a reality independent of man to the objects we use. We do this to connect the experiences of our senses in a reasonable way. For instance, if nobody is in this house, yet that table remains where it is.

T: Yes, it remains outside the individual mind, but not the universal mind. The table which I perceive is perceptible by the same kind of consciousness which I possess.

E: If nobody would be in the house the table would exist all the same—but this is already illegitimate from your point of view—because we cannot explain what it means that the table is there, independently of us.

Our natural point of view in regard to the existence of truth apart from humanity cannot be explained or proved, but it is a belief which nobody can lack—no primitive beings even. We attribute to Truth a super-human objectivity; it is indispensable for us, this reality which is independent of our existence and our experience and our mind—though we cannot say what it means.

T: Science has proved that the table as a solid object is an appearance[4] and therefore that which the human mind perceives as a table would not exist if that mind were naught. At the same time it must be admitted that the fact, that the ultimate physical reality is nothing but a multitude of separate revolving centres of electric force, also belongs to the human mind.

In the apprehension of Truth there is an eternal conflict between the universal human mind and the same mind confined in the individual. The perpetual process of reconciliation is being carried on in our science, philosophy, in our ethics. In any case, if there be any Truth absolutely unrelated to humanity then for us it is absolutely non-existing.

It is not difficult to imagine a mind to which the sequence of things happens not in space but only in time like the sequence of notes in music. For such a mind such conception of reality is akin to the musical reality in which Pythagorean geometry can have no meaning. There is the reality of paper, infinitely different from the reality of literature. For the kind of mind possessed by the moth which eats that paper literature is absolutely non-existent, yet for Man's mind literature has a greater value of Truth than the paper itself. In a similar manner if there be some Truth which has no sensuous or rational relation to the human mind, it will ever remain as nothing so long as we remain human beings.

E: Then I am more religious than you are!

a   Mind → Truth

b   Mindⴰruth

c

d

Figure 1.2

In their conversation, Einstein and Tagore found each other's positions perplexing. As a realist, Einstein's conception of the relationship of mind to reality was one of a fixed reality and a separate, searching mind, trying to discover the truth of that reality (a). Tagore, on the other hand, saw reality as something mind-dependent: a fly's reality would be quite different from a human's. So, for Tagore, truth is dependent on the qualities of mind that intersect with it (b, c, d).

Externalist and internalist views of perception

Seeing happens so easily for us that it is hard to believe that the process itself is a matter of intense debate. No one knows exactly how we do it. There are several competing fundamental theories of what is happening when we look at the world. We cannot elaborate them in detail here, although each view rewards the student who contemplates the mysteries of this, our most primary sense.

The various theories about visual perception break down into two broad tribes, externalist and internalist accounts. With Einstein, externalists hold that visual objects are mind-independent. Things are as they are out there in the world, and it is our perceptual system's job to reveal them to our consciousness with as much fidelity as possible. Sometimes our perceptual system is not quite up to the task, in which case we are fooled by what we call "optical illusions."

Externalists   There are two branches of externalism: direct and indirect. Direct realists believe that there is a "furnished world" of balls, chairs, trees, and other objects. This is the simplest and most commonsense form of metaphysics, but it is challenged by every other form.

Indirect externalists, which fall into representational and critical realist factions, hold that it makes no sense to speak of a furnished world as if we were able to simply "pick up" the information that is out there in any kind of pure and unsullied way. The indirect perspective holds that we can never know the external world directly because all contact with it is mediated by our bodies as we do the perceiving. Perception may be *caused* by an external world, but the process is "filtered" through a perceptual process that owes much to our particular needs as organisms. Representationalists argue that what is perceived is not the ball itself (Kant's *ding an sich*) but the swarm of sense data that has already been gathered from it. Perception is for them a two-stage process: we gather data, and then we form a representation of a world—such a world is always a construction of the sense data. So in the narrow sense, by the representationalist account, we do not perceive objects in the world but rather representations of our sense data of them.

Critical realists add another layer of complexity. For the critical realist, perception is not a mere re-presentation of sense data, but rather the feed from senses is combined with a critical filter, still at the unconscious phenomenal level but utilizing a portion of our higher conceptual faculty.[5] Part of this process may involve a small set of prestored templates or schemas called "geons" which sort and classify incoming data.[6] Here we have what is essentially a dialogue between sensation and conceptualization, so that unconscious raw sense data is "critiqued" by our conceptual levels in light of what they expect to be seen (though all this is still subliminal and nearly instantaneous). In our contact with the world though our senses, we are never aware of this continual exchange between the unconscious phenomena and subliminal dialogue that under-girds perceiving itself, but instead are only aware of the resulting decision: the output of the transaction. This results in our quite mistaken belief that we are directly perceiving objects in the world, when in fact an active exchange has been going on in the basement before we receive the report upstairs.

Internalists   This brings us to the internalists' camp, which is Tagore's. Among the internalists, there is general agreement that it makes little sense in perception to speak of an external reality at all. For the internalist, the object of visual perception is mind-dependent. That means, regardless of what may or may not be out there in the world, that the important things to study are the qualitative aspects of the sensation itself. Speaking of perceived qualities as if they are attributes of the objects out there in the world is not only unnecessary but is likely to lead one into error. In the perception of a red cup, it is not the cup in the world that is red, but the perception you have in your mind of redness and cupness. What counts for internalists is the sensation itself, and there is no need to look beyond.

There are a couple of different varieties of internalists. The adverbialist takes perception to be an action, not a static state, and all that can be said about "the reality" of redness lies in precisely the felt quality of seeing-in-a-red-sort-of-way. These states of feeling or sensing are called *qualia*.

In the most extreme version of internalism—idealism—everything's very existence is dependent on mind. Unperceived things are simply nonexistent.[7] If a tree falls in the forest and no one ever sees or hears it, then—"What tree?" Notice that the adverbialist doesn't go quite as far as the idealist. For the adverbialist, there may well be existent things out there, but we simply cannot hope to experience them, because it is the qualia that are fundamental to experience. With no chance of getting beyond qualia, what is important for us is the qualia we are presented with, which is all we can study.

There is another conservative variety of internalist, one that, like the adverbialist, allows a place for the something outside of the perceiver. For the phenomenalist, the external world exists, but simply as clusters of perceptual possibilities. Some phenom-enalists even see the external world as sets of information, "memories"[8] awaiting actu-alization in the act of perception. In perception, the set of possibilities is collapsed into a single internalized way of seeing.

Physiology and Cognitive Psychology

Many of the studies of the psychology of visual perception today involve looking at the physiology of the eye and brain. The psychologists who conduct these studies, although generally not noting the fact, are usually working from the standpoint of direct realism, in which objects are mind-independent, with visual perception being the study of experience. In many of these methods, the metaphysics of perception is considered irrelevant: objects may exist unperceived, but these are of no interest to the researcher.[9] In any case, important lines of scientific investigations in recent years have often bypassed the larger metaphysical questions entirely and concentrated instead on what is happening in the brain.

Top-down or bottom-up?

One paradigm for the processing of visual perceptions, held by R. L. Gregory and others, suggested that our prior experience in the world helps shape our perceptions. Since we are accustomed to seeing sunlight emanating from above us, we tend to see certain patterns as being raised bumps instead of depressed divots based on how light coming from above would illumine such objects. This theory, which assumes the importance of memory, is called the "top-down" hypothesis. However, an opposing theory, first put forward by the psychologist J. J. Gibson, views perception as an immediate uptake of information encoded from and within the environment, not requiring mediation by prior knowledge. This is often called the "bottom-up" hypothesis.

Today, a hybrid view seems to be winning out. fPET brain scans show that when we attend to something, activity flows within two particular regions of the visual cortex. These two areas of flowing activity are known as the dorsal stream and the ventral stream. The dorsal stream seems to play a role in our space perception, and in telling our body how to respond three-dimensionally, whereas the ventral stream has a greater part to play in recognition. When we gaze at an object, there is a constant major dialogue between these two areas of the brain, as well as weaker interactions in other areas of the brain. This seems to suggest that the physiological processing of the information coming through our eyes includes a process of sorting, of making guesses and reaching likely conclusions, so that what is eventually perceived is the result of a series of "most likely case" judgments. We are not idly "receiving" information; rather we quickly ascertain the most likely scenario for what the environment is confronting us with.

This is an active view of the process of perception. In the 100–500 milliseconds[10] it takes to recognize or respond to a "percept"[11] (as if the percept is a stationary thing and not an ongoing process), we have made perhaps thousands of decisions at very low levels of unconscious mind, involving both feedback and feedforward processes. There is a veritable crescendo of clandestine yakking going on up there that we end up simply experiencing as "a red apple."

But in seeing the red apple, we are not perceiving the signals themselves. The perception we have is of the "object of our attention," what the psychologists refer to as the "attended stimulus." We experience not the signal, but the message.

One way to think of this process is as two pathways leading to a common destination (figure 1.3). One path is for the brute signals impinging on the retina, which are being evaluated, filtered, and result in the phenomenon of "something registering attention." The other pathway is a conceptual pathway, and it addresses particular questions: What is it? Where is it? Is it coming or going? Does it resemble anything I've seen before? The crosstalk is mostly between these two channels, one largely dorsal and the other largely ventrally located in the brain, with other regions adding occasional commentary. The result is that we have a conceptual apprehension of what we see. From the standpoint of perceptual metaphysics, this physiological picture seems to be in fairly close alignment with the critical realist's position. In perception, we are literally figuring things out, using a host of resources, and coming to best-guess hypotheses.

Of course, our hypothesis could be wrong, as illusions remind us. In an optical illusion, we see something that we take to be x only to determine later that it is y. Or we

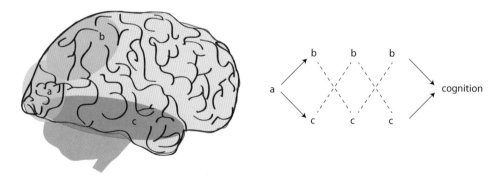

Figure 1.3
When signals from the retina reach the visual cortex, they split into two streams. One stream travels through the cortex dorsally, the other ventrally. The cross talk between these streams and resonances in other locations of the brain indicate that perception is a process that involves decision making. The decision is experienced as cognition. (Goodale and Milner, "Separate Visual Pathways for Perception and Action," *Trends in Neuroscience* 15 [1992].)

a   b

Figure 1.4
The duck/rabbit (a) and Necker cube (b) illusions are figures that cannot be resolved by the perceptual system. Both remain ambiguous. These illusions were both discovered in the nineteenth century and are reminders that perception is fallible.

see something that seems to flicker between x and y, and, no matter how hard we try, we cannot resolve the confusion. A famous example is the "duck/rabbit" illusion (figure 1.4a). We may see a ducklike form, but then it "flips" to a rabbitlike form. The form itself, the visual entity, has not changed; it is our perception of it—what we take it as—that has shifted. Try as we might, we cannot resolve the fact that the single figure is both a rabbit *and* a duck to our cognition (though never both simultaneously). A similar dilemma confronts us with a "Necker" cube (figure 1.4b). We cannot decide which face of the cube is in front. These illusions are evidence that our conceptually determined perceptions are always fallible.

Stepping from the perceptual rung of the ladder

I can imagine a theory of graphic design starting off from a number of the metaphysical positions on the perception rung of the ladder, but we will tentatively begin our climb by taking a largely critical realist perspective, viewing perception as consisting of a complex dialogue among higher and lower cognitive functions in making sense of the information gleaned from our eyes in a "viewing situation" (figure 1.5). As designers, this position feels natural because we are always aware that we are making something to be placed out there in the world, to be displayed to others. We think of that visual entity that we construct as independently existing, awaiting presentation to sight and then interacting immediately with the mind of the eventual perceiver who encounters it.

As we begin to explore the visual entity, however, we find that a strict critical realism can be supplemented with one aspect of the phenomenalist approach to perception: the notion of something in the world that is conditional, a set of possibilities for perception. There is nothing contradictory between the phenomenalist's and critical realist's viewpoints. The phenomenalist projects on the outside world a set of potentialities that are not a part of the actual experience of perceiving, while the critical realist takes up the story from inside the process of experiencing. These come together when we examine more closely what is meant by a visual entity.

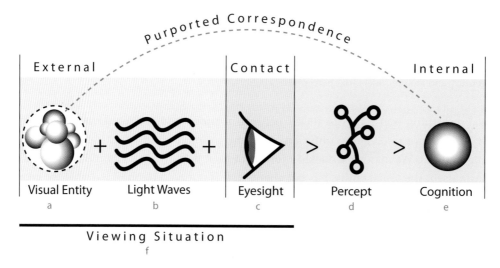

Figure 1.5
The viewing situation in critical realism with a phenomenological twist: In a viewing situation (f) a visual entity (a), which has metaphysically existed as a set of potential perceptions, affects the mapping of light waves (b) that strike the eye (c). An almost instantaneous series of unconscious resonances in the brain (d) results in a decision that is experienced as a cognition (e).

2 The Visent

Let us look more closely at this idea of a "visual entity." It is a term that will be used often in this book, so often in fact that it is useful to abbreviate it and invent the portmanteau "visent."[1] What is the visent? The visent is simply an individual visual entity, something that can be seen, something visually perceptible. In a manner of speaking, as graphic designers we are essentially visent designers.[2] The principal aspect that is helpful to adopt from a phenomenalist approach is that visents, as perceptible things, can be thought of as entities *waiting* to be perceived—sets of potential perceptions. Think of them as ingredients waiting in the cupboard for the right moment to be fully "cooked" into awareness. Flour and eggs are pressed together into strips and then cooked in hot water: the result is linguini. Visents and light are brought together, pressed through the eyes (the perceiving is the cooking): the result is cognitive content.

Being visual

What this means for us as graphic designers is that the things that we make are not fully realized until someone's actual encounter with them. This cooking situation, this encounter, requires three ingredients: light waves, a receiving visual apparatus, and something to produce differential in the field of light waves. That third thing, the something that produces a differential in the field of light waves, is the visent.[3]

Let's reduce the level of abstraction here a bit by taking an example. Returning to the red scribbling I made on the piece of paper, the marking by itself is not sufficient to do the cooking of perception. It also needs light waves, and it needs a sighted person present, looking at it.[4] I've made this mark with red ink. Now I take the mark and put it under red light. In this circumstance, there is no difference in the field of light waves that reach the viewer. As a result, the mark disappears. But although my *perception* of the mark goes away, the mark (i.e., the visent) has not ceased to exist. The mark is still there, a visent with the *potential* to effect a change in the light energy reflected to the eye of some potential future viewer—as indeed happens as soon as the red source of illumination is replaced with a light source with wavelengths that extend from 390 to 700 nanometers, the range of the visible spectrum.

The key here is to realize, with the phenomenalists, that the redness is a property that exists only under certain conditions of contact between eye, light, and visent. Every time you take a sample color swatch into a different lighting condition to see what color it "really" is, you are paying attention to the situational aspects of perception. The visent can be thought of as an influencer of the "light map" that will reach an available eye. The mark I drew has the power to influence the energy map of white light so that the eye sees colors, edges, and spatial qualities. It can only do this under certain lighting conditions, certain viewing conditions, and with an operating visual receptor system in the viewing subject. But given the happy nexus of these conditions, a visual entity is perceived and becomes the psychologist's "attended stimulus."

Being an entity

The ability to influence the light field addresses the visual aspect of a visual entity. But what about the entity part? This second part of the visent's nature leads to some unusual and problematic ramifications. An entity is something that has an independent existence, can move or be moved relative to other things, can be grasped as its own whole, an individual self. But with the visent, there is the strange subjunctive implication that what makes it "a thing" is an *eventuality*: a visent, as something perceptible, is something that would be, or could be, *perceived* as a whole. Some of the mechanisms that encourage the perception of visual wholes were first explored in depth by the gestalt psychologists of the early twentieth century.

The gestaltists wanted to understand how our perception tends to group complex things into unitary wholes. From their research they formulated principles such as closure, similarity, and so on that describe the formalistic features of visents that tend to lead to perceived wholeness (figure 2.1). They found that clusters of visents, if they have certain kinds of properties, tend to be perceived as a single entity. But if several visents can be perceived as a single unified entity, then that larger, *compounded* but unified visual entity also fits the definition of a visent. So unlike physical objects that have discrete boundaries, visents are *commutational*(figure 2.2), that is, they can shift back and forth from smaller- to larger-scale entities depending on how you regard them. If you take four black discs and place them close to each other with a 90-degree angle between their locations (figure 2.1c), you are producing not only four visents but also

Gestalt principles

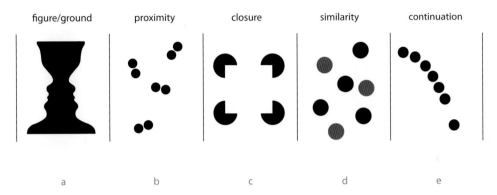

figure/ground   proximity   closure   similarity   continuation

a   b   c   d   e

Figure 2.1
The gestalt principles are techniques that allow a group of visual elements to appear whole.

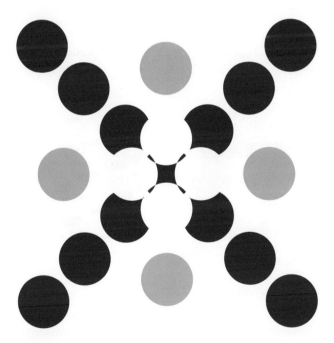

Figure 2.2
A highly commutational visent. The entire pattern makes a single gestalt, but it is comprised of both compound and complex visents, each of which can be regarded individually. Visual perception pops in and out of such complex layers. Any analysis of visual communication must take account of these elaborate perceptual dynamics.

a fifth larger square visent. If you have an illustration that uses stippling to produce gradations of gray, each of the small stippled dots in the illustration is a visent, even as those same small stippled dots are perceived as mere detail in the larger visent which is the whole figure (figure 2.3). Our perception of the two conditions toggles back and forth. If you ask, "Which one is the true visent?," the answer is neither/both. For the larger figure, the stippling is but a feature, an almost unnoticed element, but when you turn your attention to the micro level, those features and elements are fully independent and whole visents.

So we see how the notion of visents is deeply phenomenalist and cannot be reduced to simple realism. If we were to adopt a strictly realist account, the visent would be a veridical individual fact, one with certain properties and individuality, regardless of people's propensity to perceive it otherwise. In fact, the visent is dependent on the possibility of awareness. Yet neither is the visent simply the reception of sense data; it is not the array of energy on the retina, nor is it the "proximal stimulus" of the perceptual psychologists, for whom, when the red light illuminates the red-ink mark, the stimulus is negated, or when you place the mark inside a desk drawer, the stimulus ceases to be. The visent does not cease to be.

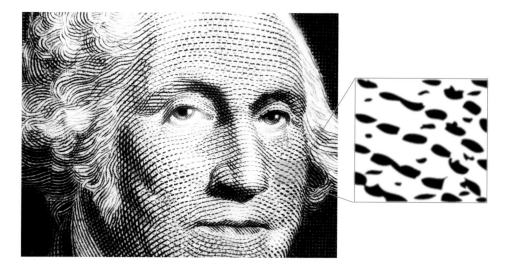

Figure 2.3
Cross hatching and stippling are commutationally subsumed into a larger image. The image of George Washington is a visent, but if you look at the stippling that combines to make the tonal gradations in the engraving, each of the stipples is also a visent. If the word "visent" seems odd, you can substitute "visual thing." The image of George Washington is a visual thing and the engraved stipples are also visual things.

Because the phenomenalist takes a visent to be a set of possibilities that would (that is, in the right situation) lead to certain perceptions, the visent still exists in the world even while it is not being perceived; as long as it is something perceiv*able*, it is "really perceptible." In other words, the concept of a visual entity contains within it an external, mind-independent reality (the power to alter a light map) *and also* a conditional ("would be") disposition toward internal, mind-dependent perceptual awareness. The concept of a visent is more in line with Tagore's reality than with Einstein's. Visents preset—as a possibility—the perception of units. The psychologist Jacob Feldman picks up this point in his discussion of visual objects when he calls them "units of our perceived physical world—*spatially coherent bundles* of visual stuff" and then goes on to describe them as "*units of mental dynamics*—the things we think of as having fixed existence in a world that changes over time" (emphasis mine).[5]

Visent: both/neither mind and/nor matter

One way to conceive of this enigmatic character is to think of the visent as a set of informational possibilities, the experiencing of which will result in the set collapsing to a particular value of information. Imagine a playing card placed face down. Like the visent, the card has a range of informational states it could possibly deliver—a set of fifty-two to be precise. Upon turning the card over, the fifty-two possible states collapse to one specific informational state: an ace of clubs. Upon encountering a visent, the infinite set of "could be" percepts collapses to the single actualized, experienced percept.

In figure 2.4, the set of possible percepts of the visent is shown as a straight line of disks which is meant to extend infinitely to represent the ways the visent could be perceived. The actual perception of it is shown as a single disk. The horizon of possibilities has been localized to a singular experience.

An amplification of this view is that the collapse can be predicted ever more adroitly and accurately through time. Imagine that there is a rare flower in a forest and that you are taking a friend to see it. At first, the number of ways that flower could come to be seen would be almost impossibly large. The odds of you and your friend coming to see it in any one specific way are small. It could have been winter, or a rainy day, or sunnier, or it could have been swept low to the ground by wind: in short, the number of ways the flower could yield itself to your friend's eye is at first incredibly vast. But now you are in the forest and it is this mostly sunny day and the light is trickling across the path before you and you can be quite confident of how your friend will face the flower. Of course, it is your friend's experience of it that collapses to a single experience of first

the visent as possible percepts

the visent upon actual perception

Figure 2.4
Upon being encountered in a viewing situation, the visent collapses from a "would be" set of infinite possible percepts to one actually experienced percept.

sighting the flower. You are having your own experience of the flower, from a slightly
different angle, so it is not exactly the same as your friend's, although extremely similar. But for both of you, individually, the horizon of possibles has collapsed to a single
actuality.[6]

The three visent types

We collapse a visent's possibility space every time we open our eyes. When we atten-
tively gaze, we collapse the manifold possible percepts that a visent has to offer to a
single one (for me, in this place, right now). But while it may seem as if the visent can
be pinned down by seeing it, in other ways it often remains impossible to pacify. For
instance, imagine that instead of flowers in a forest, the flowers in question were pictographs printed on a page so as to make a gestalt pattern (figure 2.5). In that case, the
visent(s) would be both the large overall gestalt pattern as well as each of the individual
flowers. Should the individual flowers be designed such that each petal is a distinct
visual entity itself, then each flower is a gestalt visent of the arrangement of its petals,
the floral pattern is a gestalt visent of the arrangement of the flowers, and so on; the
game need not end. In these examples, it is impossible to say, from the standpoint of

Figure 2.5
Visent hide and seek. Rieven Uncial Pro is a typeface that includes a set of ornamental toys suitable for making patterns such as the one shown here. The ornaments make use of several of the gestalt principles to make intricate and ever-changing larger visents. As you look at the pattern, it becomes very difficult to see the individual "flower" module. Instead, white shapes emerge, combinations form, and the eye scans the entire surface without being able to settle on a fixed reading.

awareness, what the visent has collapsed to become. The percept itself is fugitive at any but the briefest instant. A superb example of this is the pattern developed by Mexican mathematician José Luis Marroquín in 1976 (figure 2.6), in which dozens of quixotic figures seem to appear and just as quickly dissolve.

Simple visents

There are three kinds of visents when considered according to their likelihood of being perceived: simple, complex, and compound. When it is likely that a visent will not be seen as anything but a single thing, it is called a simple visent. In figure 2.7, column (a) shows inorganic forms (the square and the circle), an organic form (3a), and a letterform; all are simple visents. In these cases it is unlikely that you will see anything other than a single figure against a white background.

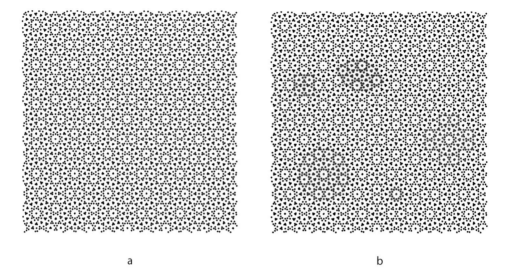

a   b

Figure 2.6
Marroquín pattern. Mathematician José Luis Marroquín created this pattern in 1976 as a study of the visual perception. To an even greater extent than the Rieven ornaments, the Marroquín pattern gives the perceptual apparatus a workout. In addition to the small "atoms" that are combined to make the pattern, the eye sees several combination structures including the ones shown in red (b).

Compound visents

But sometimes visents are likely to be "articulated" so that larger visents are comprised of smaller sub-visents. There are two kinds of these more complicated visents, *compound* and *complex*. A compound visent is mathematically one figure in the sense of having a single coterminous boundary,[7] but to the eye it appears that there are two or more "objects" of vision. For instance in figure 2.7, 1b is seen as two squares instead of a single more complicated shape, and we see 2b as a back disc and a white triangle, while 3b splits into a "dumbell" form and two white penetrating shapes, and the inter-stroke counter (enclosed element) of 4b begins to take on its own "hot doggish" independence.

Complex visents

Whereas compound visents are one shape that looks like two (or more) figures, complex visents are groupings of two or more discrete visents (simple or compound) that, when combined, appear as a single larger visent. With the floral pattern of figure 2.5 we have already seen an example of nesting visents inside more developed visents. These

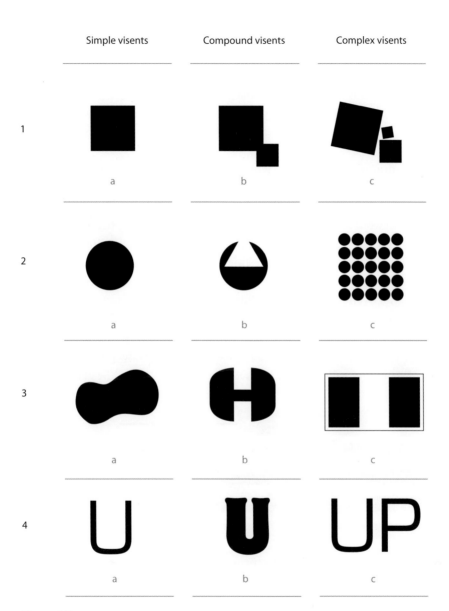

Figure 2.7
Visents can be identified as simple, compound, or complex. Simple visents (column a) trace a single contour and appear to be a single visual unit. The edges of compound visents (column b) are also simple (they can be traced from start to finish without lifting your finger) but usually follow a more convoluted path and produce the illusion they are more than a single visual unit. Complex visents (column c) are gestalts involving multiple discrete visents, yet appear to be a whole visual unit.

visents also are a product of gestalt principles. The result of the grouping procedures is that the eye has a difficult time distinguishing the individual component visents because the ordering of the ensemble is an organized whole gestalt. In the examples in figure 2.7 column (c), it is very difficult at first to see the smaller visents that comprise the whole, because the way in which they are composed forces the larger grouping as a unit into our awareness. Here, in each case, the whole really is greater than the sum of the parts.

It is worth mentioning here that 4c, which combines the letters U and P to form a word, illustrates the salient graphic feature of typography: each letter is a visent but the entire word is also a visent (becoming a visual unit if the letterspacing is handled well). In typography, the word is a complex visent, as is the sentence and the entire textual page (assuming these are composed in such a way as to maintain a unitary ensemble and gestalt). With complex visents, the nesting of visents within visents is a Russian doll game that continues all the way down to the micro level of each letter.[8] In logo design, to aid distinctiveness and memorability, a designer often manipulates the form so that compound or complex visents are emphasized (figure 2.8). When a designer is planning a piece, much effort is expended in composition to make the entire assemblage of graphic material become a single complex visent. This is the principle of unity or harmony, of which we will say more later.

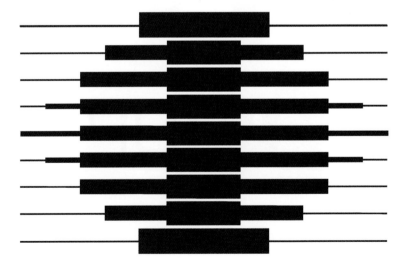

Figure 2.8
The logo for Integrated Marketing Systems is a complex visent made up of a series of linear elements, each of which in turn is a compound visent.

It is important to keep in mind that the visent is not the full experience of something that is seen. The visent is not the beauty you feel when you see an orchid; it is not even the full recognition or knowing that you are seeing a flower called an "orchid." The visent does not contain the emotional or conceptual content that happens when you see it or the associations it elicits. The visent is simply what the pronoun "it" denotes in the preceding sentence and in the following clause; it is the thing your sense of sight is capable of cutting out from the scene. The higher informational states such as feelings, memories, implications, and conceptual content will be explored in our discussion of a fully fledged semiotic interaction which the visent engenders. Therefore, we properly use the word "visent" to refer to the general thing, the object of sight, that which, in and through experience, takes on the role of the sign.

But now, when we speak of signs, we must leave the rung on our theory ladder that deals with the psychology of perception and step up to the rung that deals with semiotics, the study of the sign. There we will discover waiting for us the semiotic moment, its contexts, and the classes of sign relations.

Part II   The View from Within Sign Action

3   The World of Signs

Chapter 1 explored visual perception from the standpoints of physiology, psychology, and metaphysics, a discussion that led to the notion of the visent. The next chapter looked in more detail at the concept of visents, bringing us to the point of visents being experienced. By moving the discussion to the experiencing of the visent, we go from discussing something existing apart from us to speaking about our internal, subjective awareness. The device that allows us to connect stuff that is outside us to internal experiences is the *sign*. The study of signs and their action in the process of signification is the discipline known as semiotics, and it is the basis for the ideas put forth in the rest of this book.

Semiology or semiotics?

Semiotics refers to the study of signs, their functions and effects. But there are two branches of semiotics, and before we proceed we need to make clear which branch we will be pursuing. One branch, founded by Swiss linguist Ferdinand de Saussure, conceives the sign as a two-part construction, the union of a signifier and a signified. The signifier is the sensed image and the signified is the conception that one has when seeing the sensed image.

The other branch derives from the work of American philosopher Charles Sanders Peirce (his surname is pronounced like "purse"). Instead of Saussure's dyadic (two-part) system, in Peircean semiotics a sign is one member of a three-part relation. This system will be discussed shortly. To distinguish the two methods, the Saussurian branch is called *semiology* while the Peircean branch is called *semiotics*.

Semiology has had great influence over the course of the twentieth century and into our present century, leading to branches of study such as structuralism, poststructuralism, and deconstruction. However, there are inherent roadblocks to applying semiology to the visual arts. As noted in the introduction, because it is founded in linguistics, a code-based system, semiology has proved difficult to adapt to the non-code aspects of subject matter such as visual communication.

While Peircean semiotics faces no such barriers, it has been slow to be adopted beyond the most superficial level because of its complexity and the abstract terminology Peirce chose to employ. Nevertheless, I have chosen to work within a Peircean system in developing semiotics for graphic design. What dangers it presents in complexity are more than compensated by the enormous opportunities it presents not only to fit our experience as designers of visual messages, but to illuminate aspects that we may not have noticed. As for the difficulty with the jargon, it will be my job to translate the Peircean lexicon wherever possible into terms designers already employ and to make the system amenable to design practice in every possible way.[1] I'll do my best.

And so, onward to semiotics. Semiotics furnishes us a means to bypass the physical/ mental dualism often found in the psychological and physical sciences. The bypass is accomplished by regarding something else as more fundamental than the dualistic concepts of mind or matter. This more basic concept is the notion of relatedness.

The sign and relations of the third order

The idea is deceptively simple: in how many ways of relatedness can something stand? When Descartes thought "I think therefore I am," he was speaking of a single order of relation. He was relating to nothing but his own self (expressed as thought). In a first-order relation, something is considered solely by itself, without comparison to, or even discrimination from, anything else. This relational order of one is monadic, a singlet.[2] Of course, something can also be related to something else—perhaps a background against which it stands out, or another object with which it comes into physical contact, as one billiard ball striking another. These are second-order relations, dual, dyadic in their relatedness. Finally, something can relate to something else via the mediation of a third thing—as when you know from looking at a clock that it is time to pick up your friend. In such a mediated case, the relational order is three (a triadic relation): your friend who is in need of picking up, the clock face, your understanding to go pick up your friend.[3] This third-order relation is the sign relation. Neurons firing across synapses can be described in terms of second-order relations, but highly complex and sophisticated systems, such as the network of neurons we call our brains and which we experience as mind, rely on third-order relations. When signs emerge, minds emerge. Everything we know comes through sign work— *semiosis*, the action of signs.

It is sometimes difficult to leave behind the physical/mental, mind/body dualistic way of thinking. But to work with semiotics, it is helpful to try to think beyond these dyadic constructs. Rather than thinking of sign relations as strictly physically real or mentally real, think of them as what Floyd Merrell calls "semiotically real."[4] The third-order sign relation is like a hinge (figure 3.1). Just as, from the hinge's standpoint, both door and doorjamb are equally available (and equally peripheral), so from the standpoint of the sign relation, both mind and matter are states that are available but peripheral. From a semiotic point of view, it is the mechanics of the hinge's operation—and what those mechanics reveal—that are central to the analysis, not whether that operation is considered physical or mental. Language often fails to render the shifts of perspective as precisely as we would wish. When we allude to that entity in the world that is the source of our perception and cognition, we use terms

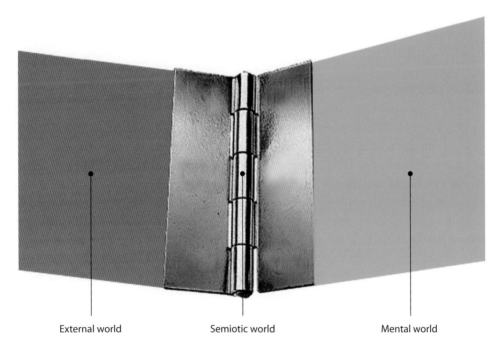

External world   Semiotic world   Mental world

Figure 3.1
From the standpoint of semiotics, both mind and matter are peripheral concepts. Semiotics allows access to that which we call physical and that which we call mental, but in the semiotic world neither concept is central. Instead, the focus is on the actions of signs, and that focus ties together the external and the mental, bypassing the mind/body dualism of psychology or physiology.

such as "visual object" or "visual thing" or the term I use here, "visent." When we refer to the *experienced* visent in the act of performing its relational semiotic function, we refer to it as a *sign*.

The sign has one function, or role to play, in a third-order relation. It stands for something else. That something else for which the sign serves as surrogate is called the *referent* of the sign. In doing this proxy work, the sign also has an effect upon the interpreting system (e.g., your thoughts). The effect it has on the interpreting system is called the *interpretant* (you can use the word "interpretation" as long as you think of the term as a noun and not a verb, and as long as you allow interpretations to be preconscious artifacts as well as conscious ones).

All of this standing-for doesn't happen in a textbook or some idealized situation—it happens in the here-and-now of experience, in this place, in this instance. This localized signing context is sometimes called the *ground* of the sign relation. It is this conditional, situational, localized context that reminds us that sign action is malleable, fugitive, transitory, and highly dependent upon circumstances. So the fundamental third-order relation is that in any given grounding context, a sign stands for its referent to an interpretant.[5]

The semiotic moment

So here you have the third-order relation: the tripartite relation of sign, referent, and interpretant, all occurring necessarily with each other, and in a particular contextually grounded situation. This is happening all the time, both in our everyday unconscious experience and in our explicit attempts to analyze or critique what we are aware of in experience. In the flow of our awareness we are not conscious of these three interrelated elements, and seldom are we aware of the context in which the triadic relation happens. But when we practice semiotic analysis, we must split the continuous flow of experience into discrete frames or brackets. A given frame of analysis, in which the grounded triadic third-order relation is snipped out from the flow of experience for the purpose of study, is called the *(semiotic) moment*. A moment consists of the selected sign situation, expressed by the excising or framing of a single triadic relation of a sign, referent, and interpretant, each performing its interdependent function with the others (figure 3.2). If you wished to study the use of hand gestures by a political candidate, you might choose a sample speech (the time and place constitute the contextual ground) and study video (the video recording functions as the sign) in order to see the action of the candidate's arms and hands, and then extrapolate from those movements what they signify. The significance you

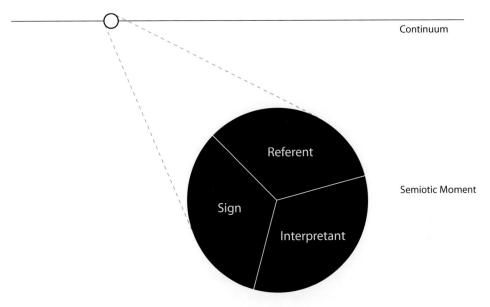

Figure 3.2
A semiotic moment is a cut into the continuum of life for the purpose of analysis. The "size" of the cut (how large the framing of the subject or time span to be analyzed) is variable. The moment is composed of three elements: a referent, a sign, and an interpretant.

ascribe to them is the referent, while the entire understanding that you have of them is the interpretant.

In saying that each element—sign, referent, interpretant—has an interdependent function or role, I mean that each of the three derives its status (as sign, referent, or interpretant) merely by the function it performs in relating to each of the other two.[6] A sign's status as sign is completely determined by its role within a given moment; it is not univocal, universal, or permanent. You may look at a flower and rightly say that it is a sign of spring, but you cannot rightly claim that it is *only* and *always* a sign of spring, for it may also be a sign of peace, a sign of hope, a sign of joy, a sign of life, a sign of death, a sign of love, etc. Nor can you claim that the flower is only and always a sign and not a referent or interpretant; if I were later to draw a picture of the flower to show you what I saw on my walk, the flower I saw would be the referent of my draw-ing, while the drawing, in that moment, is now functioning as the sign. More broadly (perhaps in the extreme), the same flower, if considered as an effect on the complex system that is the garden ecosystem, is a kind of interpretant the garden makes to the longer days and warming weather of early April. The garden, through the blossoming, "understands" it to be spring! This last instance may seem a metaphorical play, but it actually is possible to extend a Peircean semiotic analysis beyond the limits of strictly human experience to phyto- and bio-semiosis, although, for the remainder of this book, the discussion will be limited to "*anthro*-semiosis."[7] The central point for now is that the analysis of a sign, its referent and interpretant depends upon the particular instance that is being focused upon; that is, analysis depends upon the framing of the semiotic moment. The semiotic moment is a conceptual tool that is either implicit or explicit in every study or critique of visual communication. It frames the discussion and allows us to move from moment to moment as we parse the various elements and functions of a design solution.

For a graphic designer, the semiotic moment has to do with the three questions we confront in every design problem: What is it that needs to be communicated? What visual thing might be devised to carry that mission forward? Who are the waiting minds that will receive the communication and how can they be expected to receive it? The first question captures the issues surrounding the referent: the intended content, the semantics of the message. The second focuses on concerns surrounding the creation of the visent that will be sign: the form, the syntactics of a visual display. The third addresses the interpretant: the pragmatics, the likelihood that the audience will properly understand the message.[8] In the language of basic communication theory, these questions concern the message contents, the message as signal, the message as received. Put into design studio practice, they are echoed in the project brief, design, and ensuing feedback.[9]

The process of any semiotic analysis involves the continual shifting of perspectives, constant reframing, the movement through a series of moments. We pull in close to frame details of a piece, and pull out to take in a larger context; we discuss the way something works at a great distance and at an intimate reading distance, how something changes when seen from various angles, when seen by the elderly or by the young. In each of these reframings, we are making new cuts in the analysis, we are bracketing new semiotic moments. Now although this constant scale change, contextual shift, and creation of new contexts is taken for granted and seldom remarked upon, it is important to recognize that each move implies a discrete and important semiotic structure. Every analysis implies this kind of framing action, and it is helpful to make it explicit in performing an analysis or in understanding someone's critique.

Deeper dive: referent and interpretant
Before continuing, a couple of points of clarification may be necessary to clearly distinguish the referent from the interpretant. First, it is helpful to think of the referent as

something for which the sign is acting as a kind of servant. The referent is any "content" at all that is able to be communicated, and it, in a sense, *determines* a sign that is able to stand in its stead as substitute. Putting it this way reverses the way we usually think of primacy: here, the sign is not determining what its referent will be, but rather the referent helps determine the sign. The referent can be thought of as imposing limits or constraints upon those things that can successfully act as proxy for it. For example, if the referent is the concept "halt," many kinds of visents may successfully function as its sign—perhaps an outstretched arm with palm facing oncomers, or a red octagon, or the letters S-T-O-P; however, a bright green disk or a green light is unlikely to do the trick—at least, not in the United States or Europe. The referent—that which is to be conveyed—is said to be determining certain possible visents that might successfully do the work of conveyance.

We are used to thinking of meaning as starting from the thing we see and then unpacking it to get to the "contents" it provides, as if the power resides in the sign alone. It is illuminating to realize that, within any given cultural and environmental context, the referent—what is waiting there as content—is actually exerting a constraining influence on those possible visents that can do the work of signifying it.

The second point of clarification is to stress that the Peircean triadic sign relation treats the interpretant and the referent as independent players. This is not the case in the Saussurian semiological system, in which the signifier—roughly the equivalent of the sign in the Peircean system—is distinguished from a signified, the latter conflating referent and interpretant. In the Peircean system, the referent is a separate element from any particular understanding that one might have of it—that is, it is distinct from the interpretant.[10] This allows for misunderstandings. The referent may be "halt," but if you use a green disk the more likely interpretant may be "go."

The visent becomes sign

So how does the visent fit into this system? Let's say you and I see something in the distance. "Do you see that yellow thing?" and I reply, "Yes, it looks as if it is waving back and forth in the breeze." Here, the visent is the subject of our conversation, the purported thing that we agree we are seeing. It's yellowness and waving movement are qualities it seems to possess. Our conversation about it helps us to agree about its nature—that it is there, that it is yellow, that it waves.[11] But the visent, properly considered, is neither our conversation, nor our mental thought of it, nor even our initial (precognized) perceptions of it; the visent is simply the set of perceptual possibilities that is collapsing to a singular perception for me—and another singular perception for you. It is the visual entity making itself available to our sight, what Peirce calls an "actual thing or event."[12] As it happens, as we will soon investigate, actual things are one of three classes of things that can act as signs.[13]

Let us return for a moment to our imagined conversation. Let's say that you and I are having this conversation on a golf course. That waving yellow thing in the distance is now taken to be our objective: the flag marking the cup. In this case, the visent (that thing to which we point and which we call "that yellow waving flag") is the sign, the referent is some equivalent of "the cup is here," and the interpretant is the understanding that we should shoot in that direction.[14] The visent is now taking on a role, acting as a surrogate, a sign, for the cup. The sign is a function, an office. A visent performs the office of sign in the way Rita is president of the local chapter of the Honors Society. Each performs a role.

We both agree that the flag we see is the same "thing" (i.e., the same visent), but although my percept and your percept of the flag may be similar, they can never be identical. If you are nearsighted and I have perfect vision, perception renders the sign differently to us. You and I do not occupy precisely the same position on the fairway. Beyond matters of perception, other aspects of communication are similarly variable. For example, our interpretants are affected by our previous experience and what we know about the game of golf. If we are both experienced with the game, we might share the understanding, "That flag-waving place is where we should aim," but if I am an utter novice, I may have a completely different interpretation, "Why is someone waving a flag over there?"[15] Our negotiations with the world and with each other in ferreting out what we agree upon about the world are always, to some degree, tentative. One of the tasks of semiotics is to highlight this relative tentativeness, to suggest a basis for greater or lesser confidence in acting on the tentative conclusions we draw, and to provide a way to dissect the process.

The semiotic moment is analytical

As a stage in a process of knowing, the semiotic moment carries within it a mechanism for analysis, for rendering judgments. Consider this process at two extreme scales. In the first case, the moment is happening at the scale of perception, a microsegment of the process of engaging with the world through our senses. In the second case, it is a part of a studio dialogue in which a candidate design solution is being reviewed and commented upon. In the former case, the moment is but a subconscious pip in the perceptual process. We are not even consciously aware of it, only of the other end of the perceptual flow manifested as awareness, cognition. Contrast that situation with the latter, larger-scale instance, in which we find ourselves passionately debating a particular design and fashioning a critique of it. While the former is preconscious and seemingly automatic and the second is a product of willful and logical argument, in both a cut is being made in the flow of experience, and within that single referent-sign-interpretant triadic moment conclusions are made. In one case, the conclusions appear as the patterned firing of neurons; in the other, as persuasive arguments reaching a determination of how a design project should go. Either way, regardless of scale, some act of analysis or judgment, no matter how fallible or tentatively held, is inevitably made. This analytical judgment is inherent in the interpretant: it is implied in the very notion of understanding.

The semiotic moment is synthetic

If the moment is a kind of cut into the continuum of the world, either at the micro-perceptual level or at a very large scale of communication, it begs the question, What are the limits to the size of the cut? The answer is that the size is potentially infinitely variable. It can be as small a cut as the optical array on the retina at a given instant of time, or as large as an appraisal of the design of the Bauhaus with respect to modernism. Semioticians have studied the act of visual awareness in infants, and the responses of ecosystems spanning centuries. The key is that every moment is an intentional act of framing, and that act of framing is part of a vibrant decision-making process.

Like when you are framing something in a camera, you can back away and get an overview of the landscape, or you can come in close for a tight-cropped close-up to emphasize this aspect or that aspect of a larger picture. The moment is not only the analytical "frame" that we use to semiotically dissect what is occurring in a graphic display; it is also flexible to our needs. For that reason, a typical semiotic analysis will pop in and out of many semiotic moments.

Take, for example, the well-known analysis of the ad for Panzani pasta that Roland Barthes published in "The Rhetoric of the Image" (figure 3.3).[16] In his analysis, Barthes successively discusses the color palette, the use of text, the compositional qualities, the webbed shopping bag, and the selected objects including the packaged product promoted by the ad. Although Barthes does not use the term, each of these framings is a distinct semiotic moment of analysis. A further moment is the study of possible connections between these framings. Every time you change the subject or scope of analysis, you are reframing, entering a new moment, with a new, or reconsidered, sign, referent, and interpretant. Because the moment's framing is seemingly at the whim of the analyst rather than an objectively fixed thing, it is said to be *synthetic*.[17]

The semiotic moment is a consciously extracted bit of interplay that we make use of in analysis, but it is also decision making as determined in experience itself. Our experience of the world is developed with, built upon, synthesized from, thousands of

Figure 3.3
Roland Barthes devoted several hundred words to a critique of this ad for Panzani.
In the process he moved among many moments, frames of analysis.

micropercepts, an interplay between the phenomenal input of the senses and higher-level concepts resulting in judgments (interpretants) that we experience as cognitive awareness. Cognition is the coming-to-a-conclusion about what we are seeing, the result of a string of experiential triadic moments involving beneath-the-threshold-of-awareness signs, referents, and interpretants. The mind is always searching, casting moment after moment about the world (as well as in our interior thoughts), culminating in an always provisional sense of "how things are." And how things are will always remain, at least for us finite beings, equivalent to the best we can make of it—that is, fallible. Semiotic analysis, by making this largely unconscious process conscious and deliberate, allows us to penetrate deeply into the nooks and crannies that connect a visent (out there) with someone's feelings and actions (in here), thus spanning the Cartesian divide.

This constant moving between moments and rescaling is found in experience itself. Semiosis, the process of all of this sign action, is a great roiling current of flowing moments, combining, segmenting, and recombining to provide the world as we know it—or we should say, the world *in the knowing* of it.

As is the case with experience itself, any design analysis is going to be fallible, suitable to future correction, never complete. But the process of making the analysis opens up possibilities of interpreted meaning that would otherwise have gone unremarked and perhaps unexperienced. It's a valuable process, one that designers actually unconsciously practice in every evaluation during the creative act and afterward as well. Making this process conscious, detailing the subtle parts of it, reveals a beautiful structure of critique. As we are about to see, it also suggests new conceptual tools that not only can be used to evaluate candidate solutions after they are evolved, but can be plugged in to the front end, the creative process, and can aid in the evolution of design solutions. To do that, we need to step away from the abstract view of visual perception and semiotics as subjects seen from the outside, and climb further inside the turbulent current of semiosis itself.

4   Sign Classes

Once a visent has undergone the metamorphosis from something potentially perceptible to an actual experienced unit of perceived visual stuff, it emerges as a sign in a semiotic moment. Our task, from here on out, is to discuss the ways visents-as-signs interact, move us, inform us, addressing our eyes and influencing our thoughts, leading us to order in a chaotic world. The discussion now turns to specific contributions semiotics offers. We begin with the concept of the display.[1]

Displays

Consider these two examples: (1) During a walk, I see an acorn lying on the sidewalk. (2) During a walk, I see a picture of an acorn on the sidewalk (figure 4.1). I will likely regard only the second example as an act of communication. It is a *signal*, an attempt from someone to reach out to my gaze, to get my attention, to show. Visents that are interpreted in this second way are *displays*. Signaling is the act of reaching out; the display is the visent considered as a proffered message unit—sign as intended message. All displays inherently carry, as if in their DNA, the (inferred) attempt to communicate, the (implied) agency of a sender.[2] All displays are visents, but not all visents are displays. In analyzing works of graphic design, the display usually becomes the central inclusive unit of the analysis, and it is usually a complex visent composed of a host of sub-visents such as typography and graphic elements of one kind or another, all of which we will be discussing in due course. The display is often called "the page," "the piece," "the work," "the design," all such terms referencing some totality of a message unit.

Displays are signals
If a display is interpreted as being a willful attempt to communicate, there must be some kind of framing device to tip you off—something about it that sets it apart from

 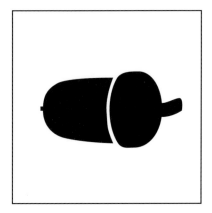

Figure 4.1
An acorn, as an actual object in the natural world, is a visent. If you see a representation of an acorn (even the photograph of a real acorn), that representation is a display. All displays signal an attempt to communicate a message.

those contextual nearby visents that, while certainly being interpretable semiotic signs, happen *not* to be taken as intentional communicative acts. The difference will be clear if the picture of an acorn on the sidewalk happens to be near several acorns that have fallen on the sidewalk. The picture is a display, while the acorns are simply acorns that have happened to drop from the oak tree overhead. But if the acorns are lined up on the sidewalk, instead of appearing to have randomly fallen, then they begin to acquire the status of a display.

Of course, connections can be made between the two circumstances. One might interpret the display as a way of identifying that the area is known for large numbers of dropping acorns: "Watch your footing—acorn zone!" We will return to this point soon in a discussion of the different kinds of sign classes, and again in chapter 11, but for the moment, simply be aware of the necessity that every display must be carved out, discriminated from non-display space. That the display is a visent requires this move. It is one of the most fundamental requirements of every successful piece of graphic design— that the viewer recognizes it to be a *signal*.

Astronomers monitoring the radio signals received as part of the SETI program to discover extraterrestrial intelligence are looking for precisely such a framing device: some feature that can discriminate the natural, nonintentional random background information from possible signals that would be regarded as an outreach of intelligent life. But let's be careful here: not every marker of intelligent life is a signal. If it were discovered that all intelligent beings naturally emit a telltale biological pulse, say a radio signature of a certain frequency, detecting it would be a sign of intelligent life, yet such pulse-emitting aliens would not be signaling. The pulse would be a sign but not a signal. But to reverse the situation somewhat, if aliens on some extrasolar planet begin to receive radio wave patterns from broadcasts of early Marconi radios, those would indeed be signals, though the attempt to reach out was never intended *for them*. While the intercepted signals were never intended for the aliens and the aliens were clueless about the content of earthling radio programs, as long as the aliens take the transmissions to be the result of some communicational intention, an outreach, then these are rightly interpreted as signals, and the radio broadcasts are the nonvisual equivalent of displays.

A signal, then, by the definition used here, is any sign or set of signs understood to be a willful or intentional attempt to communicate. The presence of a signal is a critical feature in interpreting a visual sign as a display. A display is a sign that is interpreted to be a visual message unit—a more or less whole message or message segment.

Privileging the receiver

Throughout this book, rather than privilege the sender, I place great emphasis on the receiver—the interpreter of the sign. A designer (working from the sender side) must always remain aware of and work toward the possible receptions of the audience. Even the understanding that a sign is a signal, and therefore a message-holding display, is ultimately in the receiver's hands. For something to be a display, it is irrelevant that the displayer *actually* intends to communicate at all (imagine, in this respect, the unfortunate untimely twitch at an art auction). Nor does it require that the contents of the message be *accurately* transmitted to the receiver. That I do not understand Latin very well does not prevent me from knowing that the medieval manuscript page I am holding is a display. If you take something to be a willful bit of message sending, then the visent, operating in its role of sign, is a display.[3]

As a result, there can be disagreement: you could interpret something as a display while I don't pick up signaling behavior at all.[4] There is no objective, neutral place of judgment when it comes to determining whether a sign is a display. The determination is made upon every encounter with, every experience of, a visent. Is this visent a signal? The answer is made by the beholder, and whatever the conclusion, it is always—at least for the moment—correct.

Graphic design and allaying "term anxiety"

Making displays and systems of displays is what we, as graphic designers, do. Graphic design work is centered on the formation of display elements, entire displays, and systems of displays. Most of the time, our displays are broadcast to large audiences through the aid of various technologies, so we tend to link our work with the instruments of dispersal, such as digital devices, video, web, print, and so on, but such production and distribution mechanisms are not the essential determinants of our field. The essential work that defines us as graphic designers is simply that we plan effective visual displays, regardless of how they are produced and distributed.

Words can be blunt instruments. So, before moving on to a discussion of the kinds of sign relation, let me pause to allay the "term anxiety" which inevitably arises. Remember that words are, in some respects, insufficient when we attempt the fine distinctions that we want to draw here. On one hand, I would assure the reader that the precise terms are not the most important thing: the most important thing is to be aware of the conceptual distinctions that the terms point to. The terms need not be a stumbling block, and there are no word police to enforce compliance. But on the other hand, in any complex discipline, which graphic design is, a technical lexicon can emphasize and clarify important distinctions, distinctions that are lost or glossed over without the guideposts terminology supplies. I hope the nomenclature is an aid to discriminating these subtle distinctions.

A review: Call something a *visent* and you refer to any visual entity in a general way, especially when considered as distinct from the visual perception one has in the experiencing of it. For "visent" (which is an abbreviation for "visual entity") you can substitute "visual object," "visual element," or simply "visual thing" with only the venial sin of slightly increased ambiguity. A visent is a *display* when it is taken to be a signal, an act of messaging. When referring to a visual display, you can alternatively call it a "work," or a "piece" or a "graphic," and you are not so much incorrect as possibly slightly less precise, and more likely to confuse these references with other ones that will arise in our discussion. Context will usually take care of any imprecisions. A *sign* is the visent within experience, especially when one focuses on its semiotic function within the frame provided by a given semiotic moment. Every sign has a referent that it is standing for, and an interpretant that is the understanding one obtains, however fallible.

Deep breath. We are now ready to move on to three trichotomies which allow us to classify signs.

The three trichotomies

Now it is possible to provide a framework for understanding different types or categories of signifying relationships. The discussion will begin with a matrix of the possible ways signs function in relation to their referents and interpretants, then move to the ten Peircean sign classes which are logically derived from them. The sign classes will permit our discussion to begin to move away from abstract logical theory toward specific, concrete instances of graphic design in action.

Three fundamental questions arise at this point: (1) What kinds of things are fit to function as signs? (2) What kinds of relation can a sign have to its referent? (3) What "authority toward action" can a sign/referent have upon understanding in the interpretant? Peirce considered these questions across the three orders of relation: first-order singularity, second-order dualism, and finally third-order, triadic relations.[5]

When we ask these questions across the three relational orders, we obtain three trichotomies, which produce a matrix of nine cells—the basic semiotic interrelational possibilities.[6] We will work our way through each, but one may be already familiar to you. The one aspect of Peircean semiotics that has already embedded itself deeply into graphic design education is the second trichotomy—the distinction between icon, index, and symbol. But it is only one of the three rows of the matrix, and the others deserve consideration as well. The matrix furnished by the trichotomies then logically extends to reveal ten classes of sign, which will provide the discussion for the remainder of this chapter.

The first trichotomy—fit to act as signs: qualities, visents, and systems
The first trichotomy answers the most basic question: What kinds of things can function as signs (figure 4.2)? Peirce is not speaking here only of physical things like chairs, stars, balls, and dogs. Instead, Peirce the master logician, using his orders of relation as

First trichotomy: fit to act as visual signs

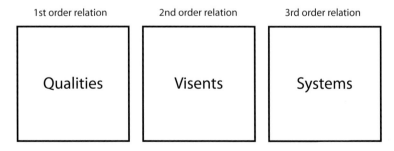

Figure 4.2
Things that can act as visual signs. The first trichotomy classifies the three broad classes of things— qualities, visents, and systems—that have the power to function semiotically as visual signs.

a guide, intends in each case to find the most fundamental *kind* of thing that fits the position in the matrix.

Therefore, the first cell, which asks what can be a sign and—in itself—be one undiscriminated whole, is occupied by something so primary that it does not even hold a distinction such as figure against ground. This is quite a riddle, because we are used to thinking of the "thingy-ness" of things, the physicality and solidity of objects. Such solid tangible things already require extension in space, a background to be figure against. But Peirce, following a long line of Western philosophers going back at least to Aristotle and working through Kant, realizes that there is something deeper that fits the bill here: mere qualities. Qualities, considered in the abstract, such as redness, roughness, and other -nesses, considered by themselves before being embodied in any particular instance or physical manifestation, can yet work as signs. The color red can act as a sign of danger or a sign of fire. That it will eventually require being painted on something does not prevent it from being significant in itself, considered in the abstract. If you were to be making a painting and it came time to paint the sky, your choice of blue or gray would be significant. The sky would be the same in every respect except the quality of its color. It is precisely quality that you are selecting as a sign when you load your brush with pigment.

It is not until we reach the second cell of the first trichotomy—a cell reserved for that which is separated out from a background, capable of contrast and opposition to another—that we find what Peirce calls "actual things and events." For us, since we limit our discussion to visual communication, this can only be the visent itself, now considered fit to function as sign. Examples include glyphs, graphics, visual elements, typography when considered solely as visual (not verbal) form, photographs, illustrations, logos, and trademarks—the world of the graphic display (itself a visent) and all the sub-visents that comprise it.

The third cell asks what it is for something to be fit to function as a sign and yet be already in some kind of third-order relation, a relation that necessarily involves prior fully semiotic participants. Cultures and societies are such relations, as are codes and handbooks, laws and procedures of etiquette, games. These are all examples of rule-, custom-, or habit-based practices. They are systems. In graphic design practice, here in this cell of the matrix we find corporate identity systems, rules for formatting, layout regularities, the grid, color standards, and all other codes that establish repeated, consistent, and functional regularity.

The three cells of the first trichotomy are continuously active in our lives; the cells are just so fundamental and ever-present that we are rarely conscious of them. Suppose I pull up to a stop sign at a street corner (figure 4.3). The qualities of a certain

Figure 4.3
A stop sign illustrates the three parts of the first trichotomy. The *quality* of hue (that particular red considered in itself, apart from its actual appearance on the sign) is capable of signifying (danger, urgency, halt, attention); the *visent* (i.e., the placard) appearing on the street at an intersection is able to act as a sign to stop; the *system* of road laws encodes the signing by stipulating that this kind of placard be placed at intersections in order to give a command to stop. Also, the system that is the English language allows the letters to communicate typographically.

hue of red and octagonality are about to be embodied in an experienced visent. The actual experienced visent that is the stop sign, standing there in its native environment, a display of a certain height and placed in proximity to a busy intersection—all of this works together to tell me to stop. And we should not forget the set of customary traffic laws that systemically encodes the signification of these things, so that upon learning to drive I learned what these qualities and these particular physical placards signify. Would the placard have functioned if it were a green circle? Would the red octagon have been successful if it were lying flat against the ground? Would the placard have meant anything to me if I were unfamiliar with traffic laws and the English language?

The second trichotomy—sign referent relations: iconic, indexical, symbolic
The second trichotomy is the most widely known, although it is often misinterpreted. Having specified, in the first trichotomy, the kinds of things that can act as signs, the second Peircean trichotomy specifies the kinds of connections a sign may have with its referent (figure 4.4). This relation may be iconic, indexic, or symbolic. Iconic relationships are relationships based on resemblance between a sign and its referent. Your passport photo bears a strong and clear relationship to your appearance. Anything that signifies something on the basis of similarity or likeness is an icon of that thing.[7]

Second trichotomy: relation of sign to referent

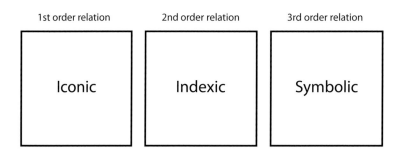

Figure 4.4
Sign/referent connections. The second trichotomy classifies the three kinds of relationships a sign can have with its referent. Iconic relations are based on similarity and resemblance. Indexic relations are connected through physical or environmental contact. Symbolic relations are stipulated or agreed upon but otherwise arbitrary.

An indexic relation is one in which the sign has some sort of environmental contact or contiguity with the referent. Smoke as a sign of fire, a windsock as a sign of the strength and direction of the wind, pointing with your "index finger" to the door are all examples of indexes. Page numbers are indexical. The key to understanding an index is to realize that it is a marker—it is tied by its physical proximity or environmental influence to that which it stands for. In a directory map, the "You are here •" is an indexical device. So is a sticky note when it is stuck to an item to remind you to do something with that item (but not when the same sticky note is on the refrigerator), or a bookmark stuck in a book (but not when it is lying on the table). A yellow ribbon tied around a tree may be an index to the lumberjack that that particular tree is to be felled. Indexes often require attention to their context in order to function. An "Exit" sign only gains its indexical function when it is mounted in proximity to a door.

Symbolic relations are simply based on consensual agreement that "this" will stand for "that." Symbols are often the result of an explicit code, linguistic or otherwise, and always the result of either habitual or repetitive cultural practice. Symbols make culturally agreed-upon connections between the sign and its referent. Virtually all words in a language are symbolic (the exception being onomatopoeic words—they are iconic). In a symbolic relation, there is neither a resemblance nor physical/environmental connection, but simply an agreed-upon relation. We saw that a yellow ribbon tied around a tree was an index for the lumberjack, but the same ribbon is a symbol for a US family with a son or daughter away in the military. In South Korea, yellow ribbons are used to remember the lives lost in the disastrous sinking of the ferry *MV Sewol*.[8] Symbols almost always require education, a learning process in order for the audience to be made aware of the sign/referent connection since it is based solely on convention. In semiotics, the convention-based symbolic relationship is said to be "arbitrary" and "unmotivated" (these terms are not pejorative). Your printed name on your passport functions symbolically: the letters do not look like you, nor do they require proximity or contact with you in order to work as an identifier. Typography works through consensual agreement—for readers of your language, these particular glyphs stand for certain speech sounds, and those speech sounds (also symbolic) stand for you.

One of the important things to take away from this is that it can be misleading to use the noun forms of these relations, that is, to say something is "an icon" or "a symbol." We have seen how a yellow ribbon can be an index for the lumberjack and a symbol for the military family. A sign may relate iconically to one referent, while *simultaneously* relating symbolically to a second referent. Take the little picture many of us have on our computer screen that portrays a small file folder. True, the visent that we know as the "file folder icon" is indeed iconic (it resembles physical paper file folders). But as that little pictograph sits on your desktop, it is also indexic of precisely *where* the directory for items can be found (you drag files to it and you navigate to it and click to open it). Furthermore, when Macintosh developed their operating system in the 1980s they decided to make it a standard that directories would be designated by that little picture, so that the picture—done in that consistent, repeated, identifiable way—has become an agreed-upon, that is to say consensual, symbol for the act of saving stuff on a computer. First designed by Susan Kare, then distributed with all Apple computers, it acquired a symbolic signification as a digital file repository once the public became accustomed to its use (figure 4.5). Because of its widespread transmission through the culture, that file folder "icon" can now be used independently of a computer screen to symbolize "computer repository." All symbols require such repetitive experience or explicit education of the audience in order to be understood. But the central point is this: in practice, a single visent often serves all three sign/referent relations—icon, index, and symbol. What changes is the situation: the framing of the semiotic moment, its context, and the person who is receiving the message. So rather than proclaim "this is a symbol," it is often better practice to use the adverbial form: in the situation before us, something is iconic of this, indexic of that, symbolic of such and such.

The third trichotomy

The third trichotomy addresses how much import, weight, or what we might call "authority toward action" a sign/referent incites in the interpretant (figure 4.6). There are three degrees of authority, and they are to some degree reflective of what the

Figure 4.5

Icons that are actually icons. Mac O.S. X "icons" include representational images for file folder, printers, sound, and trash. Not all GUI visents are truly iconic in the semiotic sense, but these four do relate to their referent through resemblance.

Third trichotomy: authority toward action of sign/referent to the interpretant

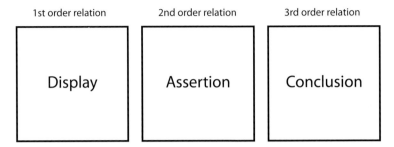

Figure 4.6
Motivation to act. The third trichotomy has to do with authority toward action that the sign/referent incites in the interpretant. One can take something as simply a display, in which case the analysis stays within the boundary of the work—its subject and its form—or one can move to the assertions and claims a work makes about the world. The third element of this trichotomy is usually the goal of a piece of graphic design: the conclusions one draws from it after the encounter. But this resides in the mind and behavior of the audience, not in the piece of design itself, and the evidence for it comes from feedback after the design is distributed.

analyst wishes to examine. The sign/referent could be considered only in its being a *display*, in which case the discussion centers on a description of the arrangement, qualities, and subject matter of the display. Or the critique could move beyond the display and involve *assertions*, propositional claims the display is making about the world, including methods and strategies the display employs in making those assertions. Finally, a discussion could center on how a receiver draws a *conclusion* and acts once a display has been seen. In the latter case, the receiver walks away with a conviction or belief of some kind that was not present beforehand. Once receivers have reached a conclusion, they are predisposed to act in accordance with it.

Let me give an example of what I mean by "authority toward action." If I consider the display alone simply as a formal composition or aesthetic artifact, or even as, say, a portrait or subject, I am not, solely on that consideration, urged to take further action of any kind. Take, for example, Leni Riefenstahl's film *Triumph of Will*. I could examine it simply as a piece of cinematography, in which case I am simply looking at it as a functional display. But I could go further and look at it rhetorically, as a powerful piece of cinematic propaganda, how it asserts a kind of truth, makes a case for a particular political point of view, understand how it manipulates an audience's sympathies; in such a case I would be thinking about its claims about the world and I would be asking

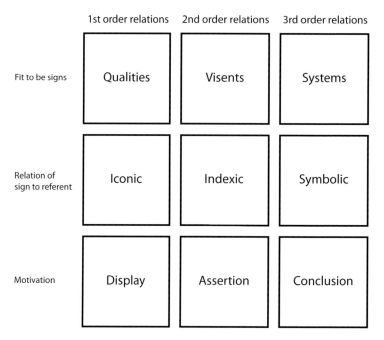

Figure 4.7
The three trichotomies arrayed together provide the basic matrix for the taxonomy of signs in ten general classes.

myself if I agreed with those claims. Finally, if I study those who are actually persuaded by the film toward sympathy to the National Socialist cause, or, conversely, led by the film to revile that cause, I would be looking at the conclusions. All conclusions involve an assent, a kind of belief. They are usually what a piece of graphic design is intended to produce. We will have more to say about conclusions after we look at the ten sign classes suggested by these trichotomies. Figure 4.7 shows all three trichotomies. It will be useful to refer back to this diagram as we move into the discussion of the sign classes.

The ten general classes of visual sign

From this armature of the three trichotomies, Peirce named and analyzed ten classes of signs.[9] It's important to note that although Peirce and later writers have referred to this schema as the ten sign classes, what are being described are actually the ten classes of sign-referent-interpretant *functional interactions*. Figure 4.8 shows the sign classes that are derived from the trichotomy matrix. The following discussion will explain each.

Feature (1.1.1)[10]

A feature is any quality or visual part of a larger unit, considered only in its affective, emotional, sensed manner (figure 4.9). A feature is not a visent, but it is a quality possessed by a visent (recall that a visent must be seen as a visual unit, a perceptible whole). Features are the formal attributes something possesses and hence the source of expression. Features may be shared by multiple visents, as indeed is the case when a visent is repeated as a motif, or when a style emerges. Features are the local attributes, characteristics, traits. As they are not independent entities but must find embodiment, features are the only one of the classes that are not actual displays and which do not include a display (although every display does include features.)

The five display types

Displays are the inferred message-bearing unit of a graphic communication.[11] When we do analysis at the level of display, we will often be looking at graphic elements that are composed to form larger, complex displays. The analysis is at the display level because these elements are parts working ultimately in concert to form a single, whole, message-bearing unit. The display is always eventually studied in terms of its ability to relay its subject, which it can do in one (or in some combination) of five ways. These five display types are the fundamental classes of graphic design vehicles. Of the five, image, mark, and symbol (especially the symbolic word) will prove particularly important in our further discussion, while format and diagram are systemic combinations of the other three.

Images (2.1.1)

The word "image" comes from the Latin *imago* which means an appearance or likeness (figure 4.10). Its dictionary definition is an imitation, likeness, resemblance, representation, or "optical counterpart" (generally produced by some device).[12] In studio practice, the word "image" is often used to point to elements, such as photographs, that have fully tonal features as distinguished from other kinds of elements that are nonfigurative, high-contrast, and graphically abstract. But I will use it here to refer to all instances of *depiction*. An image is a kind of display that represents by virtue of some visual likeness or similitude; an image is always representational. All images have

The Ten Fundamental Sign Classes

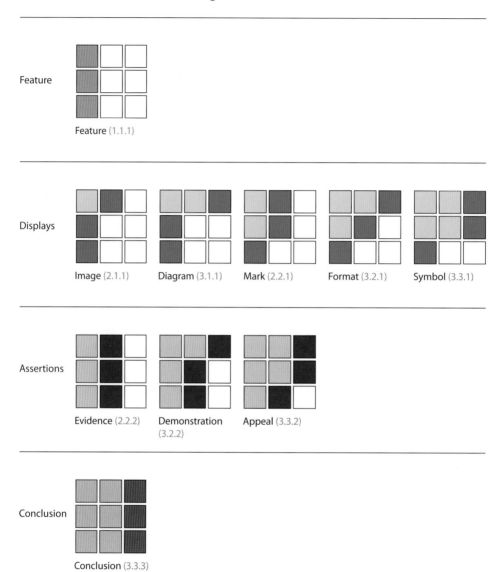

Feature

Feature (1.1.1)

Displays

Image (2.1.1)   Diagram (3.1.1)   Mark (2.2.1)   Format (3.2.1)   Symbol (3.3.1)

Assertions

Evidence (2.2.2)   Demonstration (3.2.2)   Appeal (3.3.2)

Conclusion

Conclusion (3.3.3)

Figure 4.8
The ten fundamental Peircean sign classes. Combinations of active cells of the three trichotomies yield ten fundamental classes of sign interaction. Each nine-cell diagram shown here refers back to the attributes assigned in figure 4.7. Color is used to indicate the active cells for each sign class. So, for example, an *image* is a *visent*, relating to its referent *iconically*, and being regarded simply as a *display*. The numbers in gray indicate the orders of relation (of the first, second, and third trichotomy) that are definitive in determining each class. The cells in a lighter shade are reminders that although that cell is not definitive of the class, it is nevertheless still active for it. So, for example, an image (2.1.1) is primarily defined as an iconic visent, but the visent still includes qualities (signified by the light blue cell). Cells that are not filled in are not active for the class. For example, evidence (2.2.2) is highly indexic, but does not require systemic or emblematic functions.

Figure 4.9
The hue that a color swatch represents is a feature. When the color appears on an actual swatch, the color is an embodied feature of the visent that is the particular paper swatch.

Figure 4.10
Images function iconically, by resemblance to the referent. As an image becomes increasingly graphic, eventually becoming "line art," information is lost and the image begins to be more abstract. Photograph by Margie Woods.

subjects, whether the subject is clearly or vaguely denoted, tonal or high-contrast. Images can be tonal or line art, chromatic or monochromatic. Tonal images include shades of gray or hue, while more graphic images are typified by hard-edged boundaries and do not have gradations of value or hue. Chromatic images, as the word suggests, use more than one hue (whether tonal or graphic), while monochromatic images use one hue but may vary in value.

Images are one of the most common forms of visents, and although they can stand at the level of display analysis, they are rarely found to comprise a display by themselves, being much more likely to be accompanied by typography or other more graphic devices. Images form one of the three apexes of the visual gamut that we will be exploring in a subsequent chapter.

Diagrams (3.1.1)

Diagrams reveal systematic processes and relationships. The key aspect of diagrams, the thing that makes them diagrams, is that a system is being signified—that is, a diagram's referent is a set of processes, conceptual relations, or some other principle-cohesive set of facts. Diagrams are often complex visents with many interacting elements (each element of which is also a visent). What makes the diagram a display is that the entire network of interacting parts constitutes a message. As opposed to sets of data composed typographically in a table, diagrams are iconic; the composition of the diagram resembles in some way the system it represents. This is true even though diagrams may contain symbolic components such as words and numbers.

Notice that the iconicity of a diagram does not imply the use of simplified pictures (although a diagram may happen to contain them). In Peircean semiotics, the word "icon" is used whenever the sign/referent connection is based on similarity or resemblance. In a diagram, what is being represented is a process or logical set of hierarchies that the display mimics graphically (figure 4.11).

Marks (2.2.1)

Marks tend to have a sense of physicality about them; they reference the locale in which they exist and often the enacting source of their own creation. Back in the days of hand correspondence (lamentably rapidly becoming ancient history), marking was a major part of being "in touch" with someone. The handwriting was physical evidence of the feelings of the writer, indicated by the pressure and speed of every stroke. A wax seal on an envelope conveyed two vital bits of information: its stamped seal indicated that the sender personally attended to it (for the stamp was a carefully guarded possession and proved identity), and the unbroken seal was assurance that the letter had

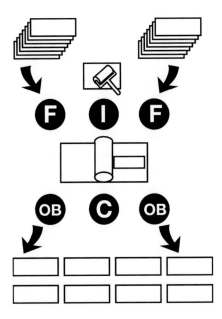

F FEEDER

I INKER

OB OFF BEARER

C CRANKER

Figure 4.11

Diagrams always function through iconicity, although they often employ elements that are symbolic (with a key or legend to inform the viewer of the symbols). This diagram shows the presumed layout of the print shop that printed the parole passes for the surrendered Confederate forces at Appomattox in 1865. There has been a mystery about how almost 30,000 passes could have been printed in a day using a single field manually operated single-impression printing press. This diagram suggests that six operators could have done the work, feeding the press from both ends.

not been previously opened. The first mark—the impressing of the seal in the wax—
spoke again to the physical contact of the sender, that he or she was in personal touch
with the act of sending and that the contents were intact from that moment in time.
The second mark—the rupturing of the seal upon opening—points to the fact that a
recipient had opened and read the letter. In both cases the mark is giving indexical
information.

There are two basic kinds of marks. Place marks are used as navigational devices to
guide wayfinding. Navigation bars on web sites, page numbers, a printer's crop and
register marks, hash marks on a football field—all of these are examples of place
marking. The marking of product by a logo or trademark is a special instance of
place marking, indicating the place of invention or fabrication a product comes from.
Contact marks, on the other hand, derive from actual physical exchange between two
surfaces. Scuff marks, handwriting, bloodstains, and vapor trails all are examples of
contact marks.

Of the contact marks, one variety, gestural marks, is especially important, as these
are derived from the movement of the human body (figure 4.12). Handwriting and
other gestural marks, such as crosshatching or line quality made in drawing, are

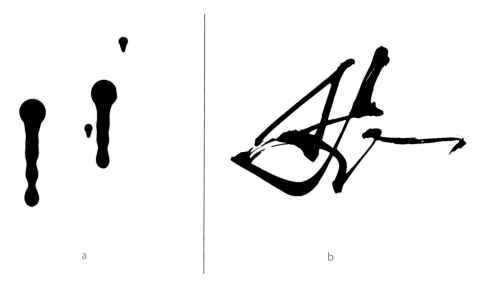

a   b

Figure 4.12
Two contact marks. The mark set (a) betrays its mechanical/physical nature. Drops of paint are
allowed to run. The laws of physics acting on the marks are unchanging. The gestural mark (b) is
unmistakably human, evoking rapid changes of direction, pressure, the restless current of thought.

particularly powerful kinds of marks. We will return to examining these kinds of marks when we take a closer look at writing and scripts in chapter 9.

Formats (3.2.1)

A format combines the regulation of a system with the locational directives inherent in an index. A format determines where things go, how the displays and elements are visually ordered and made consistent (figure 4.13). A format is a scheme for holding together disparate elements, or for finding common features among several graphic parts. Sometimes the format itself is not immediately visible, or only visible as

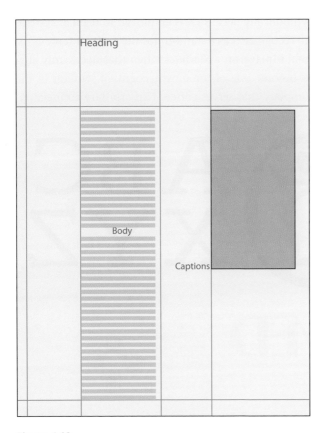

Figure 4.13
Formats are the systematic plan for determining the visible structure of visents. Formats themselves are only visible in two ways: through the visible grid layer that determines, for the designer, where elements are to be placed, and through the systematic consistency of the actual placement of visual material when viewed on the printed page or screen.

evidenced by the positioning of graphic elements. Examples of formats include grid and raster systems, style sheets, magazine layout templates, and corporate identity style formulations.

The format itself can become a powerful symbol through repetitive use within a culture. We will see this in action later when we discuss styles and genres.

Symbols (3.3.1)

As its name suggests, in a symbolic display, the connection between the sign and its referent is through symbols, that is, by consensual agreement. Symbols are often called emblems, and the two words can be used interchangeably when it comes to applying them to displays. A logo works symbolically because it is employed in regular, systematic ways so that a public comes to recognize it as a stand-in for the entity it represents. There is nothing about the mermaid image on a Starbucks logo that necessarily suggests what Starbucks is, yet it has become one of the most recognized symbols in the world, standing as proxy for a company that serves coffee. This arbitrary connection,

Figure 4.14
Symbols are ubiquitous in our lives. Here are four. Clockwise from top left: Blackthorne Press logo, Maxular (typeface), the state flag of New Mexico, Duramed pharmaceuticals logo. Blackthorne and the New Mexico flag adopt highly abstract images: pictographs of a leaf (with thorn) and sun respectively. They are, therefore, *images* of leaf-thorn and sun, but they are *symbols* of a printer and a state.

reinforced by decades of marketing and exposure by the public to its products and services, allows it to symbolize Starbucks as well as the spelled-out word itself (the typographic rendering of which is yet another symbol).

Logos symbolically represent a company (figure 4.14). All typography is symbolic in that the glyphs only relate to speech by virtue of tradition, the letters assuming their form largely through long historical practice, conventional rules, and habits.[13] The glyphs are symbols of the sounds they represent. Any abstract graphic element can become a symbol of any referent. All it takes is the informing of a public, teaching them to recognize the connection which, initially, is completely unmotivated and arbitrary. The Nike swoosh, a country's flag, pictograms which come to mean something other than what they depict iconically, musical notes in a score, all of these are functioning as symbols.

The three kinds of assertions

Before moving on to assertions, let me reiterate that these distinctions between classes are not so much a case of either/or, but of this *and* that. It is a matter of emphasis and of noticing how each of these classes helps you unpack what is going on in the tangled world of interpretation. So now as we approach the three classes of assertions, remember that it is not as if something is either a display or an assertion. Every visual assertion does its work through a display, which it logically envelops and extends. When you look at assertion, you are seeing displays, but you are taking the analysis a step further, to a consideration of what claims the display is making about the world, and how it goes about making those claims.

Evidence (2.2.2)

Evidence, as might be expected from the alignment of second-order relations, is assertion by means of physical contact or environmental contiguity. A postmark is evidence a letter passed through a post check at a certain place (figure 4.15). When a package is marked with a company's logo, the imprinting of the logo is evidence that the product inside was manufactured by the company whose logo it is. That is why counterfeit products always take care to reproduce the pirated company's logo so faithfully—and also why companies guard the trademark and copyrights for their logos so carefully.

When a court takes an object as physical evidence, it is because something about that object is linked directly to the crime scene. Evidence is often a mark of some kind, some visent left behind that, by its very existence in a given place and time, leads one toward a conclusion. This leading one toward a conclusion is what makes something an assertion. Assertions make some claim about the world, and evidence is that claim

Figure 4.15
Evidence. It is interesting to compare the classes of signification that occur on even such a small surface as the corner of an envelope. The stamp asserts that the sender has paid postage (it is a token, a receipt, that is evidence of the exchange) and the postmark cancellation is evidence that the letter has passed through a particular post office at a particular time. With the cancellation extended across the face of the stamp, the stamp is now no longer usable as evidence of payment of postage. Meanwhile, the colorful picture on the stamp makes no assertion at all—one of the few instances of graphic design in which an assertion is not present.

made physical (or in our case, visual). A visent is evidence when it is suggestive of a conclusion simply by being in a certain environment, place, or time.

Demonstration (3.2.2)
A demonstration makes an assertion by modeling. It is a run-through of what, it is asserted, will occur. If evidence is a kind of marking of the environment coupled with an assertive implication, then demonstration is the more active side of that process, as well as one that involves more moving parts in the operation of a system.

The scientist and entrepreneur commonly make such demonstrations in experiments in miniature and then "scale up" to production level. The scientist has a

Figure 4.16
Screen shots from a 1950s Wisk laundry detergent commercial asserting the product's value through demonstration.

hypothesis that under certain conditions a particular predicted outcome will occur. A situation is devised that resembles those particular conditions. Tests completed and observations made, the assertion is borne out if the predicted outcome comes to pass. Marketing consultants do something similar when they shelf-test three potential package designs. The shelf test carefully models, on a limited basis, the retail situations that will be found in many markets and larger stores. Should package design number two sell better than numbers one and three, the expectation (and the implied assertion) is that number two's design will also sell better in full-scale production practice.[14]

Demonstrations used to be a major form of persuasion in the advertising industry. Laundry commercials in the 1950s and '60s purported to show a kid's grass-stained trousers being put into identical washing machines and treated by a competitor's detergent and the client's detergent (figure 4.16). Cut to the pull-out, the client's remarkably clean, the competitor's still bearing the dark green streak of a home plate slide. Such didactic demonstrations are not in fashion now, perhaps because the public has grown more skeptical of the veracity of such edited tests, but more importantly because being instructed involves the viewer less than emotional identification does. Today, the more sly demonstration is the "demonstration by identity"—the consistent linking of a product with a certain demographic or personality type. Over dozens of exposures, the implicit assertion, which happens connotatively, demonstrates that these kinds of people use this product: if you aspire to be like those people, use that product.

Appeal (3.3.2)
An appeal is the most frequent kind of assertion. Words and images are used to make a direct claim (figure 4.17). Testimonials are made by people who claim to have experience with a product or service. A morning newspaper story tells you what happened overnight. A crawl at the bottom of the screen updates you on the latest scores. In our

Coming Soon!
(We promise...)

Figure 4.17
Appeal. An appeal asserts through the use of symbols, including the typographic word.

discussion of assertions, we should not neglect the message that promises neutral information rather than a sell.

No information is benign. What comes to us as objective, informative data not only asserts something about the world; it also is asserting its own neutrality and veracity. The assertion of neutrality is hidden, but it works by taking on the form of the dry and denotative statistic, the direct and supposedly unproblematic observation, or the authority of a trusted source of news. Such hidden appeals function through the banality of habit. They are what things look like that make no waves, have no power to startle, voice a claim in the most matter-of-fact declamatory rhetorical manner. These are the appeals that we see most often and accept without much thought, and which are therefore most capable of influencing our convictions and beliefs. Our guards are down.

All appeals make use of symbols, systematic habit, consensual practice, and usually involve the use of language. Often, the most successful appeals find ways to unite verbal text and image in ways that startle us, amuse us, and prompt reflection (figure 4.18).

Conclusion (3.3.3)
A conclusion is the coming to a belief in something, a sense of the veracity of the communication. It will almost always involve not just the assertion, but also contextual cues and prior experience of the receiver. With conclusion, the graphic design piece, as a bit of communication toward the effect of an end, ceases.[15]

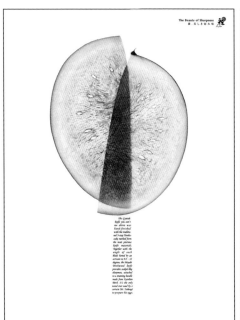

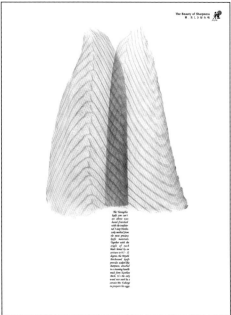

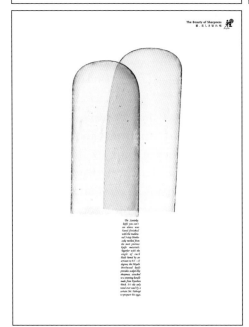

Figure 4.18

Assertions in combination. In this ad campaign for a brand of kitchen knives by the agency Herezie (Paris), thinly sliced foods overlap to give a profile of each type of knife. The ads demonstrate that the knives are good, because of the success of the cuts. The text copy that forms the handle of the knives asserts through appeal that the knives are of fine quality. A second appeal is made metaphorically through the ads being beautiful images: the tag line for the product is "The beauty of sharpness." Photograph: Baölen Pierre. Ad agency: Herezie. Art direction: Nicolas Dumeril, Jacques Derain, and Andrea Stillaci.

When I conclude that the film is successful, I am going beyond the analysis that is internal to the work, and I draw upon my understanding of the world. It is not until I compare this assertion with my knowledge of the world, usually from other sources, and draw a conclusion from it that I am moved to action by the film's rhetoric. My action may be to protest the film, or it may be to ally myself with the film's cause, but in either case this last situation involves reaching a *conclusion*. In the latter case, I am induced to a belief or an action based on assimilating that conclusion into my worldview. In the case of the Riefenstahl film, an American's reaction in 1935 may well have been wariness or even fear rather than sympathy for the cause. The reaction may have been quite different in Germany. In either case, fearfulness or fervor, the conclusion that one draws develops into a belief and inspires action in accordance with it. All design asserts—makes an argument, pitches a case, claims how something is—but only the receiver can complete the process by being moved to thought and action.

Martin Krampen, one of the first to apply semiotics to graphic design, said that graphic communication has two basic purposes: to inform or to persuade. "The process in which the source attempts to shape (or increase) the *state of knowledge* of a receiver we may call *information*. The process in which the source attempts to shape or change the *attitudinal state* of the receiver may be called *persuasion*" (italics in the original).[16]

It is both the *being persuaded* as well as the *being informed* that constitute conclusion, and these only happen within the context of a person's worldview and life experiences.[17] Displays are studied first as visual forms; that they attempt to inform or persuade entails that they inevitably make an assertion, but no graphic display or assertion has the power, strictly on its own terms, to conclude. That is a power afforded to the interpreting mind alone, an attribute only of the interpretant. It is made on the basis of more than just the content of the sign/referent, as it relies on the context of what else we know about the world. The incoming sign/referent "matches up" with the prior contextual understandings that constitute our worldview, and that matching process can result in the same information being accepted by one receiving mind's worldview or rejected by another's, the acceptance or rejection constituting the conclusion. As a result, while graphic displays considered in their formal qualities as visents are publicly available for viewing, and the assertions they make are subject to public discussion, the conclusions we draw from experiencing them are, in a particular way, inevitably private. Our perception of a visent is a result of our negotiation with the world; the conclusions we draw from the messages we receive must inevitably result in negotiations with other people who are drawing either the same or differing conclusions;

meanwhile, the only vehicle we have for performing all these negotiations is more sign exchanges. We live in a pervasively semiotic world.

Focus on displays and assertions

In these ten classes of signs, the two groupings that hold a single member—features and conclusions—are, in a sense, entrances and exits for the other eight. Features need to be embodied within displays, and so while they are important, they have less independence. Features are covered within the discussion of the display. Meanwhile, conclusions, as we have seen, involve stepping back, making judgments based on contextual prior knowledge from outside the local moment. While drawing the conclusion is usually the goal toward which graphic design is bending its energies, coming to that conclusion really requires bringing in context that lies outside the display itself. Foreseeing these contexts is largely the job of research that leads to the creative brief, and the feedback at the tail end of the design process will eventually give the designer a sense of how well she foresaw them, but drawing the conclusion and acting on the ensuing belief is paradoxically absent in the world of the display itself. All the display can do is make an assertion. The conclusion is outside the province of a visent, even a message-bearing display.

Hence, the meat of design analysis is found in the critique of displays and assertions. That critique inevitably involves features as an included critical element, and it assumes an eventual resolution in the conclusion, for which feedback is required in order to judge a design's success. The display as complex composition and the assertions the display makes are therefore the principal actionable components of graphic analysis, the decision points of the process of graphic design, and they become the focus of our ensuing discussion of specificity.

5   Syntax and Semantics

In the mid-twentieth century, Charles W. Morris made the first attempt to apply Peircean semiotics to functional communication studies. He divided semiotics into three general areas—syntactics, semantics, and pragmatics—which are roughly equivalent to form analysis, content analysis, and cultural-personal (human factors) analysis. All three must be integrated in design practice, but they must be understood as semiotically distinct, and two of the three will prove central to developing semiotic design theory.

Overview of syntax, semantics, and human factors

Syntax explores the visual/physical qualities of the visent and systems of visents. Syntax includes, but extends, what artists know as *form*. Syntax goes beyond the creation of features of a particular visent to include the formal relationships among all visents in a display, and ultimately a display's relationship to other displays within its environment. For the designer, attention to syntax directs the creation of a graphic element, the composition of elements within a display, the wholeness or unity of the display, and the coordination of specified relationships that unite displays in a system.

Semantics is concerned with the effectiveness of a display as a conveyor of meaning. Traditionally called *content* by artists, semantics is roughly equivalent to the sense and meaning of a piece. If syntax is the structuring of that which in the semiotic moment will act as sign, semantics is the connection between that sign and its referent. In design, semantics considers, for any given unit—that is, for feature, visent, or system—its relation to the referent. Syntax is manipulated in order to provide an appropriate semantic response.

Syntax and semantics depend on the interpretations made by the message's receivers; as a result, an audience's receptivity is a third consideration. Morris rather confusingly called this dimension "pragmatics," but in today's terms this approach is known variously as "consumer-driven," "human-centered," or "human factors." Human factors analysis looks at the user-interpreter, as individual and as group, to see how a sign is likely to be construed, the display navigated, and the message ultimately decided and used, in terms of individual and cultural variance. Psychology, demographics, and ethnography all come into play in human factors research—as well as ergonomics when the issues are strictly limited to how the body interacts with the sign.

A graphic designer is rarely an expert in assessing all the aspects of human factors, and we frequently team with other disciplines, especially when working on a large project with a diverse, perhaps international audience. In semiotic-driven design, the pragmatics dimension reminds us that the audience must be brought into the discussion, even if the expertise in studying the cultural and ethnographic details of that audience belongs to a marketing consultant, an anthropologist, or a demographer.

The data such research provides supplies important contextual background for the decisions regarding syntactics and semantics. In most cases, the designer is not working with a completely alien audience but with her familiar home base, the designer being a member of the general group that is the intended audience. In such cases, the human factor is often "assumed," if not completely taken for granted and overlooked. But an awareness of audience expectations is always necessary, and differences of perception arise even among members of a single cultural milieu due to differences of age, gender, race, language, or other cultural dimensions. When the message is intended for a mass audience or one that is international, advice and data from experts are especially vital.

Human factors: a supporting role for pragmatics

Having just stressed the importance of pragmatics and human factors, I now argue for narrowing the perspective, so that—for the purposes of semiotic research—human factors become a secondary concern (occupying a different rung on the theory ladder), while syntax and semantics are the focus.

This is so for three reasons. The first is that, as we have mentioned, other disciplines have already developed extensive methodologies, techniques of investigation, and a large body of research in human factors. In a sense, this portion of semiotics—at least what Morris thought of as a semiotic concern—has already been adopted, developed, or hybridized in various social sciences. What advertising campaign or product development does not make use of demographics? What marketing maneuver fails to account for segmentation, gender differences, and other subcultural nuances?

Secondly, at this point, with human factors well established, the development of a semiotic theory of design is better off developing the other two semiotic arenas—syntax and semantics—areas in which our understanding lags and which also happen to be the areas in which graphic designers spend most of their time. Designers put things together (syntax) to relay meaning (semantics) to a group of people (pragmatic human factors). We do the first two in service of the third. For any given project, let us be informed (by others) of the details of that third thing, hold the human factors as parameters and the goal to be reached by the project, then devote our attention to the first two as a way of satisfying that goal.

Lastly, it is often the case that the designer can anticipate and respond to many of the human factor variables simply because she is, after all, human. While human factors vary across cultural groups, there is also considerable stability within one's own culture, and although the apprehension and comprehension of any display by two different receivers can never be precisely the same, effective communication does not require complete unison. In design as in a game of horseshoes, close is often good enough, and the requisite precision is readily attainable when one works within a familiar social environment.

For these reasons, in the ensuing discussion human factors will not be emphasized as we develop a semiotic theory for design. Human factors will not be negated either (far from it), but the emphasis will be on developing concepts around syntax and semantics, understanding the interactions between form and content, a sign and its referent. We will essentially consider human factors as a control. We place our focus on what the graphic designer manipulates (syntax) to achieve an expected interpretation (semantics), assuming that the human factors research has been completed and the targeted audience is already understood. But even as I hold sociocultural human factors constant (most of the time) in order to explore the dynamics of syntax and semantics, it is important to remember the sleeping partner and realize that any interpretation will ultimately demand that we account for the receiver of the message, who is, after all, the one doing the interpreting.

Syntax

Syntax is the form of a visent and the arrangement of visents in a display or system. The word "form" is already in common use by designers, and it will undoubtedly continue to be used, but the word "syntax" is preferable for two reasons: it connotes not only shape but arrangement; and it suggests a linkage to semantics, which it indeed enjoys: every change in a display's syntax can be expected to create a change in the semantics of the display.

Design studio instruction, at least since the Bauhaus, has been essentially formalist. Two of the most successful texts on graphic design for studio are Richard Poulin's *The Language of Graphic Design*[1] and Alex White's *The Elements of Graphic Design*.[2] Figure 5.1 presents an outline of the topics covered in each work.

Between the two texts, there are a total of thirty-one topics. Twenty-three of these are concerned only with the formal structure of the display. Five of the topics deal with affective, emotional, feeling-inducing qualities that form elicits. Significantly, Poulin lists the remaining three topics as word, image, and abstraction. This is very close to the framework of the visual gamut that will be introduced in chapter 8.

The key point I wish to make now, however, is that with the exception of Poulin's suggestive trio of graphic strategies, all the topics have to do with aspects of form. Such formalist accounts of design are terribly constrained, for, at its heart, graphic design is never solely about form, but rather how form is used to *in*form or influence content. Form is an instrument for information.

When you think of form as a means to an end, a strategy and instrument, you are thinking of form as syntax. If form is an instrument, then thinking through the implications of syntax, we should be able to say something about the kinds of instrument available, relate them to the kinds of effects (interpretants) they excite, and raise questions about how and why those connections happen. Whatever is going on with such items as shape, texture, color, and hierarchy, the purpose has something to do with meaning. Meaning, taken in its broadest sense to include feeling and intimations, mood and power, information and aesthetics, memory and expectation, is the whole point of the enterprise. How strange, then, that our graphic design curricula and texts tiptoe around the subject of meaning (if they do not avoid it entirely) and stay in the calm formalist harbor.

One reason for this, I suspect, is that we think we know what something means without having to develop additional, refined powers of observation. It seems so natural that such-and-such display simply *has* this particular meaning, almost as if nothing were being constructed by us, the receiver, and as if nothing were shaped by the designer. It seems easier to revert to nourishing the powers of observing form alone, which art schools, from life drawing class onward, are famously able to accomplish.

But maybe this is not the only reason meaning gets slight treatment. There may be a more subtle and somewhat pernicious play here: it could be that by taking a formalist tack, the profession of graphic design can be shaped toward particular values, both aesthetic and social, without having to explicitly address the modeling. I am not claiming a conspiracy here; I merely say that if syntax always affects content, then pushing

	Poulin	White	
Point	■	■	
Line	■	■	
Plane		■	
Shape	■		
Form	■		
Light	■		Formal Attributes
Color	■		
Texture	■		
Space	■	■	
Symmetry	■	■	
Asymmetry	■	■	
Pattern	■		
Scale	■		
Contrast	■		Formal Comparatives
Hierarchy		■	
Gestalt		■	
Unity		■	
Figure/Ground	■		
Closure	■	■	Formal Wholeness
Continuation		■	
Direction/Movement	■	■	
Frame	■		
Grid	■	■	
Balance	■	■	
Proportion	■		
Emphasis		■	Form and Affect
Tone	■		
Tension	■		
Abstraction	■		
Image	■		Graphic Strategies
Typography	■		

Figure 5.1

Most works on graphic design take as their subject matter the formal aspects of the work. In this comparison of two popular current books, semantic principles are almost completely absent. Expression (affect of form) and the graphic strategies of abstraction, image, and typography are given some space in Poulin.

a particular syntactical family, a certain "look," a favored graphic style, has the effect of subtly influencing the messages of the culture, indeed *becoming* the visual culture. Such stylistic genres carry an ideological weight. This possibility, at least as a mechanism, will be explored further in our discussion of genres and styles in chapter 11.

Semantics

The word "form" is usually paired with "content," as indeed I did just now. While "form" and "syntax" are *almost* synonyms (syntax only adding the implication of compositional relations and the notion that form influences the interpretant), the word "content" seriously muddles several distinct categories of interpretation. If we use the word "content," it sounds as if there is an empty box and information stuff is just placed inside it, bundled together and ready to be pulled out, intact and entire. There are different shades of semantics, and therefore how semantics functions during interpretation is quite nuanced, something that the catchall "content" completely misses.

But where is meaning?
Before plunging into the world of semantics, we should mention "meaning," another problematic word. Although we used the word a few paragraphs ago, most contemporary semioticians avoid it.[3] While we all use it colloquially, on closer examination it can be a very confusing and ambiguous label. The reason is that "meaning" may be referring to the referent of the sign—the thing the sign stands for—or it may be referring to the interpretant, an *understanding* that someone has about what a sign stands for.

Think of the triadic relation of sign/referent/interpretant as a physical structure, something like a triangular leaf (figure 5.2). When a visent acts as a sign, it bends the referent and interpretant toward each other. It is this coming together of the referent and interpretant that is the meaning of the sign: *an approach* of the referent and interpretant. The character of this approach, this proximal engagement, through the agency of the sign will be discussed below when we look at specificity.

Terms such as "content" and "meaning" are best tabled for the most part, because while they seem explicit, they hide more than they reveal. If I use the word "meaning" it will be as a familiar gesture toward semantics, content in general, indicating broadly and in tandem the referential and interpretative aspects of the semiotic moment. But the great advantage of a semiotic system such as the one presented here is that the preferred terms are used in a much more precise way, which can illuminate a

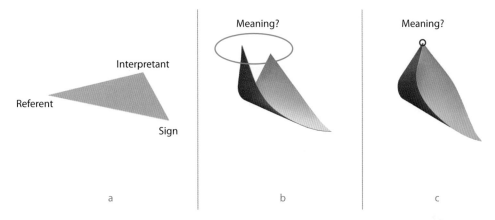

Figure 5.2
If we think of the triadic relation of sign, referent, and interpretant as a flexible leaf of paper, a sign's work can be thought of as an attempt to bend the interpretant toward the referent. One hopes that the understanding approaches the referent. Complete contact, however, is regrettably impossible to achieve. There is always a gap in certainty.

communication event in finer detail. With that in mind, we continue now to look at the semantic side, the "bending of the leaf" between the referent and interpretant.

Affective and conceptual semantic registers
There are only four ways we can have an effect on a receiver, four ways we can "bend the leaf." They are *presence, expression, denotation,* and *connotation.* The first two are affective registers (or means), the latter two are conceptual.

The affective register has to do with feeling and emotional qualities, the conceptual with the cognitive and intellectual aspects. The affective register is divided into presence and expression. Compared with the cognitive register, both presence and expression are more instinctive, which is to say, less influenced by culture and previous conscious personal experiences or beliefs, operating from the parts of the brain that deal with reflexes, motor responses, fight or flight, and universal attraction or revulsion responses. Of the two, presence is particularly instinctive. While presence sits just inside the liminal level of attention, expression includes affective sensibilities that engender deeper investment, leading ultimately to conscious reflection, at which point affective semantics is handed off to the conceptual semantic register, where the character of the interpretant, now fully conceptual and cognitive, is dependent on prior knowledge and heavily marked by its degree of specificity. We'll look at each of these grades in turn.

Presence

Presence is the ability of a visent to be prominent enough in its environment to become an object of active attention. Usually presence is considered a positive attribute that a designer will strive to engender. After all, a display that lacks presence risks being overlooked completely. Presence is the power of a display to attract the eye, irrespective of its aesthetics, subject matter, or conceptual content. Stripped of whatever conceptual content the display may have, presence is strictly a result of the display's syntactical features standing out against the background on which it is seen. Presence is the visent's ability to command initial attention. As a semantic element, presence is the most fundamental kind of interpretation, the most limited effect on a mind, barely an interpretation at all—the mere coming to awareness of a subject of vision. A display with great presence (advertising people like to call it "impact") has the ability to command the room, step forward in a world of competing visents calling for your eyes.

We come now to a predicament that is endemic in semiotics and every other discipline that attempts to dissect the world into parts: how fine a slice to make in the degree of presence? One could devise a spectrum with five, ten, or a hundred gradations of presence, a fader switch with which to classify a display's presence in a given environmental situation. For ease of use and because there is no way to measure the degree of presence beyond a few steps, we can imagine presence as a simple ranking with two steps, high or low. High presence is a display that is difficult to overlook and that stands out in a crowd; low presence is a display that tends to recede, to hide in plain sight.

How to hide a battleship
We generally want to design a display so that it will have high presence.[4] But in order to get a sense of how to do that, we can look at the opposite situation, at techniques to hide an object.

How to do you hide something that is very large and cannot be covered up? It will be in plain sight, and it will be completely exposed to vision. That was the problem faced by early twentieth-century naval officers as their battleships prepared to go to sea in World War I. It's also a problem faced by many animals in nature. Turns out, there are two main strategies: either blend it into the background, or fragment the object's surface so that the eye cannot register it as a single whole entity.[5] These two techniques specifically deny presence; inverted, they point toward ways to highlight presence. We will take a brief look at how to hide a display in order to learn how to better expose it; see how to fragment a display in order to learn how better to unify it.

Blending in and standing out

In order to see something, you have to be able to distinguish it from a background. This figure/ground discrimination is a basic mechanism of perception. Battleships were painted an ocean gray.[6] Countershading is added to the disruption to thwart the effect of seeing volumetric shadows against a background.[7] In each technique, the decisive factor in hiding a display is to diminish as much as possible its edges and its surface contrast with other visents in its immediate environment.

So in order to expose a display and provide it with a high degree of presence, prominent surface and edge contrast with its environmental background are essential. A visent cannot be seen without boundary edges marking it off from all that is not it; the more distinct the boundary edge, the more presence a display has. Indeed, a strong contrastive boundary edge is often what is meant by the word "graphic." An edge is most prominent when it is a disruption from one surface to another, a massive surface ending abruptly.

Given prominent boundaries, how do you make a display striking? It's often accomplished by strategies such as making it brighter, bigger, or closer, but the key is to make the display appear, at a glance, even out of the corner of the eye, *different*. Attention is drawn to anything that is out of the ordinary. This sort of looking is not a conscious decision but a built-in genetic survival practice. Our sensory system is geared to be on the lookout for anything that changes or disrupts the steady flow of expected experience. As a result, something that is not like anything else in the visual environment, that disrupts the flow, attracts a "check-that-out" gaze.

To acquire maximum presence for a visual display, create a distinctly bounded unified figure against a contrastive background. Whether the display can *hold* the gaze is a question for the higher registers of semantics; presence is achieved by simply getting an eyeball *to* the display. Displays that have high presence are attended to; displays with low presence are barely seen at all and easily dismissed.

Fragmenting and unifying

Back to battleships. As it turns out, it is very difficult to find one color that approximates all the shades of sea and sky against which a huge battleship is likely to be seen. But there is another way to mess with boundaries: instead of fading the edge into the background, one can create more distinct edges within the perimeter of the object, fragment it, to produce the perception of dozens of smaller-scale edges. This effect can be heightened by making the fragmenting shapes random and unpatterned in arrangement. The effect of this is to completely mask the wholeness of the display by causing the perceptual apparatus to search among smaller clusters of coherence, clusters that will inevitably include details of waves and sky that are "out of bounds" of the battle-ship's contours. This is the camouflage technique known as "dazzle," and it works extremely well in all kinds of lighting conditions.

To create a prominent presence, then, one can do the opposite: instead of frag-menting a display, make it whole by making a coherent harmonious surface. When that happens, the display has a quality that has long been recognized as an important aesthetic value: *unity*. Unity presents the eye with subparts that complement each other, leading to the edges of the whole, where there is great contrast with the background.

But notice that in hiding or exposing, part of the equation necessarily involves thinking about a background environment. Paradoxically, the background environ-ment is not itself a part of the display. So, requiring a framing of the semiotic moment to include the immediate contextual environment in which the display will appear, presence is never only about the display itself. For that reason, presence only margin-ally qualifies as a semantic variable *of* a display, being something of a fundamental a priori semantic requirement *for* the display; in any event, it certainly lacks the nuance of expression, denotation, and connotation. Presence is the gatekeeper: without it nothing further can happen semiotically with the display.

From battleships to tea and baseball bats
These principles can be used to ensure that products stand out in the environment in which they operate. In figure 5.3, the various packages of tea must compete with a very complex visual context. The central problem is how to project one's own product against a backdrop of competing products that have the same mission. In a large gro-cery store, the lighting is usually dreadful (both in color balance and in intensity). The size of the packages is quite small. In figure 5.3a, the price tags show up better than the packages themselves (rhythm, hue, saturation of color), while the most visible thing in the picture is the very black (unified) hole where there is no packaging at all! Attempts

Figure 5.3
Commercial products need to stand out against their backgrounds. When they face very competi-tive visual environments, this can be difficult. In (a), the hole where there is an absence of product is more prominent than the packages themselves. In (b) a similar problem was studied with regard to aluminum baseball bats. The question concerned how many individual clusters of information a bat barrel should contain if it wants to stand out in the field of play. The study showed that the more visually fragmented the barrel becomes, the more recessive and likely to blend in to the crowd. Except for the gray bat, the solid colors were far more successful in having a high level of presence.

a

b

by some brands to show details and create a distinct visual environment merely fragment the surface further. The problem is no doubt recognized by the maker, and an attempt is made to run a "ribbon" element across the packages so that the alignment of the ribbon from one package to the next has an effect of making a larger whole, but this move is thwarted by the multicolored backgrounds.

Figure 5.3b shows an experiment conducted for a manufacturer of aluminum baseball and softball bats. How to help their product show up in use on television or in live collegiate games? By taking photographs of crowds and distorting them as a background texture, bat silhouettes were tested in different colors and patterns. The solid colors showed up the best (except gray). The experiment suggested that the manufacturer should try to limit the amount of graphic information on the barrel of a bat and paint it a uniform color. The more messages employed, the greater the barrel fragmentation. Edges soon become broken into small parts, and dazzle causes the bat barrel to recede even when the individual colors of the messages are bright.

These are the kinds of research that must be done when high presence is important. The display can never be considered in isolation of its environment. Whenever possible, the actual surround must be carefully studied. Anything that opposes the surrounding environment and creates a sense of unitary wholeness will be able to attract the eye. But what happens with the visent's syntax within its boundary edges (as opposed to between its boundary and its environment) will be due to the expression of the display.

Expression

Expression is emotion due to form. Expression is the sum of the feelings, tonalities, and sensibilities that are due to a display's syntax—the powerful jolt of the dramatic graphic form, the whisper of a soft palette of colors, the understated elegance of a page of typography.

Expression has two aspects: quality and degree. Quality is the particular flavor of emotional feeling, such as "elegant," "happy," or "calm,"[8] while degree is the amount of feeling, the distance from an imagined mundane and emotionally neutral zero point. In figure 5.4, displays (a) and (c) both give a high degree of expression despite having quite different flavors to the feelings they elicit. The first display appears sedate, while the third composition is frenetic. The second display is at the zero point: quite devoid of expressive influence.

Usually, a goal of a design project is to provide a highly expressive experience, and we try to design a display that is not only highly expressive in degree but also has just the right quality of feeling.

a   b   c

Figure 5.4

Expression is the affective influence of a visent based on its form. Display (b) has little expression, while (a) and (c)—qualitatively very different—are each much more expressive than (b).

Both presence and expression have to do with interpretant effects due to the form of a display. The difference between presence and expression is that presence requires a comparison to a display's physical environment, while expression is internal to the form of the display itself and its resonance within a cultural system. Presence is physically dependent on environment while largely culturally independent, while expression is independent of physical environment and somewhat culturally dependent.

The conceptual semantic register

Whereas the affective semantic register is primarily concerned with the emotional impression of the form of a display, the conceptual semantic register brings us to those aspects of meaning that have to do with cognitive and intellectual attributes. Presence and expression are often difficult to put into words, while the conceptual register—especially denotation—is more readily translated into language. The semantic register is characterized by an inherently conceptual factor: specificity.

Specificity

In the metaphor of the leaf mentioned earlier, the sign has the agency to bend or inflect referent and interpretant toward each other. The degree of proximity of the corners of the leaf is known as the degree of specificity.

In actual experience, there is no objective independent observer watching the process to verify that the contact has been made. We can never step outside semiosis, we can never be sure that the kiss is perfect. So while we can imagine the ideal communication event in which the referent and the interpretant come together and meaning is perfectly revealed, we can never be assured of the contact. What you are trying to say and what is understood are never completely identical.[9] Meaning is a *bending toward*, but certain contact is always withheld; referent and the interpretant are always separated by the gap of uncertainty, a blurry indeterminacy.

The corners of the meaning leaf can never touch and perfectly match because ultimately all interpretation is fallible: "fallibilism is the doctrine that our knowledge is never absolute but always swims, as it were, in a continuum of uncertainty and of indeterminacy."[10] No one ever has an understanding that is unambiguously certain; even if one feels certain, meaning is never absolute.[11]

We always have to act on partial information, on the best understanding we can construe in a given situation. Instead of untarnished access to pure Truth, we derive or *construct* a meaning. What we do have is belief, conclusions, confidence that an interpretant is persuasive *enough* to direct our actions accordingly. Over time, we might move closer to what we might all agree is the truth, but it would require an infinite amount of time—literally an eternity—to get there. When it comes to signs bringing referents and interpretants into contact, absolute specificity is an ideal, and unreachable, limit.

In order to tease out the possibilities and ramifications of specificity, we need to turn from the leaf metaphor and concentrate on the referent/interpretant gap. We begin by plotting the unreachably perfect referent/interpretant contact (the complete, fulfilled, "factual," specific union of referent and interpretant) as a point standing at a hypothetical limit (figure 5.5),[12] a single vibrantly infallible point at which the interpretant and the referent are identical. Call this point the *absolutely specified*.[13] At absolute specification, there can only be a single reading of a display, only a single possible understanding of the sign, and that reading is absolutely true.[14]

Now entertain the opposite idea: a state of complete befuddlement, in which there is no emergent interpretation coming through the fog of uncertainty, a place where the interpretant is completely and utterly *un*specific and infinitely hazy. This is a place of zero belief and infinite doubt, where interpretation is so nebulous that everything is totally undecided, fragmented, incomplete, slippery, open, an indeterminacy beyond which nothing could ever be more vague. One might think of this as a place where there is no actual interpretation at all or, ironically, a region where, since no referent is foregrounded, an infinite number of referents is equally possible for an interpretant. This is an inchoate land where sense collapses and triadic mediation reduces to brute dyadic relations, where signification fails and mind falters. This liminal place of unbroken ambiguous fog is the *threshold of semiosis*.

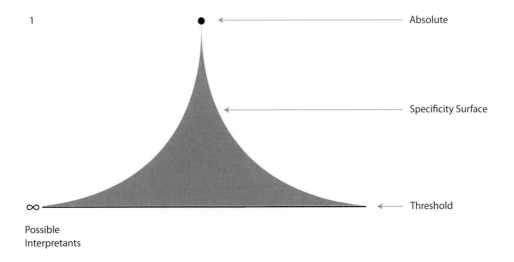

Absolute

Specificity Surface

∞

Threshold

Possible
Interpretants

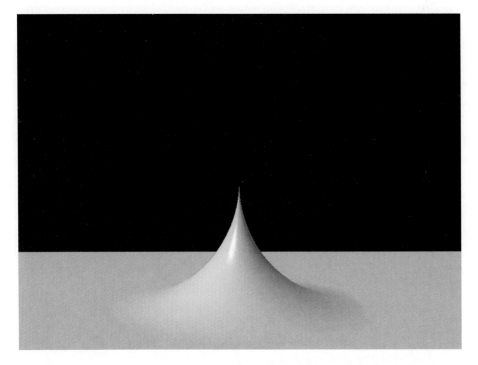

Figure 5.5

The specificity surface. Between two ideal and unreachable endpoints—one representing absolute specificity and infallible interpretation, the other complete uncertainty and vagueness—there exists a region of potential specificity. This "specificity surface" maps how an interpretant will regard a message in terms of its definiteness or clarity. More definite interpretations narrow toward the absolute certainty, while obscure interpretations are so hazy they do not resolve into any particular interpretant (which is equivalent to saying the interpretant could be anything, almost an infinity of possibilities). The bottom diagram shows how this situation would appear as a three-dimensional surface.

Interpretants near the absolute give us the impression of being clear and distinct understandings, separate from other meanings, definite. As we slide down the surface into greater *un*specificity, we entertain multiple competing interpretations; approaching the threshold of semiosis we sense an amorphous, hazy "smearing" of meanings. It is as if, near the peak, the specific interpretants possess a crystalline, particulate individuality, whereas toward semiosis's threshold, the unspecific relata melt together, blend into a mash of vagueness.

The space between these two limits delineates a *specificity surface*, the range of specificity of the interpretant, the "bend zone" of the leaf, mapping where the fully triadic mediational dance of signification occurs, a dance patterned by, inflected with, varying degrees of certainty and specificity for any given receiver in any given semiotic moment. For any moment, an interpretant's position with respect to the referent will fall somewhere along this specificity surface. You might feel so confident in your interpretation, the meaning so definite, that you would place your highly specific understanding (almost) at the absolute peak. On the other hand, the meaning of something could be so vague that you are not even sure that you are looking at something that *has* meaning, in which case such a vague interpretation would be placed near the threshold horizon.

Specificity is a designer's primary consideration when planning a display that must be clear and distinct to the public, such as an airport directional for the baggage claim area (figure 5.6). It is equally important to be aware of specificity in situations where it is desirable that the receiver be left with some ambiguity between two or more possible meanings. What is critical is that the location of an interpretant along this specificity surface be carefully accounted for in the process of designing. Some designers, such as Tom Geismar, are known for tending to work the highly specific region of the surface, while others, such as David Carson, are known for preferring the radically polysemous area closer to the threshold. All designers, however, must have the ability to move up

Figure 5.6
Some applications, such as airport wayfinding, require solutions that strive for utmost clarity and specificity.

and down this continuum as required. And in every design project, some thought must be given to how specific a display needs to be.

Denotation

Highly specific, direct and immediate meanings, in which there seems little doubt in the interpretant with regard to the referent, are *denotative*. Denotations are stable, seemingly obvious, and convergent.

Denotations are said to be stable because no matter how many times they are seen, they will tend to produce the same interpretations. A house number sign will tend to have the same denotative, highly specific meaning whether you look at it this year, next year, or forty years from now.[15] By contrast, in the case of a display that is vague, one's interpretation is uncertain. Precisely because it is vague, indistinct, "nothing in particular," it has the potential to be interpreted, if interpreted at all, in numerous ways. An active mind begins to offer various associative guesses and hypothesized or hinted connections between the sign and the referent. These interpretations tend to be fugitive. Although you may think the ink blot looks like a dragon and that interpretation will tend to strengthen and in time become habit, if someone shows you how it is more like a vase of flowers, your interpretation can change and you will find yourself suddenly seeing the flowers.

However, a display that is highly denotative, because of its high degree of specificity, is not only stable but is interpreted as immediately obvious. We think of it as unremarkable. Even as we may logically concede that our understanding cannot be infallible, we nevertheless *feel* we are 100% spot on. In a highly denotative situation, we wonder how anyone could possibly conclude anything other than what we conclude. High specificity settles the internal debate about what the sign is representing: our sense is that *we know what it means*, $x = y$. We have full conviction, a belief we are prepared to act on, and it appears entirely obvious that everyone should be in agreement on the matter.

Notice there is an inverse relation here regarding interpretant specificity and range of referents: you can have a very high number of potential referents (low specificity) and be really unsure of any of them, or you can be quite certain about single one and lose the abundance of other denotative possibilities.

Convergence

This sense of immediate obviousness implies that as you work your way up the specificity incline, closer to the absolute, and approach the strong conviction of clarity in the understanding a sign/referent, the interpretant essentially closes off debate. You have the sudden strong sense of knowing. This tendency toward knowing is *convergence*. The desire to settle on a single meaning is so great, it is almost as if the sign has a magnetic force attached to it which begins to focus your interpretive energies toward a specific rendering. Sometimes convergence is due to arriving at a "story" that seems to make the best sense, a unified whole, out of multiple alternative loose ends. At other times, convergence is simply a matter of overcoming physical or sensory parameters and constraints, in which case the specificity will seem to snap suddenly from vagueness to a single interpretant.

To experience this leap to convergence, try this simple experiment with a design partner. The goal is to design a standard-sized automobile license plate (US standard is 6 by 12 inches, European standard is 520 by 110 millimeters) that can be read from about 150 feet (figure 5.7). Your partner selects a random set of seven letters and

Figure 5.7
Observing a license plate with random letters and numbers from a distance is a good test of the collapse toward felt certainty. Like an eye chart, the license plate will provide no denotation at a great distance, then as one approaches, it will snap to clarity and provide complete confidence in one's reading.

numbers and designs a plate, and you do the same. The license plates you design will have no information on them other than the number/letter combination. You can use any color for the numbers and letters and any color for the background of the plate. Start with your friend's plate. You stand about 75 yards away as your friend mounts the mocked-up license plate over the license plate of a car in a parking lot. Once ready, you begin taking slow steps toward it. For several steps, perhaps twenty yards, you will not be able to distinguish the characters. Then, suddenly, usually within a single pace, you will be able to read all the characters. Occasionally there may be one or two recalcitrant ones and you briefly debate whether you are seeing a 3 or an 8. But one more step and they are all very clear. Try this again using your plate design and your friend as the pacer. Then each of you repeat the exercise, pacing toward your own plates. Usually you will be able to read your design one or two paces further back than your friend can read yours (and vice versa).

The key here is to notice the seeming abruptness by which the numbers become legible. The fact is, they hardly seem to *become* at all: they simply are not legible, and then in one more pace they *are* legible.

What is happening? You are constantly trying to match the plate's figures, which start out very blurry and unresolved, with known numbers and letters. At some point, the acuity of vision is sufficient to resolve the edges of the visents (each character) and to differentiate them from each other. At that point you are able to read, and the entire set becomes very specific. You do not experience this as a gradual march upward toward absolute specificity. You experience it as complete vagueness and then, in a flash, complete certainty (figure 5.8).

You strive to interpret, and then all at once you do. But in your brain, the process is continuing all along, and it is only when the letters and numbers reach a high degree of probability that your conceptual mind, your cognitive executive brain, is given the answer and you become aware of the correct reading. The brain rarely permits the hazy unspecific stuff to filter through to awareness. As very mortal animals, we are too busy surviving to be consciously burdened with the vague; we attend to vague things only to discern their relevance to our lives. If something is judged relevant, we do the further work of interpreting it.

This biological advantage of clarity produces a kind of inward flow or bias toward specificity and away from ambiguity, which causes the leap toward the denotative interpretant.

Another everyday example of this is our tendency to see representations in ink blots or in natural objects like clouds, rocks, or walls. Leonardo da Vinci remarked on this in one of his notebooks: "If you look at walls that are stained or made of different kinds of stones … you can think you see in them certain picturesque views of mountains,

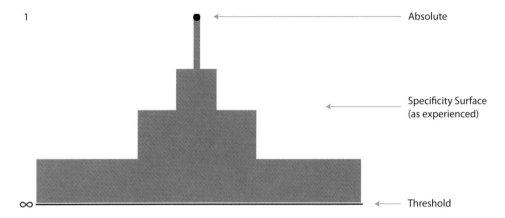

Figure 5.8
The specificity surface shown in figure 5.5 is an idealized situation, as if viewed from a third party's perspective. As the license plate test reveals, in practice the even slopes of the specificity
surface feel more like a ziggurat of only a few terraces. We think we are completely sure of an
interpretation when we could well be mistaken, and we often take complex messages to be completely ambiguous when certain interpretations become favorable upon closer inspection.

rivers, rocks, trees, plains, broad valleys, and hills of different shapes."[16] We always
try to make sense of the world. Meaning making is a survival practice—ambiguity is
usually something we strive to overcome.

Although a highly denotative interpretant allows quicker action and gives the
impression of a more settled and definite meaning, this is not to say that high
denotation is always to be desired. A certain degree of mysterious ambiguity can be
a means to slow the viewer, attract attention, create involvement. Roland Barthes
makes a distinction between highly denotative displays, which he calls "works," and
more open interpretive situations, which he calls "texts."[17] The closed, conventionally
guided interpretation of the highly denotative "work" is transparent to the receiver,
quickly processed, often barely regarded consciously. By contrast, confronting enigmatic "texts," the receiver plays a more active role in the process of interpretation.
"Texts" move the emphasis from the author to the active reader/viewer—a hallmark of
postmodernism.

A parallel theme was investigated by Katherine McCoy in the 1980s in her distinction between reading and looking.[18] The largely unconscious process of reading is
governed by long-standing conventional norms, while the process of looking requires
an active search for clues in order to interpret what at first seems highly ambiguous.

Encouraging the active involvement of the viewer, by purposefully ambiguating a display, has been a major tactic in design for a generation.

Connotation

A display, even if it produces a highly denotative interpretant, may also suggest, hint at, or imply other related referents. Connotations rely on *associative* connections; they are less specific, certainly less specified by a specific code or program, more dependent upon the life experiences and memories of the individual perceiver. As a result, connotations are less stable, more personally variable and divergent, than denotations. In figure 5.9, the specificity surface has been expanded into an elaborate shell shape, with the central denotative peak now surrounded by all the possible associations (each potentially falling somewhere along a specific/vague continuum). This specificity shell is a 3D map of the entire spectrum of conceptual semantic events that could be triggered in an experience of a display.

The word "connotation" derives from the Latin *connotare*, meaning to "mark in addition to or along with." To distinguish connotations from denotations, the "in addition to" and the "along with" are key. Connotations seem to arise from the happenstance of time and place, even the vagaries of personal life experience, whereas denotations seem obvious and "true" for everyone—at least those who share a language or general culture. Consider a picture of a political figure. Political figures, for good or ill, become known for their actions in the world. For a portrait of Joseph Stalin, the portrait "means Stalin" as its denotation. That the same portrait "means genocidal dictator" is a connotation. The nature of connotations means that for every denotation there can be multiple connotations, each of greater or lesser specificity, which is what is being indicated in the specificity shell shown in figure 5.9.

Divergence
Denotations converge toward clarity and the absolute, but connotations are *divergent*. Whereas a strong denotation will tend to push away and exclude competing denotations, connotations are much more cooperative, and you can entertain many of them simultaneously from various arenas of experience.

We see this with typefaces (figure 5.10). The word "hate" set in Times Roman (a typeface that has become generic) denotes a strong feeling of revulsion. The same word, set in the typeface Bickham Script, still denotes a strong feeling of revulsion, but now, because of the "full dress" of the script typeface, this is suddenly ironic. The form of the script suggests tenderness and beauty, qualities that are opposites of hatred. As the

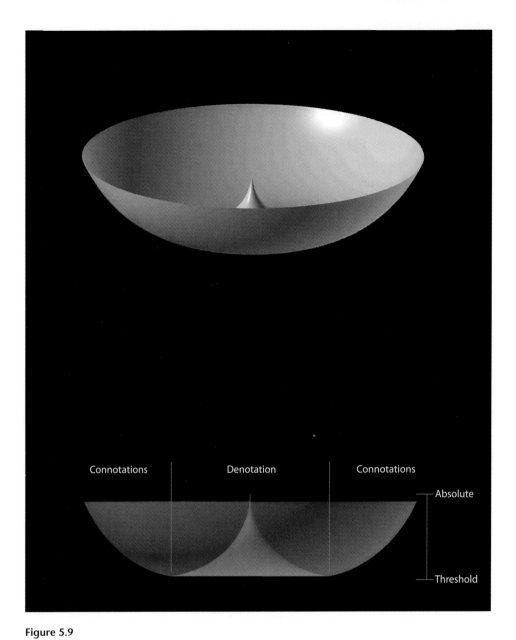

Figure 5.9

Specificity surface with connotations (specificity shell). Envisioning the full range of denotations and connotations in terms of specificity, these diagrams show how the entire surface appears as a set of possibilities. For every denotation, converging toward the peak of the absolute, there are various connotations, each with its own degree of specificity. An interpretant that is completely vague falls at the base of the bowl, being neither a denotation nor a connotation. Very specific interpretants, whether denotative or connotative, rise toward the top. It's unlikely that a connotation is ever as specific as a clear denotation. In working on a design problem, one must take into consideration the likely connotations that will be excited by the solution.

a   b   c

Figure 5.10
The connotations of cultural associations of the love letter and the destruction of distressed typography interact with the verbal denotation of the word in these examples. The irony of (b) and (c) is completely due to the use of letterforms that have their own cultural associations. The connotations of the love letter (b) and violence (c) almost negate the denotative verbal message which remains unchanged from (a).

viewer begins to think of the contrast between these interactions, more memories and associations arise. The list of connotations expands. If denotation were the only content factor in typography, there would be no need to have more than one, supremely legible, typeface. That there are now tens of thousands of typeface designs is evidence that the factor being manipulated in almost all typeface design is not the denotation of the word; it is the connotation of the form of the word.

Whereas denotations are usually culturally determined, coded, with tight sign/referent bonds, connotations can be quite idiosyncratic, personal, and difficult to predict. I was once part of a team that designed a corporate identity program for a family-owned auto-servicing business. The company was having difficulty being visible in the marketplace, and our design research pointed to a solution that was minimal, bold, and (at the time) distinctive: a white "M" in a red diamond (figure 5.11). The presentation of this proposed logo design was going fine until the youngest member of the family—a twenty-something Texan the matriarch introduced as "Baby Bill"—arrived (late) at the meeting, saw the proposed logo, and pronounced, "Them's the Devil's horns" to a stunned room. The red diamond also reminded him of the deadly sin of gambling (playing cards), and this was confirmed for him by a red arrow that unmistakably pointed the way to Hell. There was no recovery: we packed up our materials and went back to the office to attempt to revise the mark. These were all conceptual connotations for Baby Bill, whose particular life experiences no doubt paved the way for his impressions. The point of this story is that it doesn't matter how or why someone becomes primed for associative meanings or whether the connotations are logical or not. If a receiver interprets a display and has certain connotations, the connotations are real. There are no false connotations.

Figure 5.11
An "M" by any other name … is this simply a highly recognizable letter M in a diamond, or is it a sly sign of evil?

Characterizations by denotative and connotative emphasis

Figure 5.12 shows a 3D model of the specificity shell and, below that, a variety of possible denotation-connotation combinations. If a given display can elicit both denotations and connotations, and if these can vary with respect to their specificity, then a very large number of situations can be expected. In (a) there is a denotation that is quite specific. It is positioned high up the peak of the denotative surface, mustered in a tight disk near the absolute. The interpretant in (b) on the other hand illustrates a weak, unspecific denotation, spread out and dissipated, just barely above the threshold of semiosis. This represents a very vague understanding of a display. With (c), the display has a weak denotation but a very strong connotation, which is signified by the tight bright highlight near the raised rim of the connotative shell. But it is also possible that a display can produce multiple connotations, which are shown in (d), (e), and (f). In (d) a strong denotation is accompanied by two strong connotations. Their positions represent them to be orthogonal in that they do not have any relationship between them. Another orthogonal dual connotation shows up in (e), this time with a weak denotation and one connotation substantially stronger than the other. Finally, in (f) a strong denotation has two agonistic weak connotations. I say agonistic because, being 180 degrees apart, they represent opposite or conflictive readings.

With so many possibilities already becoming evident, and realizing that one could easily decide to look at many degrees of specificity, we have to ask what level of fineness of detail is most useful to our purposes as analysts of graphic design displays—and as creators of them. I'm going to assume that having just two levels—strong and weak—will be sufficiently precise for our purposes; and if, among a host of connotations, just one of them is strong, then I will include that display in the category of displays with strong connotations. It should be noted that this move, made for the purposes of simplicity, truncates what could be a more finely articulated rendering that may prove important in some situations, so it is necessary to keep the possibility of a more detailed map in view, even as we move to elaborate the implications of this simpler, bifactor model.

We are now ready to begin a categorization of display types based on their semantic properties. In doing so, realize that the breakdown and the taxonomy that is developed do not address the individual content of the displays, but rather attempt to classify *kinds* of display strategies, regardless of their specific message content.

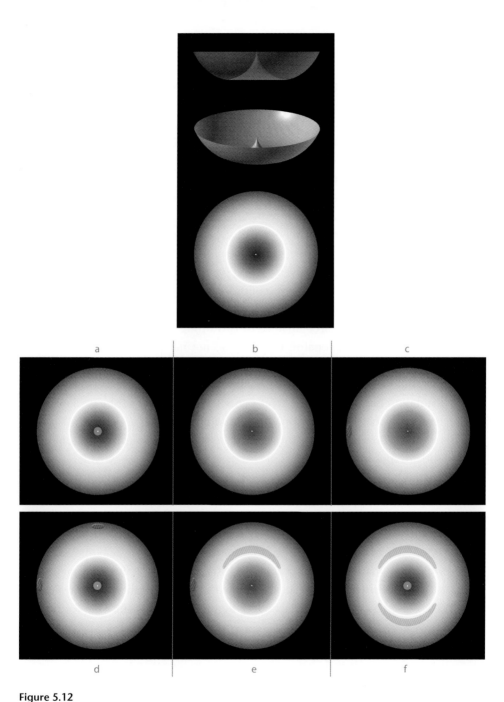

Figure 5.12
The specificity shell (from figure 5.9) can be rotated to show a view straight down from the top. From this perspective it is possible to map the impressions of a denotation and the connotations that might be present. (a) Highly specific denotation; (b) Vague denotation; (c) Vague denotation with highly specific connotation; (d) Highly specific denotation with two highly specific connotations; (e) Vague denotation with two connotations (one vividly specific, one vague); (f) Highly specific denotation with two vague connotations.

Part III Conceptual Tools

6 Semantic Profiles and Display-Assertion Strategies

In the preceding chapter, we saw how a display has the semiotic functions of syntax and semantics. We also divided semantics into two registers, the affective register of presence and expression, and the conceptual register of denotation and connotation. In this chapter, we take a closer look at the semantic register and show that it can be opened up to reveal sixteen semantic profiles. We conclude by extending the discussion from displays to assertions and noting additional strategies in which display and assertion characteristics interchange.

Valency

In the last chapter, we saw that a denotation or a connotation can range from very specific to very vague. A denotation or connotation that is highly specific has a kind of power that it exerts; it has a special kind of influence or force on the receiver. Consider an image that is denotatively weak. You cannot make the image out. The ambiguous image may excite curiosity, which is also a kind of power, but it has not (yet) proved to be informative. As we saw in the license plate exercise, with further scrutiny an ambiguous image often becomes highly specific. When it does, that high degree of felt certainty causes the viewer to reach a conclusion, to form a belief, to be ready to act on the basis of the information it provides.

Valency is the degree of forcefulness with which a display exhibits each of these semantic functions. A display with high valency in presence has more ability to gain attention than one with low presence. Highly expressive displays strongly engage the feelings, highly denotative displays have very specific referents, and highly connotative displays can be expected to evoke strong associations.[1]

A two-step scale

When we looked at the specificity surface shells (figure 5.12) we saw that the degrees of relative specificty are potentially infinite. If one had the right software, and the ability to identify valencies to a high degree of precision, one could construct finely grained ten-degree or twenty-degree scales. But even were it possible to be fairly confident of giving a display the "correct" placement on such finely nuanced scales, the sheer number of semantic types that would be generated by such a precise instrument would soon prove overwhelming (as long as they are used by human designers). Our purpose here is to construct a system of profiles that, while capable of discriminating various semantic situations, is still simple and practical to use. For that reason, in the following discussion we will use a simple two-step scale for valency. In assessing presence, expression, denotation, and connotation we will make a determination that the attribute is either powerful or weak, high-valent or low-valent. Even this rudimentary device provides us with sixty-four kinds of semantic interactions.[2]

Affective register types

The affective semantic register accounts for the effects of a sign when those effects are due to the syntax—the composition and graphic form—of the display.[3] The affective register does not include conceptual components such as subject matter, or higher-level meanings such as statements, assertions, or any kind of content other than the mere instantaneous influence of the visent as visual object.

Accordingly, we call displays that are high in presence *projective* displays; those low in presence are *recessive* displays. With respect to expression, displays that evoke strong feeling through their form, and therefore have a high valency in expression, we describe as *soulful*; or, if they do not evoke very much feeling they are *apathetic*. Since a display can be either projective or recessive in its presence, and either soulful or apathetic in its expression, we have four classes of affective displays: Projective Soulfuls, Projective Apathetics, Recessive Soulfuls, and Recessive Apathetics (figure 6.1).

A Projective Soulful display contrasts sufficiently with its environment that it claims our attention, and then delivers a highly expressive sensibility when we behold it. A Projective Apathetic display is just as effective at attracting the eye, but seems quite devoid of feeling or sensitivity when we attend to it. Recessive displays, whether Soulful or Apathetic, struggle to gain even a glance, although once noticed, a Recessive Soulful rewards with strong feeling whatever gaze it receives. We see Recessive Soulful designs in situations such as elegant book typography (figure 6.2), where the viewer is coming to the display rather than the display needing to reach out to the viewer, as might be the case in advertising. The Recessive Apathetic type, easy to overlook and

The Four Affective Register Types

Presence	Expression		
●	●	Projective	Soulful
●	·	Projective	Apathetic
·	●	Recessive	Soulful
·	·	Recessive	Apathetic

● High Valency
· Low Valency

Figure 6.1
If their valencies are limited to high and low, presence and expression can interact in four ways.

also not very interesting once seen, is perhaps best reserved for such uses as ingredients labels, insurance policies, instruction manuals, and other "small print" applications. The Recessive Apathetic is often the realm of the mundane, the unplanned, where design could simply be dispensed with. I wonder if even a legal brief shouldn't be typographically expressive of dignity, or a contract redolent of care in its graphic crafting. However, there are some valid occasions in which a simple bit of information needs to be conveyed in an understated way, and this is the proper place for a Recessive Apathetic solution. So although many Recessive Apathetics may happen to be syntactically banal, belonging to the category should not, in itself, be taken as a fault. Analysis must always relate the category or class to purpose; only then can a judgment be made with respect to appropriateness.

Use these affective register types when discussing the "feel" of a design. When planning or analyzing the manner in which a display reveals its content, we must turn to the more complex semantic profiles found in the conceptual register.

Conceptual register types
Whereas the affective register limits inquiry to the sense affects of the form of the display, at the level of the conceptual register the full contents of the work are opened to interpretation. Just as we did with the affective register, we will be judging the two attributes of the conceptual register (denotation and connotation) by whether they have high or low valencies. A highly valent denotation will be very specific and vivid,

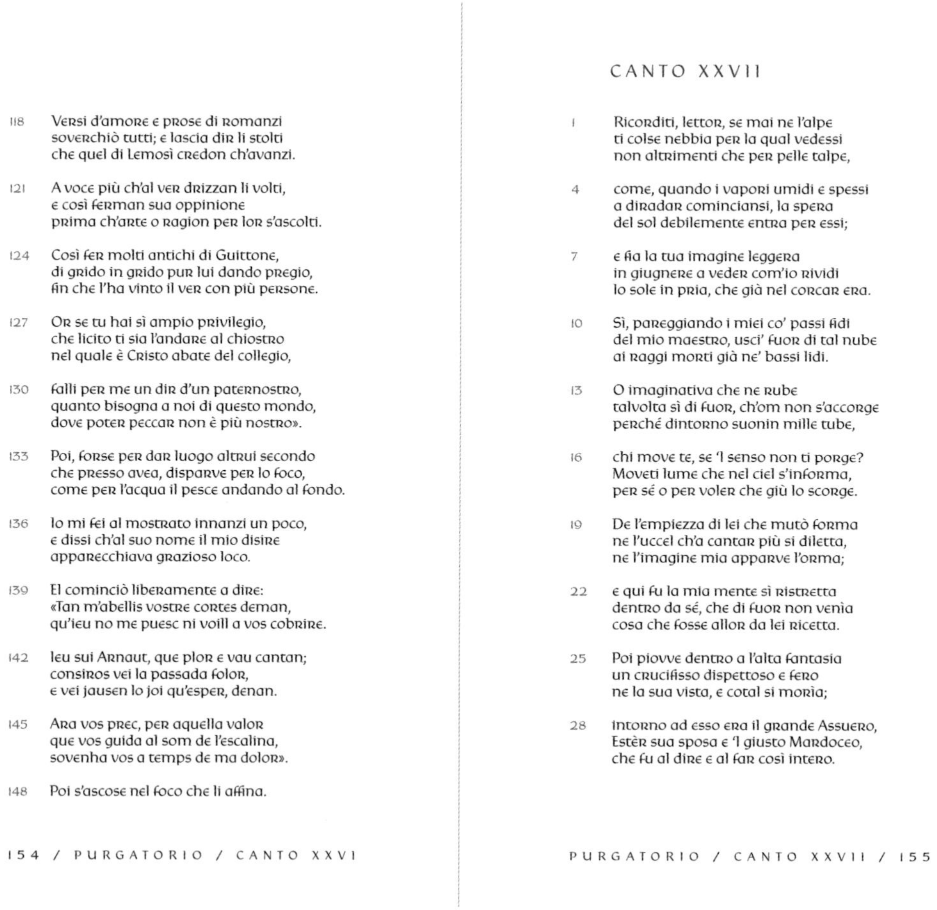

118   Versi d'amore e prose di romanzi
       soverchiò tutti; e lascia dir li stolti
       che quel di Lemosì credon ch'avanzi.

1   Ricorditi, lettor, se mai ne l'alpe
       ti colse nebbia per la qual vedessi
       non altrimenti che per pelle talpe,

121   A voce più ch'al ver drizzan li volti,
       e così ferman sua oppinione
       prima ch'arte o ragion per lor s'ascolti.

4   come, quando i vapori umidi e spessi
       a diradar cominciansi, la spera
       del sol debilemente entra per essi;

124   Così fer molti antichi di Guittone,
       di grido in grido pur lui dando pregio,
       fin che l'ha vinto il ver con più persone.

7   e fia la tua imagine leggera
       in giugnere a veder com'io rividi
       lo sole in pria, che già nel corcar era.

127   Or se tu hai sì ampio privilegio,
       che licito ti sia l'andare al chiostro
       nel quale è Cristo abate del collegio,

10   Sì, pareggiando i miei co' passi fidi
       del mio maestro, usci' fuor di tal nube
       ai raggi morti già ne' bassi lidi.

130   falli per me un dir d'un paternostro,
       quanto bisogna a noi di questo mondo,
       dove poter peccar non è più nostro».

13   O imaginativa che ne rube
       talvolta sì di fuor, ch'om non s'accorge
       perché dintorno suonin mille tube,

133   Poi, forse per dar luogo altrui secondo
       che presso avea, disparve per lo foco,
       come per l'acqua il pesce andando al fondo.

16   chi move te, se 'l senso non ti porge?
       Moveti lume che nel ciel s'informa,
       per sé o per voler che giù lo scorge.

136   Io mi fei al mostrato innanzi un poco,
       e dissi ch'al suo nome il mio disire
       apparecchiava grazioso loco.

19   De l'empiezza di lei che mutò forma
       ne l'uccel ch'a cantar più si diletta,
       ne l'imagine mia apparve l'orma;

139   El cominciò liberamente a dire:
       «Tan m'abellis vostre cortes deman,
       qu'ieu no me puesc ni voill a vos cobrire.

22   e qui fu la mia mente sì ristretta
       dentro da sé, che di fuor non venia
       cosa che fosse allor da lei ricetta.

142   Ieu sui Arnaut, que plor e vau cantan;
       consiros vei la passada folor,
       e vei jausen lo joi qu'esper, denan.

25   Poi piovve dentro a l'alta fantasia
       un crucifisso dispettoso e fero
       ne la sua vista, e cotal si moria;

145   Ara vos prec, per aquella valor
       que vos guida al som de l'escalina,
       sovenha vos a temps de ma dolor».

28   intorno ad esso era il grande Assuero,
       Estèr sua sposa e 'l giusto Mardoceo,
       che fu al dire e al far così intero.

148   Poi s'ascose nel foco che li affina.

Figure 6.2
In book design, the reader is coming to the book, so there is no need to have a high valency in presence. In fine book typography, however, a great deal of effort is expended to create a subtle flavor so that the text and its composition on the page have expression. This is Recessive Soulful work.

The Four Conceptual Register Meta-classes

#	Denotation	Connotation	Abbrev.
1	●	●	DC
2	●	•	Dc
3	•	●	dC
4	•	•	dc

● High Valency
• Low Valency

Figure 6.3
Conceptual metaclasses. When denotation and connotation interact given a low-high valency determination, a set of four possibilities results. These are called metaclasses because they comprise a repeated class unit in the subsequent semantic profiles.

while a low-valent denotation will barely register as content at all. High-valent connotations have at least one association that is very strongly suggested. In a low-valent connotation, there are not many associated ideas, concepts, memories, or other associated thoughts.

Figure 6.3 shows these four conceptual register cases. They are called metaclasses because when combined with the four affective types, this four-member sequence will be repeated as a pattern throughout the semiotic profiles we are developing. Notice that the four members are given both numbers and abbreviations to help distinguish them and act as mnemonics. These will be used as we develop and expand the system.

Semantic Profiles

In figure 6.4, the conceptual register's four combinations of denotation and connotation are combined with the four affective types to yield sixteen different semantic profiles. Given a two-step articulation by valency, these sixteen profile types chart all the ways presence, expression, denotation, and connotation can interact semantically in a display. Notice the conceptual metaclass bundle outlined in blue, and how it is repeated through each of the four affective types. These sixteen semantic profile types

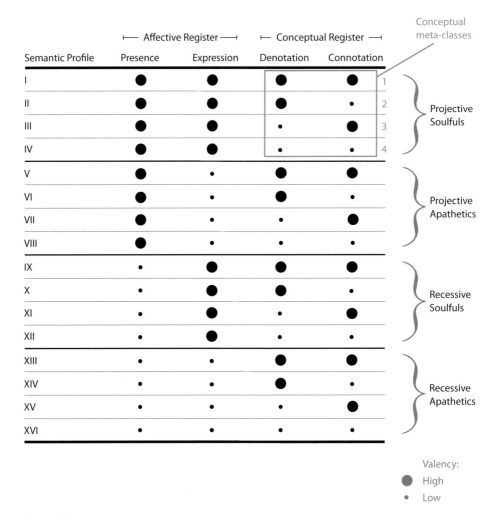

Figure 6.4

The semantic profiles. Affective and conceptual registers combine to produce sixteen semantic profiles. The semantic profiles function much like personality types, defining sixteen ways a display can deliver affective and conceptual content.

are similar to personality types, and they may be thought of as describing the graphic personality profile of an element or display.

Profiles in action

Clinique and Lancôme both market beauty products, but their brands use distinctly different semantic profiles. An image search turns up a great variety of advertising output (figure 6.5), but the displays are rigorously held within certain parameters.

Both Clinique and Lancôme individual screens have high presence. In Clinique's case, the presence is obtained by having the product itself, in the jar, being shown forcefully by means of a silhouette halftone (in which the background is inevitably white). Lancôme achieves presence by extreme close-ups of faces.

Expression is a higher valency for Lancôme screens than for Clinique. While Clinique places each product matter-of-factly center-screen, Lancôme uses the shapes of chins, shoulders, hands, and eyes to create movement and a dynamic page. Clinique uses white backgrounds and even, filtered light to accurately depict product hues; Lancôme uses chiaroscuro for dramatic effect and reduces the product emphasis.

Denotation is a primary emphasis for Clinique, and is much less strong for Lancôme. Clinique makes immediately clear what it is selling and what the object looks like. Lancôme downplays the actual product, having, in almost every case, the model as the primary visent on the screen. One works one's way from the arresting model through to the product and perhaps the typography. Clinique often tells the story with no typography except that on the package, which in Clinique's case is inevitably highly denotative.

Connotation must be broken into two parts here. If the analysis is focused on the design of the web pages instead of the product, then Lancôme has strong connotations, while Clinique has relatively weak connotations. In this respect, Clinique's images are almost invariably photographed straight on to the subject, matter-of-fact, highly denotative, while Lancôme's are off-axis, seductive, suggestive, and allude to the beauty that (by association) is the promise of the product. However, there is a second kind of connotation here—one that goes beyond the particular design of web pages: the identity of the brand. Clinique, by its very name as well as its packaging, suggests a scientific, almost medicinal approach to cosmetics. These are products that allude to health, and share with pharmaceutical packaging a declarative, expository, almost didactic presentation. Therefore, what seems at first to be an absence of strong connotation in the individual package ends up having very strong connotations as a brand; Clinique connotes science (a practice whose discourse distinctly eschews the suggestive, the allusive). Clinique suggests truth.

Figure 6.5
The look of beauty. Product lines attempt to project their brand's personality through systematic conformation to type in their publicity. In these web pages, two brands of beauty products follow two distinctly different semantic profiles. Clinique tends toward more denotation and could be profiled as a profile V. Lancôme depends more on connotation and weaker denotation and is a profile III.

From this quick analysis, Clinique emerges as a profile V (the brand's connotations of science trump the website's apparent astringency), while Lancôme is a profile III. Clinique is a Projective Apathetic in terms of affect, while Lancôme is a Projective Soulful. We see from these case studies that semantic profiles help us to map how these two brands are developing their images. Each brand strategy is unfolding in a systematic way, in response to what they perceive as their particular market segment. This kind of analysis also reveals the underlying messages, the subtle associative allusions to genres, that allow a brand to piggyback on reputations and symbols found elsewhere in the culture.

From displays to assertions

The sixteen semantic profiles are built from a simple premise: every display offers some combination of four independent variables of presence, expression, denotation, and connotation. But now, if we recall Peirce's third trichotomy, we might ask what happens when we extend this typing to include assertion. Whereas the first cell of his third trichotomy deals with questions about characteristics of the display, the second cell deals with how that display goes about making claims and propositions about the world. Here the conceptual register must be considered a second time. I can look at the conceptual guts of a display simply as a display, or I can look at how they function to make assertions, propositions, claims about the world. A display may be highly denotative in its subject matter (that is, in its manner of displaying) and yet be low-valent in denoting an assertion. Many advertisements, for example, work as a highly denotative display, but their assertions are delivered contextually, associationally, suggestively.

In light of this need to consider conceptual semantics both as display and as assertion, figure 6.6 now extends the diagram of four conceptual metaclasses shown earlier by adding two columns that label the way the conceptual metaclass functions in a display and the way it functions as assertion. A display that is high in both denotation and connotation (metaclass 1, abbreviated DC) is called an *emblem* or *emblematic* when it is considered only as a display; when a display asserts through strong denotation and connotation, it is considered a *declarative* assertion. A high-denotation and low-connotation display (metaclass 2) is *clear*; a high-denotation and low-connotation assertion is *informative*. Displays that are low in denotation and high in connotation (metaclass 3) are *stylistic*; assertions that are low in denotation and high in connotation are *suggestive*. The low-denotation and low-connotation display (metaclass 4) is simply *vague*; the low-denotation and low-connotation assertion is *ambiguous*.

The Four Conceptual Register Meta-classes

#	Denotation	Connotation	Abbrev.	As Display	As Assertion
1	●	●	DC	Emblematic	Declarative
2	●	•	Dc	Clear	Informative
3	•	●	dC	Stylistic	Suggestive
4	•	•	dc	Vague	Ambiguous

● High Valency
• Low Valency

Figure 6.6
The metaclasses can be extended to cover assertions as well as displays. When this is done, it is helpful to use verbal labels to make clear the difference between display and assertion functions.

An ironic note before leaving the nomenclature: you could have good reasons for deciding to place a display in a certain conceptual profile; but it really doesn't matter that someone else might disagree with the placement—what is important is that you, the designer, the analyst, think about *why* you assign it to that place. It is the thought itself, and the discussion it engenders, that lead to greater understanding, let you see more deeply into the functioning of the design, and pull you into new places of imagination.

Semantic display-assertion strategies

Table 6.1 maps together the display behaviors and the assertion behaviors.

By repeating these strategy types for each of the four affective register possibilities (PE, Pe, pE, pe), we obtain sixty-four display-assertion interaction profiles. These are shown in the appendix at the back of this book.

But … but … but … (some objections)
Some of these profile classes seem at first to be contradictions. Can a Soulful display be Vague? Can a Vague one be Informative?

It's important to keep in mind that the descriptors are simply devices to make discussing the qualitative aspects of the work more manageable. As verbal labels, they can only be approximations of the action that is occurring on the page.

Table 6.1

Strategy Type	As Display	As Assertion	Numerical	Descriptor
ED	DC	DC	1-1	Emblematic-Declarative
EI	DC	Dc	1-2	Emblematic-Informative
ES	DC	dC	1-3	Emblematic-Suggestive
EA	DC	dc	1-4	Emblematic-Ambiguous
CD	Dc	DC	2-1	Clear-Declarative
CI	Dc	Dc	2-2	Clear-Informative
CS	Dc	dC	2-3	Clear-Suggestive
CA	Dc	dc	2-4	Clear-Ambiguous
SD	dC	DC	3-1	Stylistic-Declarative
SI	dC	Dc	3-2	Stylistic-Informative
SS	dC	dC	3-3	Stylistic-Suggestive
SA	dC	dc	3-4	Stylistic-Ambiguous
VD	dc	DC	4-1	Vague-Declarative
VI	dc	Dc	4-2	Vague-Informative
VS	dc	dC	4-3	Vague-Suggestive
VA	dc	dc	4-4	Vague-Ambiguous

Remember, too, that this is a dissection. The semantic functionality of the visent is being split into constituent semiotic mechanisms here; an instantaneous, holistic interpretation is intentionally divided into sectors of semiotic operation, each of which may function differently—sometimes in concert, sometimes in opposition. Because this system separates the affective and the conceptual registers, and separates an analysis of the display-qua-display from analysis of the display as an assertion, the way something functions in one category may be quite different from its function in another. For example, expression is a semantic affective function produced by the display's syntax, its composition and form; how that display works in terms of its conceptual register may well be at odds with its expression and its affective partner, presence. Indeed, this dissection provides one of the potential insights of the system. Breaking down the analysis in this way allows us to see the possibility of irony, between expression and denotation for example, and also how such irony may be reconciled.

Also, we must consider that one can have an emotional experience without being able to assign it any particular conceptual content at all. Music is an obvious example of this split. We may appreciate the expressivity of an instrumental musical piece without recourse to "what the music is conceptually about." In the visual arts, one sees the

Figure 6.7
A gestural mark does not necessarily carry any conceptual content for the viewer, although it may
be very powerful in presence and expression. (Ying Kit Chan, *10,000 Things*, 2014.)

division most often not in the area of functional design but in fine art. An artist, working expressively, may make an energetic stroke that conveys great passion and life but
has no specific conceptual content whatsoever (figure 6.7).

Would there ever be a reason to produce a graphic design that is recessively and
apathetically vague? I don't know. But the semantic profiles do not make a case for the
relative usefulness of each of these "personality types." Just as one might identify a
particular kind of human personality type as "psychopath," the semantic profiles may
be used as a guide for what to avoid as much as what to aspire to. They simply are the
outcome of considering implications of Peircean semiotic concepts.

Confident discriminations
The semantic registers promise the ability to make a distinction between display-
level analysis and assertion-level analysis, but in practice these are often blended in
intricate ways and are difficult to separate. You see a photograph and recognize it as a

photograph of Marilyn Monroe. Is that recognition a display-level denotation—a representation of Ms. Monroe—or do we consider the image to be an assertion that Marilyn Monroe once stood before the photographer and was documented? Both inter-pretations are valid. In recognizing Marilyn Monroe to be the subject of a photograph, there is also an implicit assumption, with the photograph as evidence, that she was "really there" in a room before the camera.[4] There are numerous examples of this kind of blending, with a display seeming to be an assertion (and likely to be several simulta-neous assertions), so that it might seem futile to treat the display independently of any assertion the display makes about the world.

But the usefulness of this tool lies not in uncontroversially fitting things into the correct profile, but rather in the insight it offers us as we tackle messages with complex semantics. By going through the exercise of assigning semantic profiles, we learn some-thing about how a display is delivering the goods. We can also predict, after meeting with a client and doing some background research, what kind of profile to target in a prospective design. In education, we can begin to give assignments in which students are asked to take a design of a certain profile and change it to another profile. Sliding between profiles is an excellent way to feel the change of emotional and conceptual ingredients.

Speaking of discerning ingredients, an analogy that would help here is baking. If you are baking a cake, you need to be aware of each of the ingredients that go into the bat-ter. But when you eat the cake, it is very difficult to taste the egg. The ingredients have become fused in the baking; we simply enjoy the whole tasty cake gestalt. But the top bakers develop the ability to taste, in a completed cake, the action of various ingredi-ents. They may not get the proportions exactly correct, but they are able to separate the parts from the whole in their imagination. This allows them to try baking the same cake later, and in a few attempts a master baker can get pretty close. It may not be important to produce a second cake identical to the first, but learning to recognize the way the ingredients combined to create the whole is a large part of developing a cre-ative sensitivity to baking. Good designers are good bakers.

What does a portrait say?

Let's consider an example of the degrees of analysis we are proposing here. Take as an example a portrait of Queen Elizabeth I, the so-called "Rainbow Portrait" of 1600 attributed to Marcus Gheeraerts the Younger (figure 6.8). Paintings of this era, espe-cially ones whose subjects were royalty, universally employed a host of customary sym-bolic devices in order to make nonverbal assertions.[5]

Figure 6.8
Giving birth to hope? The receiver of the information determines the semantic profile. Viewers of seventeenth-century portraits who are familiar with the conventions of the genre will receive many more connotations and denotations than viewers who are unfamiliar with them.

We will begin the semantic analysis by considering the portrait as a display. Apart from its particular subject, a display (or display element) will have qualities such as size, color palette, formal attributes, and other syntactical qualities that influence presence and expression in a certain situation. These "sensibility" aspects—solely based on the syntax of the display—make up its affective semantic register.

The essential syntax of the painting is the layering of symmetries: the elaborate twistings of the headdress, the double layers of stiffened lace collars, the jewels, pendant, cleavage all reinforce stability. This stability is softened and made more graceful by the figure being at a slight angle to the front plane of the picture, so that the symmetries are not aligned with the vertical axis of the display. The result is a feeling of gracefulness and ease, yet this ease is met with the vibrancy of the color orange, picked up in the cloak and the hair as well as the central portion of the cross. Firing out of the dark background, which is a very deep orange color itself, the highly saturated orange gives an expression of activity, power, an energetic persona.[6]

These sensed or felt attributes are barely semantic at this point, being preconceptual, but they are effects on the receiver (and hence interpretants), and they open the door to the more highly elaborated conceptual semantic register.

Going deeper in our analysis, we see the display first as a portrait, second as a portrait of a woman, and we might identify the woman as Queen Elizabeth I. In these steps we are passing fully into the conceptual register of semantics. We could stop here, limiting our analysis to the display, and even so we could have much to talk about.[7]

But we might want to move more deeply into the analysis and look at the assertions the portrait makes. Here the depths of our analysis will largely depend upon our knowledge of the metaphorical symbols common to portrait painting in the early seventeenth century, and of other cultural cues. We see that the queen's crown is of a theatrical type and conclude that she is in a costume fit for a masque. By having her hold a rainbow, the painting asserts that Queen Elizabeth has the power to bring a better or a more peaceful world. If one is conversant in Latin, the inscribed motto, "Non sine sole iris" (no rainbow without the sun), reinforces the link between prosperity and the queen.

There are more subtle symbols as well. The lining of the cloak has ears, mouths, and eyes, patterned on the silk.[8] Is this suggesting the queen is sensitive to the needs of her subjects? Or that the queen's administration is vigilantly paying attention to her people in a more clandestine manner? And given the placement of the rainbow, which seems to disappear into the peculiarly rendered fold in her garment, can there be any question but that the queen is essentially giving birth to the rainbow? This allusion reinforces the primacy of the queen as source for all that is hopeful in the realm.

For someone who does not recognize the subject and is not familiar with historical iconography, the feelings imparted by the affective semantics may be similar, but the conceptual profile will be very different. Someone who understands the tradition of seventeenth-century portraiture might give it a semantic strategy of type ED (emblematic and declarative), while someone without such knowledge may find it much less clear in its assertions, perhaps assigning it to type EA (emblematic but ambiguous in its assertions). Perhaps for some it could be an SA (stylistic as a display, ambiguous in its assertions). The audience must be kept in mind.

This is not a full analysis, of course, but I want to show the lines if inquiry that such an analysis would pursue. I also want to show that there could be multiple readings for a display. In any event, it is important to remember that taxonomy is less about assigning profile and strategy types than about bringing to the work an inquisitive mind and developing a scalpel-like ability to make small semantic discriminations. The theoretical system I am proposing offers tools by which meaning can be analyzed the way formal art principles like balance, texture, or contrast can be analyzed, or the way baking can be analyzed. The theory suggests discriminations, distinctions, facets of interpretive process that offer a more subtle way of thinking about design and a more precise language for talking about it. The presence of the categories, all derived from the structure of the Peircean semiotic system, offers the possibility of insight, and as long as one can defend one's assignment of categories, the design process will be carried forward.

Envisioning conceptual relationships as 3D space diagrams

The sixteen strategy types (the possible combinations of the four metaclasses for both displays and assertions) can be arranged according to a trio of dimensions:

• Overall conceptual "fullness" (conceptual strength),
• Denotative or connotative relative emphasis,
• Display or assertion relative emphasis.

The best way of envisioning these relationships is to illustrate them with two three-dimensional diagrams, one for display-dominant types and one for assertion-dominant types (figures 6.9 and 6.10). In the figures, the display-dominant profiles are illustrated by a blue polyhedron, and the assertion-dominant profiles are illustrated by an identical red polyhedron. The polyhedrons represent the logical semantic structure between the various profiles. What we are seeing is essentially a mapping of the territory of conceptual content strategies in its simplest representation. A more detailed accounting (e.g., by progressing from a twofold division to a valency spectrum divided into eight, twenty, or a hundred segments) would begin to take the form of intricate hemispheres, but the essential relationships would be retained.

The schematic view below the 3D model shows these relationships in a flattened-out form. With the schematic view it is easier to grasp the scheme of relationships such as semantic strength, which is accounted for by the simple totaling of the high valencies (either connotation or denotation). But the 3D model is better at capturing the distance of profile types from each other. For example, a type 1-4 (Emblematic-Ambiguous) is maximally distant from all four of the nodes that have balanced display-assertion weights: 1-1 (Emblematic-Declarative), 2-2 (Clear-Informative), 3-3 (Stylistic-Suggestive), and 4-4 (Vague-Ambiguous). This is due to the strong emphasis on the display side. (We observe this display-side dominance as a characteristic in much aestheticist fine art and the balance of display and assertion in much conceptual art.) Notice that type 2-3 is somewhat transparent as it actually lies at the center of the structure; it, and 3-2 on the assertion-dominant side, are the only types that do not lie on a surface of the polyhedron.

Types 1-1, 2-2, 3-3, and 4-4 form the polyhedron's base, present in both display and assertion models, as they stress neither display or assertion. Each of the other strategies carries more semantic weight as either display or assertion (i.e., they have higher valencies as either display or assertion), and they appear on either the blue (display-dominant) or red (assertion-dominant) polyhedron but not on both.

Referring back and forth between the schematics and the 3D conceptual space diagrams reveals the beautiful network of logical relations that arise. For instance, moving toward type 2-2 is a move toward absolute denotation in both display and assertion, while moving toward 3-3 stresses the suggestivity of connotation at the expense of clarity. A move toward the peak of 1-4 pulls you into a territory of maximum attention to the display, without necessarily favoring a denotative or a connotative understanding. As would be expected, its converse, 4-1, peaking the assertion side, implies something very vague as a display that nonetheless manages to make a powerfully concise assertion.

It is also worth noting that as one moves along the x-axis from left to right, one gains a measure of what may be called conceptual vigor or conceptual strength, since the total valencies of denotation and connotation, counted in both display and assertion domains, are increasing. The maximal condition is reached at 1-1, the Emblematic-Declarative strategy. Strategy types that are toward the right and have this kind of strength can therefore be said to have conceptual fullness. On the other hand, the types toward the left side, culminating in 4-4 (Vague-Ambiguous), are weak,

Conceptual Semantic Profiles – Display Dominant Types

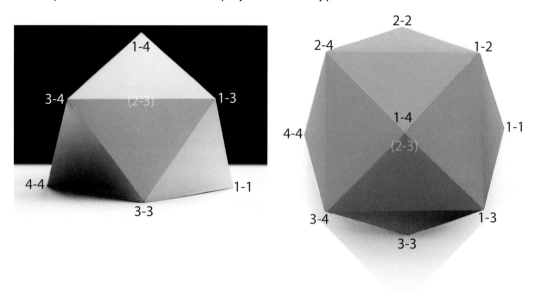

STRATEGY TYPE	AS DISPLAY	AS ASSERTION	NUMERICAL	DESCRIPTOR
ED	DC-DC		1-1	Emblematic - Declarative
EI	DC-Dc		1-2	Emblematic - Informative
ES	DC-dC		1-3	Emblematic - Suggestive
EA	DC-dc		1-4	Emblematic - Ambiguous
CD	Dc-DC		2-1	Clear - Declarative
CI	Dc-Dc		2-2	Clear - Informative
CS	Dc-dC		2-3	Clear - Suggestive
CA	Dc-dc		2-4	Clear - Ambiguous
SD	dC-DC		3-1	Stylistic - Declarative
SI	dC-Dc		3-2	Stylistic - Informative
SS	dC--dC		3-3	Stylistic - Suggestive
SA	dC-dc		3-4	Stylistic - Ambiguous
VD	dc-DC		4-1	Vague - Declarative
VI	dc-Dc		4-2	Vague - Informative
VS	dc-dC		4-3	Vague- Suggestive
VA	dc-dc		4-4	Vague - Ambiguous

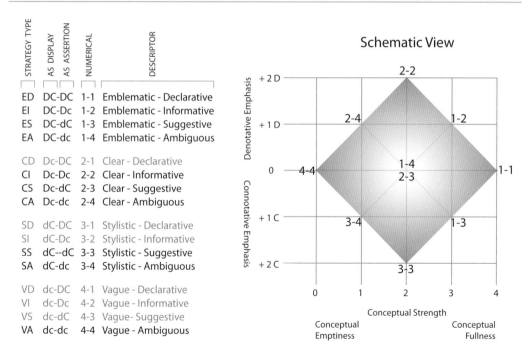

Figures 6.9 (left) and 6.10 (right)

Display-assertion strategies. Schematic and 3D diagrams showing the network of relations established by conceptual strategy type. The blue polyhedron of figure 6.9 shows those strategy types in which the emphasis is on the display or is balanced between display and assertion.

continued

Conceptual Semantic Profiles – Assertion Dominant Types

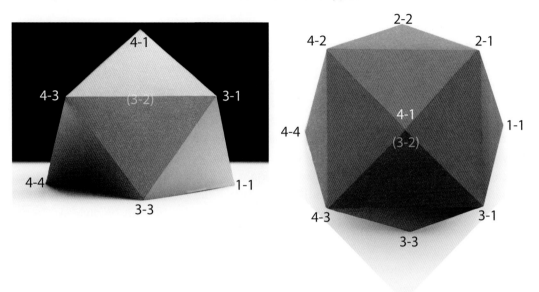

STRATEGY TYPE	AS DISPLAY	AS ASSERTION	NUMERICAL	DESCRIPTOR
ED	DC-DC	1-1	Emblematic - Declarative
EI	DC-Dc	1-2	Emblematic - Informative
ES	DC-dC	1-3	Emblematic - Suggestive
EA	DC-dc	1-4	Emblematic - Ambiguous
CD	Dc-DC	2-1	Clear - Declarative
CI	Dc-Dc	2-2	Clear - Informative
CS	Dc-dC	2-3	Clear - Suggestive
CA	Dc-dc	2-4	Clear - Ambiguous
SD	dC-DC	3-1	Stylistic - Declarative
SI	dC-Dc	3-2	Stylistic - Informative
SS	dC--dC	3-3	Stylistic - Suggestive
SA	dC-dc	3-4	Stylistic - Ambiguous
VD	dc-DC	4-1	Vague - Declarative
VI	dc-Dc	4-2	Vague - Informative
VS	dc-dC	4-3	Vague- Suggestive
VA	dc-dc	4-4	Vague - Ambiguous

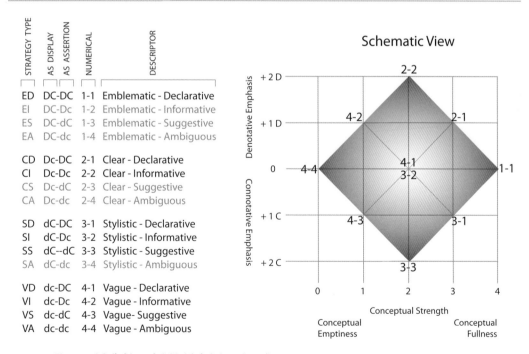

Figures 6.9 (left) and 6.10 (right) (continued)
The red polyhedron of figure 6.10 shows those strategy types in which the emphasis is on assertion or is balanced between assertion and display. The charts include details of each type. All sixteen strategy types are shown in each table; grayed-out strategy types do not apply to the model and schematic being illustrated in the respective figure.

conceptually empty. This is not to say that such displays do not have other virtues—they could be Projective Soulfuls, for instance, strong to the eye and strong to the feelings, but they are not strong as *conceptual* entities.

Conclusion

This model, starting with the semantic profiles and moving to the display-assertion strategies, suggests a way to categorize the semantic effects of a visual sign. The taxonomy is designed to be functional in a design situation or an analytical situation, but does not pretend to be exhaustive. It places a certain kind of interpretive structure on the table for those that can find it useful. The structure of the affective and conceptual semantic registers grows naturally from the premise that meaning can be divided according to specificity, and then according to convergent denotative and divergent connotative attributes. The Peircean third trichotomy, whose first two cells ask whether the analysis is to be of the display or of assertions the display makes, is then applied to these bifurcations to produce the profiles and strategies presented here.

From this point, the abstractions of semiotics begin to come down from the clouds and are brought into ever closer contact with the everyday realities of the graphic design studio. We will see this grounding process as we move to the functional matrix.

7   The Functional Matrix

As we saw in the last chapter, the semantic profiles promise a scheme for parceling various kinds of "meaning behaviors" and organizing them within the semantic registers into distinct profiles. A further way to look at the effect of a display is to bundle certain factors *across* semantic registers and syntactical features.

When we do this kind of cross-comparison, we find surprising alliances. Presence and denotation, despite belonging to different registers, share a kind of immediacy, a sense of being thus and so, a convergent sense of definitiveness or determinability. Presence is largely determined by perceptual cues and the physiology of the eye and brain, while denotation is often a culturally coded formulation. Nevertheless, they share this trait of sureness: the display stands out against a background or it doesn't, it has a specific message or not.

On the other hand, expression and connotation are somehow more indirect, indeterminate, open to discussion, subtle in their associative resonance. They depend to a much greater extent on the life experiences of the viewer, the audience's augmentation and imagination of the material.

In terms of syntax, the immediate functional and practical effects of a display's visibility within a particular environment at a definite viewing time has a similar predictive power as presence and denotation, one that can be contrasted with the slightly more esoteric, or at least ultimately abstract, aspects of its compositional relationships.

Whether at the level of syntax or of semantics, and within semantics whether in the affective or the conceptual register, we might refer to these two opposing groups of characteristics as "hard" and "soft" semiotic attributes. A hard attribute is precise, potentially definite, verifiable. A soft attribute is contingent, suggestive, in process.

The functional matrix: hard and soft attributes intersecting semantics and syntax

Crossing the syntactic and semantic levels with the hard and soft axes yields a matrix with four nodes (figure 7.1). Semantic components that are "hard" include presence in the affective register and denotation in the conceptual register. Let us call these somewhat veridical semantically hard attributes *concrete*. Concrete attributes allow for a figure to be representational, for objects to be easily recognized, and generally have to do with what one might call the subject matter of the display. Is the typography legible? Is the picture of a dragonfly recognizable as a dragonfly?

Semantic components that are "soft" include expression in the affective register and connotation in the conceptual register. Semantically soft attributes have to do with associations and sensibilities triggered by the display. This is the area that defines a display's mood or *tone*. Tonality has to do with expressive and connotative aspects of the display. What is the attitude, the "feel" of the display? What does it remind you of when you look at it? What is its style?

Syntactic components have to do with a visent's formal materiality and its interaction with its environment. In some ways, it may be less easy to distinguish hard and soft attributes in terms of syntax. The key is to regard the actual occurrence of the display in an environment as more defined, more definite, than any particular traits it might possess taken for their own sake. So, for example, hard syntactic components include contrast with specific background, sufficient size for readability, and illumination conditions. These are conditions for actual functionality in situ, or *praxis*. What are the conditions necessary for the text to be legible? How large does the display need to be so that it can be seen by people from a distance of so many yards? Does the display project well in the evening, or does it need to be fitted with lighting? These decisions can be made on the basis of empirical observations and research into the actual conditions. When one studies how a display actually appears in the environment, one is looking at praxis.

Syntactically soft components, on the other hand, include all graphic elements and visent features in their *arrangement*. These are the quintessential components designers know as *form*, and they comprise the geometry of elements and composition of the display. What are the ways to unify the physical structure of the display? What are the formal attributes that arrest the eye, create drama and interest, make it memorable?

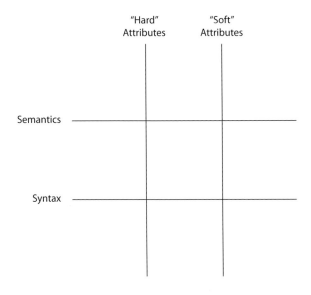

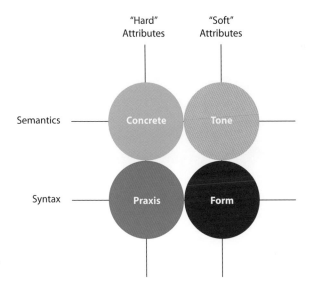

Figure 7.1

Syntactical and semantics dimensions can be organized according to "hard" and "soft" attributes to form four nodes that become the centers of focus for a design project.

Visual/verbal and mind/body divisions

Clearly, these four nodes receive a great deal of attention in the practice of design. Not only are they crucial in themselves, but their interactive relationships provide insights. One of these insights involves the apparent divide between the visual and the verbal; another has to do with the division we feel between mind and body (figure 7.2).

The visual/verbal split is a gulf so wide that our culture usually keeps the two sides apart physically. They are segregated on our college campuses, where the visual arts and English departments usually occupy different buildings; in our advertising agencies, where copywriters and art directors often work on different floors; and it is only with the recent popularity of the graphic novel that books have come to accept illustration in the way of pictorial content. The four nodes suggest a root cause for these visual/verbal tensions by indicating the ease or unease of translating factors of each node from visual to verbal.

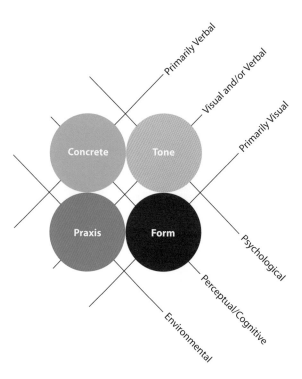

Figure 7.2
The four nodes of the functional matrix illuminate relationships to verbal/visual, and psychological/environmental (mind/body) distinctions.

To see an example of this split, try this game. Take a common picture—say, the portrait of George Washington on a dollar bill—and try to describe it to someone so that they can understand what you have in mind. You must do it by describing its visual form alone; you are not allowed to use concrete, tone, or praxis nodes in your verbal description. So saying it is "on a dollar bill" (praxis) or "a man with a curly wig" (concrete) is not allowed. In the case of the engraved portrait of George Washington on a dollar note, the most concrete thing you could say would be to name its subject, because it is precisely the function of language to denote, as is accomplished by the phrase "engraving of George Washington." What this visent is is very difficult to convey verbally through descriptions of form alone, because words are better adapted to convey hard information—the who, what, when, where—than the feelings and tonalities or compositional details.[1]

Meanwhile, at the opposite corner of the four nodes lies form. Beyond fundamental geometric structures such as square and circle, it is *very* difficult to convey form well using language. This was described a century ago in a passage assessing the problem of putting the experience of music into words.

Strictly considered, writing about music is as illogical as singing about economics. All the other arts can be talked about in the terms of ordinary life and experience. A poem, a statue, a painting or a play is a representation of somebody or something, and can be measurably described (the purely aesthetic values aside) by describing what it represents. … To describe it [music] you must describe tones and their arrangement, a task for which there is no adequate vocabulary in ordinary language, and only a clumsy jargon in the speech of musicians.[2]

It is worth noting here that the writer allows the exception of visual representation, a concrete denotative function, as something that *can* be better rendered through words, while musical pitch, texture, and arrangement (i.e., form) while understood instantly by the ears, manage to elude adequate verbal description.

Meanwhile, tone and praxis are visually and verbally balanced. In the engraving of George Washington, the tonality is the suggestion of respect, that the subject is a person of high standing in society, or that the portrait is historical, the subject being an important historical figure. Words can often best relay tonality through simile and metaphor. Simile and metaphor are rhetorical devices that point toward, rather than explicitly pinpointing, their objects. Connotative words gesture toward their semantic target.

In translating praxis into verbal language, one voices expectations of how the visent will behave when it is in various conditions in the world. How well will it show up at night, how large is it relative competing displays? Once again words are somewhat effective here, but an actual demonstration—by viewing—is far superior to anything words can foretell, describe, or define.

With both tone and praxis, a picture really is worth a thousand words; with concreteness, a reasonable translation may be obtained with just a few; while no quantity of words can adequately capture the experiencing of visual form.

The four nodes can also be seen from the standpoint of their emphasis on interior (mind) action or exterior (material world) action. In this regard, tone stands as the most emphatically psychological, praxis as that node most oriented toward the exterior world, while form and concrete seem to balance between the perceptual (the effect of materiality on mind) and the cognitive (the effect on the conscious understanding).

The combination of these four semiotic functions defines the areas that must be considered in any graphic design project. The concrete side of a project is both the easiest to discuss with a client and usually *least* likely to need a graphic designer's attention. If you are only trying to communicate that an event is to occur at a certain place and time, and you don't care to express the excitement of the event, then setting the words in Helvetica centered on a white sheet of paper is going to get the job done just fine (figure 7.3). Indeed, the most concrete element of the display is precisely the text, presenting legible verbal information on the page. There is no need to bring in a graphic design specialist to do this. However, while every project manager can attest that orally presenting to a client is easiest when discussing the concrete aspects of the design, it is rarely a project's concrete requirements that the designer was hired to satisfy, or that need the verbal explanation. While explaining the intricacies of form, expression, and connotation may present a linguistic challenge, it is precisely these areas that generally mark the visual expertise of the designer. Understanding the friction between visual and verbal as it pertains to the functional matrix is therefore as important in preparing a presentation as it is in preliminary project analysis and brief.

Fraternal clusters and antagonist pairs

Another insight emerges from the functional matrix: focusing on any one of the four nodes requires some consideration of two other "fraternal" nodes—adjacent to it in the functional matrix—while, for the time being, virtually ignoring the fourth "antagonist" node that lies diagonally across from it in the array. Figure 7.4 shows these fraternal clusters.

When you are concentrating on the concrete aspects of a display, its connotational and practical needs will be coming into your awareness as secondary factors, while the formal aspects (considered in themselves for their own sake) will be absent. That is to say, although you may manipulate form in the service of trying to attain, say, a clear

Figure 7.3
The concrete information on each of these postcards is the same. Which version do you favor as the best fit for a mathematics conference? Whereas (a) is a solution that stays completely concrete, (b) and (c) begin to explore other nodes of the functional matrix. Version (b) succeeds in standing out from its background (good praxis) but its tonality is suspect: perhaps a bit "commercial" for a meeting of mathematicians. Version (c) may come closest to meeting the objectives.

Concretist Cluster	Practical Cluster	Formalist Cluster	Attitudinal Cluster

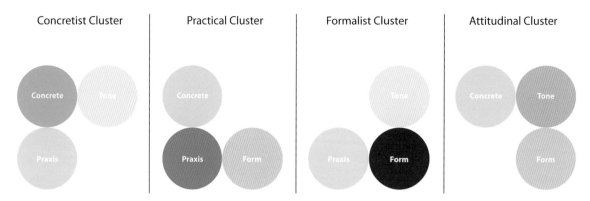

Figure 7.4
The four "fraternal" clusters: attention to any one of the nodes of the functional matrix entails some attention to the nodes adjacent it.

and unmistakable representation of a subject, you are not concentrating on form *for its own sake*. While attending to the concrete aspects of the display, you are also keeping in mind how, when, and where the display will be seen (praxis) as well as the attitudinal feeling (tone) that it conveys. These two fraternal nodes of praxis and tone are present in your thinking but somewhat backgrounded, while form is ignored. While attending to the concrete, tone and praxis are fraternal while form (for its own sake) is antagonist.

Take, on the other hand, what happens when you turn your attention to grooming form, paying attention to its aesthetics and unity. Now praxis and tonality are backgrounded, praxis because the perception of form is dependent upon it, tone because it is form's expressive and stylistic result. So while these become fraternal to form, the concrete concerns, for the moment, disappear, antagonistic to the focus on form. Figure 7.5 shows the antagonist pairs.

Now, let me be clear: I am not saying that, for the design project as a whole, you cannot be concerned with both concrete and formal issues. On the contrary, during a project, the designer moves around through all four nodes, but for that moment when he is focused on one of the nodes, two others are backgrounded and the fourth is out of his consciousness entirely. This suggests that good and efficient design practice requires some focused time on each of the four clusters, but that while the focus is on any one cluster, the designer should, for the moment, relinquish interest in its antagonist, only regaining interest in it as attention purposefully moves to another focus. This revolving wheel of attention allows, eventually, a full consideration of all four nodes, while allowing keen concentration on each one in its time.

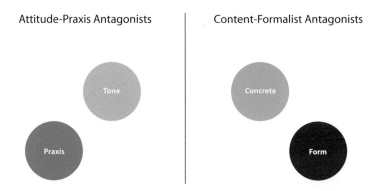

Attitude-Praxis Antagonists   Content-Formalist Antagonists

Figure 7.5
Each of the nodes of the functional matrix has an "antagonist" node, opposite to it in the matrix. When considering attributes represented by any one node of the functional matrix, the attributes of its antagonist will be repressed.

Most good designers do something like this as a matter of course, without really being aware of it. By becoming conscious of the process, one gains efficiency and sharpens studio practice.

Using the functional matrix

Let's take an example of the functional matrix applied to the design of a logo. For many years, I have used a spinoff acronym from the functional matrix to guide logo development. With attention to form, one aspires to a design that is memorable. Working to achieve the right tonality yields a design with the appropriate attitude. A concrete design will have elements that are recognizable. Attending to praxis ensures that a logo is versatile. The acronym is MARV (every logo should be MARVelous): Memorable, Appropriate (attitude), Recognizable, and Versatile (figure 7.6). These are the four goals of every logo, the only objectives to be considered during the design process. In a memorable logo, there is something about its shape, a geometrical or compositional game perhaps, that causes a second glance, a longer gaze, that catches the eye in a striking way and implants itself into memory. Appropriate attitude implies that a logo for a group called the Angels should look quite different if the Angels are a church choir than if they are a motorcycle gang (figure 7.7). Here the connotational aspects, dependent on cultural symbols and style, become important. Recognition, in the concrete, denotative sense implied in this context, does *not* mean that the logo itself should be recognized to stand for whatever organization it represents, but that the referent of any

A logo should be MARVelous:

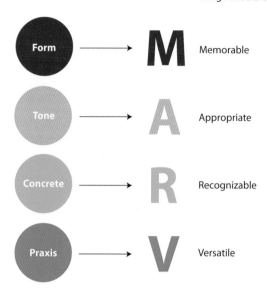

Figure 7.6
MARVelous identity design. An example of the functional matrix pressed into service in logo de-sign. There are four important considerations in the design of a logo, stemming from the four nodes of the functional matrix. A logo should be memorable, which it generally achieves through crafting an interesting form. It must have the appropriate attitude or tone, which it does through paying attention to various connotations that the visent calls to mind. Being recognizable in this context means that the images and typography must "read" properly. Versatility is a result of good praxis: being able to work small, in a variety of materials, in any situation that may arise for the logo to function in the world.

Figure 7.7
Tone (appropriate attitude) is the defining node when deciding if a logo is right for a church choir or a motorcycle gang.

depiction *within* the logo should be clearly represented and understood.[3] If you depict a rose, one should be able to tell, without great effort, that it is a rose. Versatility is praxis, the logo in use in the environment. In logo design, this means the ability to function well at a variety of sizes, in a variety of materials, and in a host of contextual situations.

The functional matrix can be used to describe or predict how and why certain displays work or fail. In the design process, it can serve as a check at various analytical stages to ensure that a candidate design is likely to succeed. As we've seen with logo design, it can be a reminder to check various conditions.

The functional matrix can also be a tool for historical-cultural analysis. For example, the Bauhaus, in rejecting earlier European traditions and ornamentation, sought to find a more pure basis for design. This was exemplified in both their method of instruction and in the emphasis on formal minimalism which developed in concert with it. They sought a fresh way of design that would throw off the cultural weight of traditions that had culminated in the Great War. The designs that they created emphasized the syntactical axes of the functional matrix and suppressed the semantic axes. They were formalists, finding a new vocabulary in exquisite proportional details and minimal compositions. This minimalist vocabulary became the vocabulary of modernism, and by the time modernism had become the predominant design vocabulary in the industrialized world, it had taken on deep cultural symbolism: that is, it had become style. What we see in tracing the development of the ideas of the Bauhaus is first an attempt, through a formalist emphasis, to eschew the conservative tonality (connotations and associations) of traditional European compositional methods, and then, over time, the eventual semiotic migration of "the Bauhaus look" so that it inevitably recovers, for a later generation, a strongly traditional, corporate, attitudinal stance. An attempt to defeat style becomes in the end a style, one that is being transformed yet again in the present day by some designers. Today, if one chooses to work in a modernist idiom, one cannot escape the fact that it is a choice among many concurrent stylistic currents, and as such carries strong connotations. One can never escape culture, either by being within it (in which case it is largely invisible) or by being outside it (in which case it is cast in high relief).

Nomenclature -philia and -phobia

Again, a note of optimism and one of caution are required here. The terminology I am using is a double-edged sword. After the semiotic distinctions I have been making in the last two chapters, it should be clear why it is far too limiting to speak of "what something means" as if there is simply one kind of meaning. What something is meaning is a complex arrangement of connections that reverberate with each other and simultaneously depend on the background of the person receiving the communication. Furthermore, something is concurrently "meaning" in both denotatively hard and connotatively soft ways, and in ways that are affective and conceptual.

To get at the complexity of the semiotic situation, we use verbal labels, each label identifying a particular important distinction. In that respect, the words we use to describe the semiotic action are important and helpful. Meaning is a many-faceted crystal, and highly dependent on the angle from which it is being examined. We use a certain lexicon as a way to point to that taxonomy, that structural complexity, to make some sense of it, maybe to predict how it will operate in a given design situation. We have no choice really. If we were to see a rainbow for the first time, we would be compelled to invent words for important hue distinctions. But how many words would we invent? The rainbow is a continuum: an infinite number of distinctions would be accurate but impossible to put into words, much less practice, while two or three distinctions would not serve the richness of a rainbow experience.

Here we face the same dilemma. I am trying to discover and label only what I sense to be major distinctions—major changes in hue. Yet there is the ever-present danger of terminological overload, of a semiotic tool that fails not because it is too blunt, but because it cuts the continuum too finely to be practicable. All one can do is attempt to steer a middle course between Scylla and Charybdis. Binney and Smith decided on eight rainbow divisions and came up with a Crayola eight-pack of crayons. They left it for later generations to expand the range of crayon colors.

I have a similar sense as I do this work: keep it as simple as possible. At the same time, we have been working with a conceptual toolbox that has failed to distinguish (at least verbally) very many semantic relations. Designers intuitively know more distinctions exist. We feel that complexity, and we respond, but we have lacked the language to speak it. That is why it is important to make these further distinctions verbally (and visually) explicit here, and to show how they relate to each other in an intricate but logical set of relations. It is better to oversupply articulate complexity than for designers to be limited to "form and content." Maybe this is the thirty-two-pack of crayons.

Just as we have shown in the previous discussions of semantic profiles and the classes of signs, the functional matrix presents intricate ways in which meaning's various facets interact. The ability to separate these multiple aspects and to speak acutely of how they interact at any given semiotic moment is the epitome of design analysis, a role that should become indispensable not only during the design process but also in explaining solutions to clients as well as developing a growing body of scholarly criticism within the field.

Now the caution: in laying out these new tools such as the functional matrix, it is important to remember that they are simply analytical tools. They contribute to a more articulate language and terminology about design, a greater degree of detail in display and system analysis, and to some extent they may enhance creative methodology. But one should not allow categorization, taxonomy, and lexicon to become the only role for design process. I have heard an analogy (attributed to the great designer Paula Scher) in which design process is compared to having two aunts, both of whom you love dearly. One aunt is very precise, a bookkeeper, and is a stickler for detail and getting everything just right. The other aunt is the "hippie" aunt who is playful, completely nonjudgmental, and fun. Design is the process of having both aunts come to your aid—just be sure to *never* let them both in the room at the same time. Logical analysis need not diminish the creative playfulness of your inner hippie aunt.

As we develop these conceptual tools, think of them as offering possibilities of insight. With them, we can investigate visual communication at very small conceptual scale, discovering new relationships in the complex interactions of the visual semiotic process.

It is far better to consider visual design in light of the new possibilities that awareness of these relationships provides than to overthink which examples fit into which schematic slots. In all schemes of analysis, and especially in considering something as seemingly fugitive and intangible as visual communication, it is good to retain wiggle room. Whether as the preparation of a new design or in the investigation of a classical work, the analysis we do needs to be done in the spirit of seeking practical enlightenment, intellectual discovery, and artistic pleasure, rather than as a purist orthodoxy. This is true even of the method itself. The method and its tools will grow and develop in time; the method and its application should always allow a certain flexibility and admit a certain fallibility as well.

Using the functional matrix: a case study

To look at how the functional matrix might come into play during the design phase of a logo, we can do a bit of reimagineering. Barr Pharmaceuticals was extant for almost forty years before it was bought out by Teva Pharmaceuticals in 2008. We can do a bit of forensic "what if" design work to study how Barr's logo might have been developed had it continued as an independent company and used semiotic principles to evolve its identifying device.

In figure 7.8, display (a) shows the original Barr logo. The hexagon references chemical bonds. It is not clear that the color blue carries any particular symbolic value, but the uniform hue helps unify the mark into a single visent, and the sans serif typeface has an affinity with the minimal drawing style of the hexagon as well. We can see how the mark would be harmed in terms of visual unity by interrupting the uniform color (b) or by employing a less harmonious typeface (c). The breaking of the gestalt in these cases would make it more difficult to see the mark as a single visent. But in all three cases (a, b, and c), legibility is compromised—a deficit in recognition (concreteness). Even in the original mark (a), reading the "b" in "barr" is forced and uncertain. The hexagon's angular features are different enough from the kind of "b" that typographically fits with the "arr" that it is likely the mark would already be misread as "a-r-r."

So the first focus in solving the problem is to address these issues of concreteness. The word should read in an easy, natural, unforced way. The obvious strategy is not to have the hexagon do double duty, but to allow the full word (b-a-r-r) to be visible. The hexagon could then perhaps simply be placed next to the word (d). There are dozens of ways the hexagon could be placed in some proximity to the word, and virtually all of them would succeed in having the viewer properly read the word and see the hexagon as a symbol; but how to choose between them?

At this point, already evident in (d), attention shifts to the harmony and memorability of the logotype. That places the focus on form, and the search for formal relationships begins to suggest aligning the hexagon with the x-heights of the lowercase letters. While investigating these formal possibilities, various treatments of the hexagon are tried, including placing the hexagon, as a figure/ground illusion, within the word (e).

Somewhere during this process, the design focus also considers the tone of the mark. Does it feel like science? Does it express an attitude compatible with innovative development? With a large corporate identity project, it is possible to check this with various instruments. One of the possibilities is to see if, within the realm of science, or more specifically the pharmaceutical industry, fairly heavy sans serif letterforms are common, blue is common, simple modernist design is common. The very features that are habitually seen in the milieu of that subculture will predispose one to symbolically and connotatively relate the new logo to the industry. Of course, if a great number of industry logos are blue, then an orange hue might better stand out in the crowd, but that is the kind of decision that will need to be made.

We might make a pun on the name's English meaning by placing a black bar over the logo (f). But it is perhaps more subtle and more harmonious to do so in the manner of (g), which, surprisingly, carries a second benefit: the bar when related in this way to

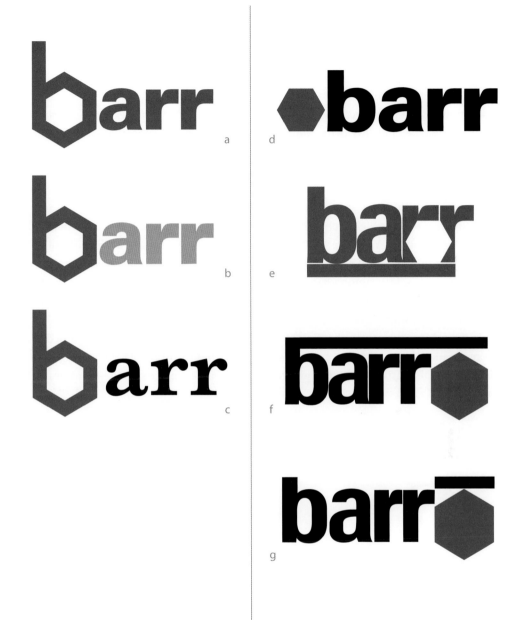

Figure 7.8

In exploring possible alternative designs, all four of the nodes of the functional matrix must be considered. Options (a) through (c) in this example each suffer from recognition issues, because the hexagon is unlikely to be easily read as the first letter of the word. It tends to be seen as a symbol followed by "a-r-r." Options (d) through (g) attempt to overcome that problem while still maintaining a sense of unity. The optical illusions that begin to form a shieldlike form in (g) hold promise for memorability of the prospective logo, while retaining superior recognizability.

the hexagon also begins to suggest a shield, symbol of service and defense—welcome connotations. This reading could easily be encouraged in all marketing materials for the company. The shield, while subtle in its gestalt, would be impossible to miss after it was pointed out just once. This is the kind of formal game that makes for memorability of a logotype, and this is the kind of connotation relationship that supports the mark on several levels.

We have considered the mark from the standpoint of concreteness, tonality, and memorable form; the last node to consider is praxis. Will the mark be versatile? A few tests of it at various sizes should give confidence that this would be a quite versatile logo (figure 7.9). It is Memorable, has attitude in an Appropriate way, is now legibly Recognizable, and is Versatile: MARV is satisfied. This might make a successful logo design. Notice, too, that if the hexagon does successfully stand for pharmaceuticals (as it likely would, at least among Barr's partial audience of chemical engineers), then the placing of the black bar over the hexagon makes a rebus for the complete brand name: Barr Pharmaceuticals.

In a real identity project, the designing of the mark might go through a hundred or more iterations rather than the handful shown here, but the principle of checking with the functional matrix as the work progresses is the same, and that is the point of this example.

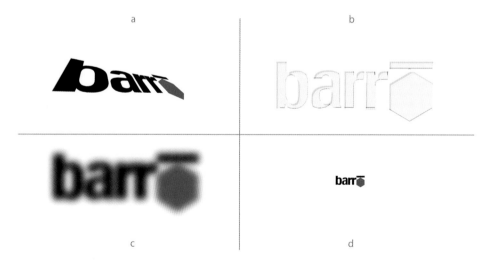

Figure 7.9
The Barr logo is taken through several tests to look at its versatility (praxis): (a) perspective and skewing; (b) molded in glass or embossed; (c) foggy, blurred, great distance; (d) reduced to quarter-inch size.

Notice, with respect to what has been mentioned about the Bauhaus and modernism, that the minimal style of the logo is itself a culturally significant symbol, connoting a certain kind and size of business. It would be inappropriate (in tone) to some groups and purposes, while perfectly suiting others. If this were a logo for, say, Barr Family Pharmacy—a small-town corner shop—the modernist, stripped-down approach might be too suggestive of large industry. In that case, a more personal, friendly, and perhaps idiosyncratic solution would need to be found in order to successfully satisfy the tone function. Remember that tone, especially in stylistic terms, is always a culturally derived construction and, of the four functional nodes, is the most variable with the conditions of time and place (only praxis is close to being so dependent, since environmental context largely determines it).

Graphic design is a semiotics laboratory

While using the functional matrix is no guarantee of success, this demonstration shows how awareness of the four nodes can assist the process of creation and design analysis. In some ways, introducing the functional matrix is telling graphic designers something they already know. But this knowledge has been largely implicit and unconscious. Semiotics brings it to the foreground, makes it explicit, gives it language and structure. We have long made decisions at a deep level, creatively manipulating semiotic structures. Now we are obtaining a language for what we have done intuitively.

Semioticians are getting something, too, from this uniting of semiotics and graphic design. Semioticians have only occasionally looked to graphic design as a laboratory that is ideally suited to active experiment and innovation in understanding visual sign exchange. Now perhaps they will increasingly do so. Graphic designers are visual semioticians in professional practice.

But how large is this visual laboratory of visual design? What are the boundaries and possibilities of the territory of graphic design? To answer that question, we turn to another conceptual tool: the visual gamut.

8   The Visual Gamut

The structure of the systems we build develops in response to fundamental questions we ask. Ask what the basic kinds of relationships are, and we discover the first-, second-, and third-order relations. Ask what relationship holds between a sign and its referent, and we are led to a discussion of icons, indexes, and symbols. If we wish to understand the precision by which a referent might be understood, we discover the specificity shell. Inquiring about the variety of ways a display might deliver its semantic contents leads us to the semantic profiles.

Now, in this chapter, we ask: What is the breadth of possible kinds of visents? In doing so, we will be mapping the territory that is the graphic designer's playground, the working space within which visual entities function as elements.

The gamut and some observations

What we will be delineating here is a gamut. Just as a color gamut is the range of potential hues, chroma, and values that are feasible for a given technical system, such as a monitor or camera, so the full sweep of possibilities of the visent is the *visual gamut*. The visual gamut is defined by three distinct extremes: mark, image, and word.[1] All elements of displays[2] fall somewhere along the edge or within the triangular territory defined by these three apexes (figure 8.1).

This gamut naturally ensues from Peircean semiotics. Recall that there are three fundamental ways a sign can signify a referent: by resemblance (iconically), by environmental influence (indexically), or by arbitrary and consensual principles (symbolically). The apex occupied by the representational image is fully iconic, a visual simulacrum resembling the referent in appearance. The apex occupied by the mark is highly indexic: some encounter or connection with its environment produces the sign. The third apex is occupied by something for which the only connection between sign and referent is the agreed-upon, consensual adherence to a system or code, a rule-based

The Visual Gamut

Image   Word

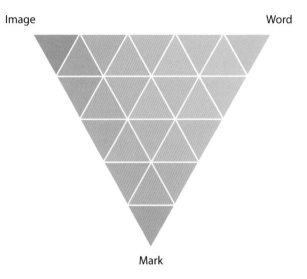

Mark

Figure 8.1
The terrain of visual work can be imagined as a triangular gamut spanning the apexes of image, mark, and word. This visual gamut defines the range of elements that can be created. Displays are usually a mixture of elements which can individually be plotted on the surface of the visual gamut.

set of otherwise arbitrary relations: this is a coded notational system, or "notational script." Since the most ubiquitous notational system is verbal language, I label this apex "word" as a handy shortcut, but it is important to realize that some notational systems, such as music notation, are nonverbal.

A passport is a visual gamut symphony
We can see these three apexes of the visual gamut at work by looking at a passport. Your passport photo is an image that stands for you because it looks like you (figure 8.2a). To specify the "realism" of the image, the lighting on such documents is usually flat, set up so that it illuminates all parts of the face—the focus sharp, the color balanced— against a background that is usually a neutral color without features of its own. The aim in these kinds of photographs is to have the camera lens become the passport control attendant's gaze, the eye of the camera substituting for the eye of the beholder. Indeed,

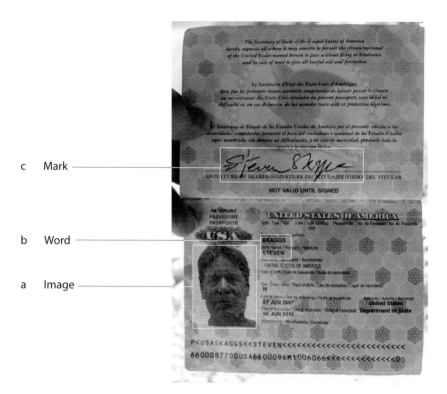

c Mark

b Word

a Image

Figure 8.2

Documents such as passports provide an excellent opportunity to see the apexes of the visual gamut in simultaneous action. A mark, an image, and a word work in unison to assert identity. A highly denotational image (a) serves iconically to denote the passport holder. The proximity of the name (b), in a highly legible typeface, reinforces the assertion that this person pictured here goes by this name. The signature (c) functions much like a fingerprint—a mark of identity based on the unlikelihood of someone being able to passably forge this gestural sequence.

the camera not only substitutes for a momentary gaze, but begins to cover an average of what might be expected in real life to be a composite of many gazes, many sun positions. The attempt is to be "objective."

But in important documents, a so-called objective photographic document is seldom sufficient. A passport or a driver's license often employs redundancy—additional means to secure the identification with certainty. A fingerprint is indexical. Your particular finger, at a given moment in time, pressed against a surface leaves behind the inky trace. The indexical apex of the visual gamut, of which the fingerprint is but one example, is the *mark*. A fingerprint mark signifies you through a sequence of reasoning:

your fingerprint is known to be unique to you and constant over time, this print matches your finger, therefore you were the one who pressed inked finger to paper to make this mark.

But just to make sure identity is well established, there is a second gestural mark on your security documents—your signature. Your signature is also a mark (figure 8.2c), the result of contact between an ink-dispensing tool and a receptive surface, but now it is the habitual regularity of that mark's pace and pressure, as well as the muscle memory path of the moving gesture, that determines the identity of the signer. Because gestural marks are almost as unique to the maker as their own fingerprints (which is why signature forgers must develop a great deal of ability to succeed in their craft), the signature acts as an identifier by being a mark. A signature is a unique kind of mark because, unlike a fingerprint which can identify its owner through a single impression, a signature's efficacy relies on it being a repeated, rehearsed, and frequently executed mark. That requirement for adherence to a pattern suggests that a signature is on its way to becoming systematic—a symbol, a recognized code.

The final apex—first hinted by the idiosyncratic loose signature, but now realized fully in the operating symbol system known as the legible alphabet—is reached when your name is typed on the document and becomes *word* (figure 8.2b). In a legible typeface such as Times Roman or Helvetica, it denotes that the fingerprint, photo, and signature—if any possible misunderstanding remained—are indeed, by bearing your name, definitely your own.[3]

In this way we see in the simple case of a passport document the interplay of the three apexes of the visual gamut, working together in concert, to deliver a particular bit of information—that you are who you say you are. Let's take a brief detour here to see how the passport embodies many of the other concepts we have discussed.

A passport as design lab

The passport allows us to see distinctions in the process by which visents do the work of identifying and denoting. We can take just a few minutes to see how some of these concepts are manifested in a simple visual document.

The fingerprint and the hasty illegible signature both identify you by virtue of being indexical marks. They're different kinds of assertions, however. The fingerprint is evidentiary; it relies on the logic that only *this* finger could have made *that* mark— match finger and mark and one can only come to a single conclusion. The signature is also a kind of evidence, but it mainly asserts by demonstration (evidence is a shadow feature in all demonstrations), which is why once a signature is attested and on file, you are asked to repeatedly mark it when you "sign for" contractual exchanges.

It is evidence of a weaker sort, and the act of signing in the presence of a witness demonstrates that you are able to execute a series of movements in a natural way. Image and word, appearing on the display in close proximity, together say "This pictured guy is that named guy." Such an assertion is an appeal. An appeal always carries a "trust me" component, an implied hint that the person in the photograph may, in fact, *not* be the named individual. The photograph, implying that it is a record from an actual sitting, has an element of indexicality to it—photograph as a marking by photons—and this indexicality lends to it an air of credibility that no typographic label can supply. That the photograph could have been conjured in Photoshop is a possibility, just as painters in the Dutch realist period often painted "tronies"— portraits that looked uncannily like a real person but were often blended features of several individuals or even complete fantasies of the painter's imagination. When the passport control officer compares the photo with your face as you stand before her, the match verifies identity.

It would be interesting to take a passport and rearrange its visual hierarchy and expression with the idea of moving it from a semantic profile XIV to, say, a profile III or profile I (check back to figure 6.4 to refresh your memory).

Meanwhile, typographically rendered names function because an arbitrary convention exists among a group of people to allow certain nonpictographic visents,[4] known as the alphabet, to be used in a carefully prescribed order to stand for speech sounds; those symbolic, graphically rendered speech sounds, now a visual word, stand to identify the individual.

This process of symbolic reference, using a system of units that are arbitrary (not resembling the referent or having environmental contact with it), is the defining characteristic of a code. With any graphic code, its graphical units can be substituted with other graphical units; as long as knowledge of the code shift is transmitted, the translation can go quite smoothly. Words (as well as the scripts of other, nonverbal systems) are an ordered, specified, and conventional linkage between some system of visents and their designated verbal referents. All codes require an educational process to teach the code. In grammar school, this is called "learning to read."

One can imagine that almost every one of the sentences in the prior three paragraphs could be the basis for a graphic exercise or further "laboratory" study.

The center of the gamut

In order to make clear the various possibilities that the visual gamut reveals, it's natural that we have immediately investigated the farthest extremes of the territory. The apexes reveal the largest contrasts and the clearest divisions in functions of the visual elements. But we should not forget that many visual devices blend aspects of these three apexes and thereby occupy an interior portion of the gamut.

An outstanding example of an identity system that occupies the center of the gamut by blending image, word, and mark is the St. Petersburg-Clearwater (Florida) system designed by Michael Bierut (figure 8.3). Here, highly stylized gestural marks resemble waves and at the same time form the letters S, P, and C. When used as a seal, the city names surround the emblem in the manner of the lettering on traditional lifesaver's buoys. It is unusual to see all three apexes of the gamut blended so seamlessly and effectively, because to be successful, each allusion must look natural, unforced, and clear.

Another artist who worked a great deal of the time at the center of the visual gamut was Paul Klee, whose late work often made use of painted marks that looked as if they could be writing, but also pictographic.

Displays: "buckshot" on the gamut

We've been emphasizing individual elements in this discussion because a display is usually composed of many graphic elements occupying various locations on this gamut, often strikingly distant from each other. A simple page containing nothing but a photograph with a caption under it already makes use of two of the three corners of the visual gamut. Plotting the elements of a complex display on the gamut results in a scattered, buckshot pattern.

This visual complexity is one of the factors that, while not a defining characteristic, often distinguishes the look of a work of graphic design from that of a traditional fine arts medium such as painting. If "polysemy" is defined as multiple interpretations for a given image, graphic design is *doubly* polysemic; it not only engenders the multiple interpretations from a single image,[5] but generally combines many informational graphic elements in clusters which operate at various far-flung regions of this gamut. A work of fine art, whether a painting, a photograph, a sculpture, is usually an exercise in image making, a whole composition in which elements cohere to a single area of the visual gamut.[6] This attribute of doubly polysemic reference does not fully define design (being neither absolutely necessary nor sufficient), but it is so commonly observed that it deserves to be noted as an important distinguishing characteristic. Graphic design almost always entails managing a complex set of submessages and composing the whole into a single display or display system, whether this is a suite of screens, the pages of a book, or a single broadside.

Because graphic design problems require this complex mix of submessages, the hierarchy of emphasis given to the various visual elements becomes critical. Displays are

Figure 8.3

Center of the gamut. Michael Bierut's design for the visual identity for St. Petersburg-Clearwater.
The emblem includes the letters S, P, C, fashioned to look like waves and to call to mind simple
sand mark drawings. When the emblems are combined with the entire logotype to make the city
seal, there is an additional allusion to traditional lifesaver's buoys. Courtesy of Michael Bierut,
Pentagram.

interpreted in stages, with each stage having a different purpose—and often a different position on the visual gamut.

The apexes and opposing baseline spectra

As with the other conceptual tools we have seen, the visual gamut is best used as a device to illuminate an analysis and need not require absolute precision. The idea is not to dispute the selection of a location for its own sake, but to use the map as a tool to spark discoveries. As we discuss particular situations, the locations on the gamut are markers that illuminate relationships and offer insight. At times the gamut simply serves to explicitly acknowledge designers' implicit knowledge of the visual world— knowledge that has remained implicit for want of an instrument to help them articulate it. For instance, the gamut illuminates some overlooked connections and antipathies between types of visual elements. In each of the three cases shown in figure 8.4, an apex of the triangle stands in opposition to a base that comprises a spectrum between two apex termini.

The image versus the graphic spectrum
An image is a highly iconic visent, one in which the immediate referent is something in the world that is itself visual. In this respect, an image is a visent of another visent "captured" in a particular time frame and within a visual frame. The capturing can be by hand or by photography, by analog or digital means. At the extreme of this apex, the image is described as being lifelike, representational (a term from fine art), true-to-life. The key to this apex is that the manner by which the image refers to its subject is through detailed and very strong resemblance—realism.

A realistic image uses depth cues such as atmospheric tonality, blurring of edges as an object recedes, texture gradients, and perspective with naturalistic colors. The apex of image realism would be a virtual world in which the experience of the image was indistinguishable from the experience of the reality itself. Actual visual images, especially static ones such as a news photo, always fall slightly short of the ideal of "capturing reality." The very act of framing a photograph, of selecting an occasion to click the

Table 8.1

Apexes	Opposing Baselines
Image (realistic, representational)	Mark-to-Word (graphic spectrum)
Word (notation, code, script)	Image-to-Mark (visualistic spectrum)
Mark (abstract, physical, syntactical)	Image-to-Word (denotative spectrum)

Apexes and Opposing Baselines

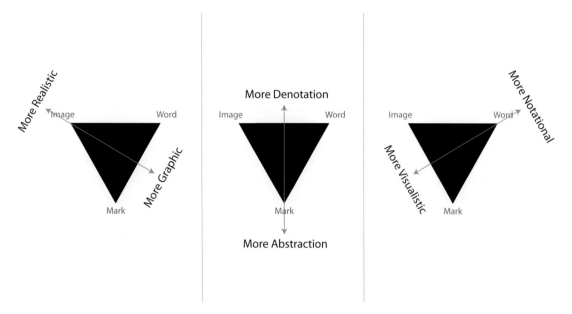

Figure 8.4

Opposite each apex of the gamut is a baseline that is a spectrum of possibilities, but for which the particular graphic quality of the apex is absent. So, opposite image is a baseline spectrum that runs from mark to word—a range of possibilities that are highly graphic as opposed to the image which is realistic; opposite the apex of mark lies the spectrum that runs from word to image—a range that is highly denotative, while a mark tends toward abstraction and connotation; opposite word is the spectrum running from mark to image—a visualistic territory opposed to the very notational and prescribed apex of word.

shutter, of setting depth of field and shutter speed, already carries the image away from a supposed total realism. All mediated recordings of reality contribute a synthetic overtone, as has been often remarked.[7]

Nevertheless, despite the mediated synthetic overlay, an image treated as a document still has the power to cause us to take the image for the thing: "That is [an image of] Babe Ruth," "There is [a picture of] the president visiting London." The omission of the phrases "an image of" and "a picture of" suggest the fading, in our awareness, of the visent-as-display and the taking of the realistic image *to be* its subject, the sign to be its referent. This transparent, ostensible directness is what Roland Barthes referred to when he spoke of the photograph as zero sign, a signifier without a code.[8] We go a step farther, and say that not only does it seemingly lack a code but it also hides its indexical character.

Standing across from image is a spectrum extending along the edge of the visual gamut from mark to word. The mark-word spectrum is called the *graphic spectrum*. Mark and word are distinguished by precisely those traits that are contrary to realism. Members along this edge are hard-edged, crisp, high-contrast, flat, nonpersepectival. These are highly graphic visual elements, where the word "graphic" alludes to the qualities that have historically typified the printing arts: the etched, clear, vivid and pronounced character of what the old lithographers called "line art."

The distinguishing feature of this spectrum, and one shared by both mark and word as well as all points between, is that the means of reference is *non*iconic. Words are symbolic, marks are inherently indexic, so any binding of sign to referent in those nodes or along that edge is based on something other than resemblance. This move away from iconic realism entails less detail, less gradation of tonality, less atmospheric scenic qualities, as these are replaced by the qualities that are more natural to words and marks. In short, what is lost in the move toward the graphic spectrum is pictoriality.[9] Picture recedes as word enters, or as marks are applied.

The mark versus the denotative spectrum
A mark is highly indexic. A bookmark locates a place in the stack of pages, an "X" marks the spot where the buried treasure will be found, a scuff mark is evidence of scraping contact. A handmade mark is almost as idiosyncratic and distinctive as a fingerprint.

Across the visual gamut from the mark is a spectrum that defines all the kinds of visents that are least marklike, and this edge extends from image to word. What members of this spectrum lack is any hint of the indexical markedness that lies at the bottom corner of the gamut. This spectrum emphasizes denotation; it is conceptual, usually having a clear and definite interpretation, and highly specific, highlighting the semantic in a direct and apparently transparent manner. Often, when viewing a visual element that lies on this spectrum, one will not be aware of the visent as a physical object at all, but only of the direct thoughts that it communicates. This is the world of conceptual art, of legible words, the world of the highly journalistic documentary photograph.

The mark, meanwhile, tends to be more open to interpretation, semantically "soft"—expressive and connotative—more abstract. It is not surprising that, from the viewpoint of the abstract mark, the map gets wider as one ascends into ever higher denotative states, as at higher levels of denotation one has to decide between moving to the left toward the strict iconicity of the representational image or toward the right and the highly coded realm of words. Marks themselves show a preference for neither.

Perhaps because it is not as denotational, as clear and transparent, the mark is often neglected in graphic design planning. Some graphic designers think of their profession as the manipulating and composing of words and images, as if mark making were not required. However, every time a designer decides to employ a handwritten title instead of a typographic one, or a loosely rendered illustration instead of a photograph, she is opting for the expressive power of the mark.

The split in western culture between the word and the image can be seen by a simple thought experiment. Imagine taking any word and emphasizing the marking of that word, as for example in handwriting or graffiti. Now do the same imagining game with an image of something; imagine emphasizing the marking of that image by making, for example, a quick gestural sketch. Again, it is easy to imagine such a continuous move down the edge of the visual gamut from image to mark. But now try imagining a move between word and image—say between the word "c-h-a-i-r" and a photograph of a chair. It is easy to place the two together, as a picture with a label underneath, but much more difficult to combine them into one visent. Word and image, both highly denotational, resist blending. Marking, on the other hand, can easily be blended into either word or image.

The word (and other notational scripts) versus the visualistic spectrum

The third apex is occupied by the word, but in a technical sense this apex should be called "scripts," because it is not limited to verbal code systems. Examples of non-word scripts are music notation, mathematical formulae, and highly technical schematic code systems such as those used in electronics (figure 8.5). Braille is a verbal but nonalphabetical script. The key feature of all these systems is that they use a symbolic system, composed of a set of explicit visual units, called characters, in order to convey clear denotative conceptions.

So in using the label "word" for this apex of the gamut, I make what might be regarded as a technical error, but I do so in the service of utility by folding these other scripts into the category that is by far the largest and most ubiquitous script: written language. The translation of verbal language into graphical writing systems is one of the major developments of our species, and it is a graphic device that is difficult to imagine living without. Nearly all displays use typography, fewer than half use an image, and far fewer than that use explicit mark making or graphic abstractions of any (nonlinguistic) kind. We are, at core, the speaking animal.[10]

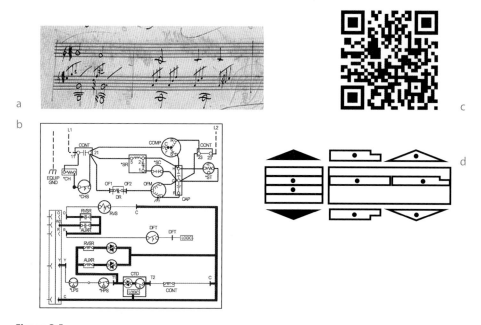

a

b

c

d

Figure 8.5
Nonverbal notational scripts. Specialists within disciplines that involve communication of complex information use their own coded scripts. Four notational scripts are shown here: (a) two bars of Beethoven's *Moonlight* Sonata in manuscript music notation; (b) a schematic diagrammatic notation for electricians, using a partly symbolic and partly iconic notation; (c) PQ codes (machine-readable scripts); (d) Labanotation, a dance choreography notational system developed by Rudolf Laban in the 1920s.

If the script is typographical, the entire set of graphic notational symbols is called a font, while an individual drawn character from the set is called a glyph. In any script, visents are used to stand for particular ideational, aural, tactile, or phonemic components that are parts of an interrelated systemic whole. A *notation* is the code system in which the nonvisual system is translated into a visual system. The code inevitably must be taught to the users, because there is nothing natural or "motivated" about this process. Sometimes the teaching of the code happens through the use of a key or legend, or, in the case of intricate systems, through formal educational means.

Opposite script, on the image/mark spectrum, one encounters visual elements that are more *visualistic*. The image-mark visualistic spectrum accounts for those elements that are furthest from words, from language, from any scripted code system. What this edge represents is the most visuality-dominant visents of the gamut, visents in which the eye is held by their features alone, not by what they may tell us in words.

It is just the inverse when we move to the word corner of the gamut. When we learn to read a notational system, the visual form of the script becomes almost invisible to us. The processing of words as language, or of musical notes as procedures for making sounds, seems direct, immediate—meanwhile, our awareness of the notational script itself in its visual detail is greatly diminished. That is why it is so difficult to see the words on this page as anything other than the concepts they convey. It is also why beginning typography students have a fondness for the more exotic typefaces which, by their compromised legibility (not *despite* their compromised legibility), are easier for the beginner to see as shapes and expressive forms. Something unorthodox (literally: unaccepted, wrong) has to happen—perhaps making the letterforms very large, upside down, overlapping, or cut off at the edge of the page—in order to induce the viewer to see material shape and form instead of reading words (figure 8.6). Katherine McCoy and the graduate students at the Cranbrook Academy of Art in the late 1980s and the 1990s became famous for challenging this read/see dichotomy by experimenting with various ways of altering textual words by layers or other compositional means so that

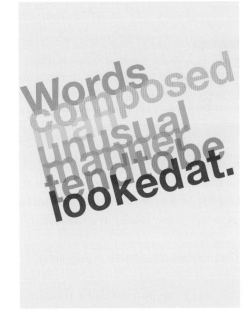

Figure 8.6
There is always a tension between the demands of verbal denotation, which require strict adherence to orthodox systemic practice, and of typographic form as expressive vehicle, which requires unorthodox treatment.

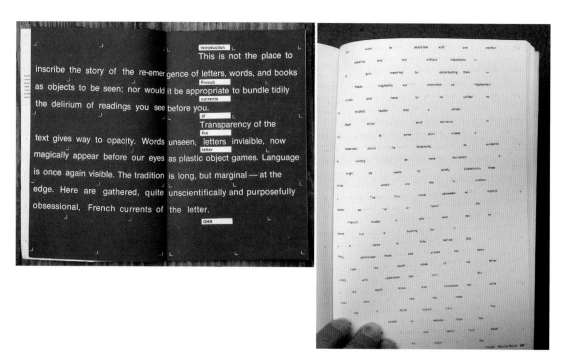

Figure 8.7

Pages from *Visible Language* (Summer 1978), one of the first postmodern typographic designs. Katherine McCoy's students at Cranbrook materially deconstructed the text of the articles, progressively taking apart the orthography until the pages were patterns of words. The text could be read—with difficulty—but the eye was so engrossed by the appearance of the page that it was impossible for the intellect to be held by the author's thoughts.

they would emerge as visual material rather than remain visually backgrounded. Doing so, of course, hindered the reading of them, precisely demonstrating the point made here (figure 8.7). When visuality is emphasized, the word *as word* disappears, and when the word is emphasized, it is difficult to notice what it looks like.

The problem of aesthetic typography

This brings up an interesting problem. If the purpose of typography is to become invisible, to disappear into the act of reading in which the verbal is highlighted and visuality is diminished, then what are we to make of the attempt to render a text in an aesthetic manner? Why bother? Wouldn't the most legible, serviceable, commonly used typeface be universally most effective in rendering language?

In the case of the aesthetic visent, attention is focused on syntax, form, and the materiality of the medium.[11] Obviously, this is difficult to achieve in typography that is meant to be read for content, as the reading makes it invisible. It is occasionally seen in typography, however, especially in private letterpress work, where the craft of type-setting and printing are carried out to such a high degree that they distinguish the whole of the typographic page as something to be felt and looked at as much as words to be read. One wonders how many of the people who have enjoyed seeing the great works of the book arts such as Andrew Hoyem's Arion Press *Moby Dick* or Donald Jackson's calligraphic manuscript *Saint John's Bible* have also actually read them. These are works that become emblems; they are not meant to be gone *into*, for they stand, as a unitary whole, for their subject. The *Saint John's Bible* stands for reverence, as "personified" (made one with the person) in the arduous action of writing out, with utmost care, a sacred text. Indeed it is an exemplification, a demonstration, of that reverence. In such works, we are summoned to the text in order to appreciate the skill, craft, and complete attentiveness of the makers. In all these ways, in private press work the text as a sign is being densely packed with features that call us to *see* instead of *read*.

But the reaches of this problem are best explored by taking apart the graphic spectrum, the edge that runs from mark to word, and studying the kinds of tradeoffs that take place as a word is located at different locations along the spectrum. This we will take up in the next chapter.

Part IV Analysis and Implications

9   The Graphic Spectrum

In this chapter and the next, we will explore insights in increasingly fine detail in a single region of the visual gamut—the graphic spectrum. The graphic spectrum is an ideal one to open up in this way as it begins in the complete abstraction of the graphic mark and terminates in the entirely transparent and legible typographic word. The graphic spectrum lies on the opposite side of the gamut from the image apex, so the attributes that enable images to signify their referents—resemblance, fidelity to something in the world, representational likeness, detail, verisimilitude—are precisely the attributes that are absent here. Iconicity eradicated, a mark signifies indexically, a word signifies symbolically. Graphic elements that lie along the spectrum between these nodes combine aspects of the abstract indexic mark and symbolic, coded reference. The central observation that is investigated in this chapter is that the progress from mark to word can not only be traced visually in terms of a visent's features (marklike or wordlike) but can be broken into distinct stages, or states, of writing.

Marklike and wordlike visents

Figure 9.1 shows a complex visent that is about halfway between being a pure mark with no verbal content and a typographic word with great legibility and clarity. When we see this graphic form, we might not see it as a word at all, but perhaps we will see in it the word "fire." Even if we do see it as the word "fire," we are still very aware of its marklike qualities. Any written word can be brought down the graphic spectrum toward markness, and when that happens, reading is forced to slow up, the awareness of the gesture is increased, and a tension is established between our desire to read and our desire to see.

These tensions between reading and seeing are brought out even more starkly through an exercise I have occasionally given to students. It's called "word for a king." First, the student must choose a word that is suitable for honoring the king. The word

Figure 9.1
A word that is difficult to see as a word because its markness is so pronounced. The graphic spectrum provides infinite choices for melting from mark to word.

must be drawn in all capitals, perfectly letterspaced. We admire the transparent, legible word and its applicability for a king.

Only after the class has labored to draw a very fine word is the second portion of the assignment given. The king has regrettably died. But the new king is jealous of the accomplishments of the old king and will have nothing in the realm that is associated with the former ruler. The edict is given that the students must now destroy the word they have just created. Indeed, they must destroy each letter in a different way.

A few of the results are shown in figure 9.2. To the students' amazement, the act of destroying their hard work becomes enjoyable and creative. The finished projects have an innate rhythm (because they are based on letterspaced capitals) and surprising energy.

Several situations tend to emerge from the exercise:

1. The student makes a vain attempt to destroy the letters, and the word is still legible through the modifications (a and b). In such a case, the relationship between the original word's denotation and the connotations of the obvious attempt to destroy it make a very powerful statement. Is the "destruction" an act of violence—or of decoration?

2. The word is obliterated; verbal content is lost (c).

Figure 9.2
The "word for a king" exercise reveals the dance between word and marking. The word is sometimes semilegible even after clear attempts at obliteration. Even when the verbal content is completely dead, the visual qualities live: indeed, they are often enhanced.

3. In the attempt to obliterate the word, new words or clear images are created, quickly making for a very complex set of word and/or image relations (d).

Along this spectrum, then, lies a rich region of interactivity between abstract graphic form and verbal content. When the verbal language is obliterated, the "visual language" not only continues to live but becomes *more powerful* in expression.

This interplay is developed further by dividing the graphic spectrum into five sectors that define distinct states of writing, which we take up now.

Five states of writing

To trace the graphic spectrum is to trace writing as it emerges from more generalized physical marking and ascends the right side of the triangle toward word (figure 9.3a).

In figure 9.3b the visual gamut is tilted back to reveal the graphic spectrum as an edge divided into five segments. Mark is the apex at the far left, and word is the apex

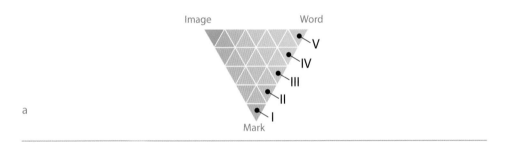

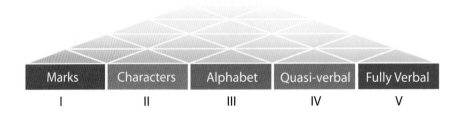

Figure 9.3
States of writing. The mark-word graphic spectrum can be divided into five segments that delineate states of writing: the five transitional stages between the abstract mark and the fully verbal word. Writing proper (in the visual sense, as in handwriting) happens from the moment a gestural mark is taken to be a character, irrespective of whether the viewer is able to interpret verbal information, which happens only when state V is reached.

labeled "fully verbal" at far right. Behind, the visual gamut fades toward the distant apex of image. The graphic spectrum has been divided here into five segments, but it is important to remember that the decision to choose five instead of ten, twenty, or a hundred divisions is arbitrary. There is a continuum here, and a division into discrete units is generally made as a convenience. In this case, however, as we trace the semiotic evolution from abstract mark to fully notational linguistic word, a five-unit segmentation happens to be necessary because there are five particular states that define the graphically written word.

As a reader of these words, you can do a quick experiment to immediately experience a shift in these states. **See this sentence as a string of graphic characters.** Notice that you have actually read the sentence first, and in so doing you "hear" in your mind the instruction to see it as a character string. When reading the sentence, you were using it as a notation, a verbal script, as words, so that you had the verbal understanding of me, the author, conversing with you, the reader. But the content of that sentence instructed you to see the sentence as visual characters. This requires going back to the line of characters, turning off the reading response, and turning on the visual abstract response. To help in this, you might try turning the page upside down—an old trick of typographers when they wanted to defeat the reading response to ensure that formal issues such as letterspacing were worked out in their typography. If you are able to see the string of characters as graphic forms instead of as a verbal instruction, then you have experienced moving from one state of writing to another. There are five distinct states of writing.

State I: marks—evidence of physical contact
The word "writing" comes from the Old English *writan*, to scratch—even its etymology references the connection to mark making. All writing is a kind of mark making, although at the mark apex it is devoid of any verbal content whatsoever, and at the other end the typographic word is so immediate in its verbal signification that we are usually unable to see it as an impression on paper or illumination on a screen; we just receive it as verbal language.

We begin our tour of the graphic spectrum at the apex of pure mark. Every mark gives evidence of some kind of physical contact. One kind of physical contact is between a firm surface and a tool that impresses into it (cuneiform for instance) or leaves a deposit upon it (ink on papyrus or paper for instance). A sprayed graffiti stroke, an inked nib, a piece of metal type pressed against handmade paper: all of these are ways of leaving marks behind which tell of the former presence of a mark maker. The graphic mark is the trace that remains; it is always evidence of a prior encounter.

Marks, by their graphic features, tell the nature of the contact that made them, the action being documented in the traits of the mark's interaction with the surface upon which it is made. One might examine a mark, such as a skid mark after an automobile accident, for the evidence it asserts, perhaps to determine a car's speed and direction. Most of the time, however, marks deliver their evidence in more subtle and immediate ways, through expression. The feeling, sensation, and intuited empathy that the observation of the mark elicits in us is due to our experience in the world, understanding its physicality, how things act and react, how they move. We can sense the impact of a splash of paint, feel the gentle press of a bird's wingprint in snow (figure 9.4). It is this second, empathic trait of marks that eventually provides the expressive qualities of warmth, urgency, violence, softness—feelings more nuanced and numerous than we can ever hope to name with a string of nouns—that we feel in a drawing's line quality and in handwriting's strokes.

Not all marks are made by human beings or by gestural movements. Some are mechanically physical—punched, stamped, crimped, torn, rubbed—or they may evolve slowly by natural processes such as the growth of algae or staining. At this corner of the

Figure 9.4
Contact marks leave a trace of expression in the notion of touch. Even when the result is partially iconic (as in this impression of a bird in snow), we sense the haptic qualities.

graphic gamut, the key attribute is simply that of contact or physical process that results in a visent. For graphic designers, marks are consciously employed to indicate conceptually that something has happened "in this place," or to produce an affective, expressive tone.

Of all these possible kinds of marks, a particular class stands out: gestural marks (figure 9.5). Gestural marks are made by the human body, usually by the arms, hands, and fingers using tools such as brushes, pens, and ink. When we watch athletes or dancers perform their well-practiced movements, our minds and bodies sense something of what it would be like to move in that way, and we perceive, at low "mirror neuron" subconscious levels, the sensations of those movements and their expressive emotional tone.[1] Because gestural marks preserve characteristics such as pressure, speed, tool, touch, and directional movement, it is likely that they are encoding information for our mirror neurons in much the same way as watching

Figure 9.5
Gestural marks, such as these made by the artist Laurie Doctor, convey emotion through the sense of direction, speed, touch, and inertia. Through "mirror neurons" we feel the dance of the mark's gesture directly in our bodies, and this expression is universal across cultures. Laurie Doctor sketchbook, 2014 (courtesy of the artist).

the action itself while it is being performed. Seeing a gestural mark, we sense the movement and affective expression that caused the mark to have its unique particular visual qualities.

State II: character marks, handwriting, and calligraphy
Neither a skid mark nor a lipstick imprint is properly called writing. All writing is marking, but not all marks are writing. Writing begins with those marks that carry the trace of human gesture.[2] Figure 9.6 shows a diagram of the major mark families.

Our particular focus here is within the family of human gestural marks. Some gestural marks may be complex contour drawings or dependent small units such as stippling and cross hatching (figure 9.7). In such cases, the gestural quality of the marking always contributes to the expressive tonality of the larger whole, but the isolated movement, the individual gesture in itself, is contributory rather than central, relatively insignificant rather than emphatic.

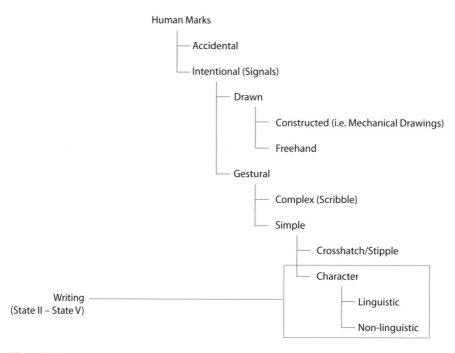

Figure 9.6
A taxonomy of marks. Marks can be broken down into several distinct categories. Only with character marks, which consist of both linguistic and nonlinguistic simple gestural marks, do we arrive at writing proper. Note, however, that writing in this view is still a more liberally applied term than often thought of, as it includes nonverbal gestural marks.

Figure 9.7
Stippling, cross-hatching, and complex gestural marks (a) do not appear as individual discriminable marks and therefore are not character marks. Though (b) is a painting that may have been constructed of individual gestures, the strokes have merged into larger shapes that are not character marks. Laurie Doctor sketchbook, 2014 (courtesy of the artist).

Figure 9.8
Made with a chisel-cut reed pen and a pointed brush, these character marks have a sense of their own independent identity, are comprised of one or just a few strokes each, and convey the path of the gesture.

In one kind of gestural mark, however, the marks are emphasized as independent, autonomous individuals, and the path of the mark itself has a replicable and powerful identity. These are *character marks* (figure 9.8). A bridge is crossed when a gestural mark is a character mark: we enter the second state of writing. It is also the most primitive state of what can reasonably be called writing proper, though it lacks verbal content.

While complex gestural marking and the gestural cross-hatching of a drawing may be considered writing-like, and certainly are expressive, the naked foregrounding of the ductus (the sequential flow of the gesture) in the character mark, brings us to something that, from a visual standpoint at least, is unambiguously writing, even when it is completely nonverbal.

As it happens, virtually all language systems use character marks as the basis for their graphically written forms. Even when transformed by technology and adapted to different means of construction, the characters of our alphabet still hold the vestigial memory of their gestured and calligraphed forebears.

Whether the character marks serve a language by being part of a linguistic graphical notational code (such as the alphabet) or are independent of any language system is irrelevant to the nature of handwriting per se.[3] Figure 9.9 shows a series of thirty-two iterations of a character mark. These characters were written in the sequence presented here, and no characters were made in between these iterations (that is, nothing has been edited out of the sequence). It illustrates how a single gestural movement can evolve through subtle manipulations of angle, brush pressure, and speed.

The question of whether each iteration shown here is a single character or two or three characters placed close together cannot be resolved. That depends on many contextual factors, including how closely spaced these characters are to other visents, whether or not the characters here are recognizable as members of a notational system (for example, you might be inclined to see letters Z, V, and perhaps R in these marks), and even the orientation (try looking at them from a 90-degree angle and your interpretation of them changes). But unlike cross-hatching, character marks maintain a sense of individuality; they require simplicity and unity in order to achieve this. Their wholeness also depends upon the relative proximity of their elements. All characters are "logoesque" in that they seem to have an individual sense of identity and personality.

As in every gestural mark, characters carry the sense of speed, confidence, emotion, and power of the individual who has written them. In other words, a character mark has individual expression, something an inanimately made mark doesn't have, and something cross-hatching has but sublimates to a pictorial end.

Unlike accidentally generated marks such as a scuff mark, character marks also imply intentionality. A character is assumed to have been intentionally made by someone whose attention was entirely focused on the making of the mark. The absolute attention of the writer increases the power of the expression through the strengthening of the intentionality, which is then conveyed in the characters. Because we sense intentionality, we see an individual character mark as a signal, a message, a display.

This infusion of concentrated attention into the making of the written form is a universal trait of calligraphy throughout the world.[4] In calligraphy, expression of the handwriting conveys deep engagement and focused unselfconsciousness. Even in a

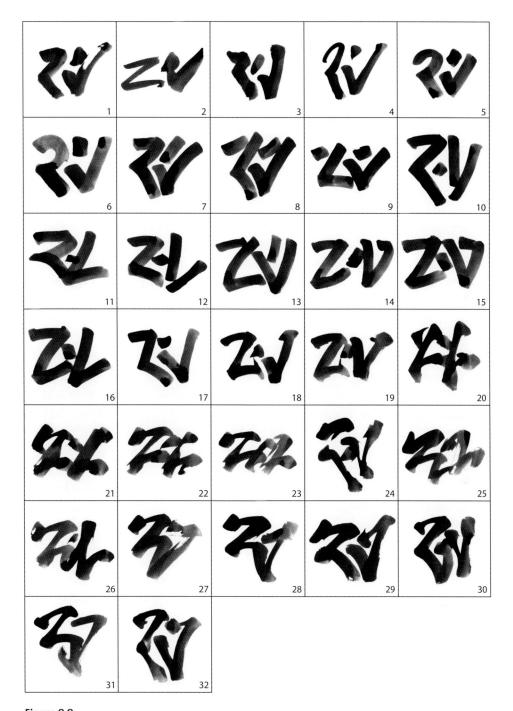

Figure 9.9
Following a character mark through modifications made in quick succession with the same tool. These thirty-two marks evolve through different expressions, breaking into roughly four groups: 1–4 (getting started); 5–19 (carefully made); 20–27 (rapid script); and 28–32 (interlocking). The viewer may easily see various letters of the alphabet in these marks, even though that was not my intent. When you see letters, you are feeling yourself move from state II to state III.

little exercise such as the thirty-two character marks in the figure, one can see the changing moods or feelings that are expressed in an instant by the brush. The sequence opens with a series of four marks that are quite different from each other in tonality, before finding a groove from 5 through 17. Then 18 and 19 begin to become looser before the drastically different 20 ushers in a series of very expressive quickly written forms which continues through 27. Then 28 through 32 return to a slightly more relaxed pace but keeping the extremes of pressure variation.

It is sometimes mistakenly thought that calligraphy is the making of fancy or decorative characters of the alphabet, but calligraphy need be neither fancy nor alphabetical. The essential ingredient in calligraphy is the ability to make gestural character marks that express unselfconscious, focused attention. It is that sense of confident movement, untrammeled by worry, tentativeness, or even intellect, that is conveyed in the calligraphic mark. Just as in a fine athletic move or in dance, it is that unselfconscious integrity that provides the "beautiful" in "beautiful writing."

State III: the alphabet and the constraints of notation
We mentioned that state II involves characters without the need to be linguistically notational. state III is entered once characters are seen to be elements of a linguistic notational system. The notational system could be logographic such as Chinese, syllabic such as Bengali, or phonemic such as the Greek or Latin alphabet. Virtually all current graphic language systems are based on character marks.[5] A roman letter might be carved into wood or metal, but the fundamental character derives from a gesturally written graphic form. Not all characters are members of linguistic notational systems, but all members of contemporary linguistic notational systems are characters.

Although writing at state III involves characters of any notational linguistic system, the following discussion will focus on one kind of notational system: the alphabet. When the marks in figure 9.9 are read as letters of the alphabet, state III is entered, and we now add a crucial additional dimension. Without losing the expressivity of the gesture, we gain the allusion to a culture, its history, a place in the world and in time, because seeing it as part of a linguistic system implies the culture that is home to that system. The choice to write an alphabetical character in impulsive brush script, or in classical roman or intimate pointed pen, connotes political and social characteristics (figure 9.10). Not only are these cultural connotations added to the inherent expressiveness of the character mark, but simply being members of a linguistic notational system carries with it the reference to literacy, books, culture, and learning—of civilization itself. Considering the power of the alphabet, it is not surprising that the possibilities of nonalphabetic writing are sometimes, lamentably, forgotten.

a   b   c

Figure 9.10
Figure 9.9 explored one gestural character mark with a single tool. If we take one of the iterations in figure 9.9 (iteration 29) as a starting point, the gesture can be explored with various tools, inks, surfaces. The tool selected will require a change of form. But regarding the gesture now as a combination of two letters of the alphabet (state III) suggests cultural overtones as well. Whereas (a) has the intensity and rapidity of the original tool, (b) renders the gestures as formal roman caps, and (c) writes the letters in pointed pen with its historically derived overtones of personal correspondence.

In figure 9.11, one of the thirty-two iterations is transformed. Iteration 29 has been "stylized" (9.11a and b) and then pulled through a number of variations. Stylization involves cleaning up "accidental" details and features that come from the whimsy of paper and the foibles of the ink. Ductus (stroke path and sequence) is retained and emphasized. You lose the idiosyncratic characteristics of the gesture, the warmth of human impulse, but you gain a sense of permanence, and the form becomes more harmonious with inorganic shapes such as perfect circles and squares. Notice how, for all its stylization, the mark retains the sense of being letters z-v until (f) and (g), in which the rotation defeats the viewer's easy reading of the mark as a letterform. It is a good lesson to realize that the mere rotation of a letterform is often enough to bring its visuality forward and to diminish the notational aspect of the mark.

It's worth noting here that with each successive higher state of writing, an additional bit of energy or learning is required of both writer and reader. The writer must make an effort to keep the forms legible so that they may be recognized as words, the reader must work through the words in a disciplined, controlled way, and of course both writers and readers, as children, have had to go through a laborious process of learning to read and write. Something is gained but also something is lost in making

Figure 9.11
Iteration 29 is taken through a process of "stylization." Stylization edits the raw gestural mark while retaining the gestural movement (a). The resulting stylized mark (b) is then explored through several more iterations (c–g). The rotated versions (f) and (g) begin to lose the association with the letters z and v and therefore slip from state III back into state II, more abstract readings.

that effort. In state III, the requirements of letter recognition restrain the writer's free-dom. Whereas state II can be as wild and expressively effusive as the writer desires, if one wishes the receiver to see a mark in state III, recognizing it as belonging to the alphabet, then scribbles must be harnessed; constraints on form come into play—the letter "A" must look something like an "A." Emotional and expressive constraints must also be accepted; the hand that writes the "A" must remain under a certain degree of emotional restraint.

When all of these factors come together in a hand-lettered title block or logotype (figure 9.12), the viewer is able to easily read the words while at the same time sensing connotations that have to do with history, culture, style, or other aspects that are asso-ciative and expressive. Unlike the smooth stylization that occurs in figure 9.11, here the edges of the calligraphy are left rough to emphasize the hand-written quality of the mark. The denotative portion of this mark consists of the words Fournier & Shaw; every other aspect of the "feel" of this mark can be attributed to expression and cultural con-notations of the visual form.

Let me remark that one of the hallmarks of the great calligraphers is that they make these constraints *seem* to vanish; their expressiveness feels effortless despite the need for great discipline. They operate under severe constraints but suggest limitless possi-bilities.[6] Throughout history, the world's great calligraphers, if they have worked at state III and higher, have always achieved this formal and expressive balance. In the march from mark to word, each successive state of writing requires more constraint on the expressivity of the writer, while providing a new set of connotations and verbal

Figure 9.12
In this title block for an article comparing attitudes on bookmaking by early French printer Pierre Simon Fournier and author George Bernard Shaw, historically evocative hand lettering inter-twines the surnames. The edges of the lettering retain the roughness of the paper, reflecting the handwriting process.

denotations. Despite this turbulent and opposing pressure, the great calligraphers continue to convey the sense of confident freedom that is essential to the art. This tension is a beautiful thing—the resistance the calligrapher feels at the conceptual level mirrors the resistance a pen feels against a writing surface. William Morris said, "You can't have art without resistance in the material."[7]

What about typography?
We have so far limited the discussion to handwriting as a gestural, immediate form of marking. But at state III the road begins to widen, ultimately to terminate in that most legible and "invisible" of graphic forms—what the great illustrator and book artist Barry Moser has called the "hearth"[8] of graphic design—typography.

As early as the eleventh century in China and Korea, typography meant the casting of individual, identical characters in ceramic or metal, for the purpose of arranging them later and making multiple impressions. Today it means any mechanical production of multiple individual identical characters. What was originally accomplished through casting in metal, and later through photographic means, is now handled through digital technology; in all cases, typography is the employment of character replicants. Although we may associate calligraphy with ornamental intricacy and typography with cool precision, the essential difference between handwriting and typography is the fact that characters in handwriting are responsive to immediate changes in the mood or intentions of the writer and can never be made the same way twice, whereas each character in typography is an identical token.

But typography, in spite of its clonal, replicant nature, is historically based upon handwritten forms, and even a rationalized sans serif font often carries a vestige of this handwritten ancestry, though many fonts have traveled a far way from their original calligraphic homeland (figure 9.13).

We must be careful of another thing in using the word "typography." It is not sufficient that typography be anything created by means of mechanical and digital replication. Today there are many kinds of digital/mechanical clones; virtually any graphic element can be easily assigned to a keyboard or other means of replication. What sets typography apart is its rootedness in language; it is no longer merely the act of clonal replication that defines typography, but the clonal replication of linguistically notational characters. By this more narrow contemporary definition, typographic allies such as ornaments and pattern elements (figure 9.14), which were historically included in typography specimen books, are no longer considered typography.

This raises an interesting paradox. While a proper understanding of calligraphy has now broadened beyond the linguistic elements to include any gestural characters

Handwritten

Garamond

Century Schoolbook

Helvetica Neue

Figure 9.13
Although the means of production are very different, typographic characters have not departed greatly from handwritten characters when words must be highly legible.

Figure 9.14
Although they are designed to accompany typography and are found in the fonts folders of graphics programs, non-notational elements such as these Bodoni Ornaments are not typography in the narrow sense employed here. Typography must be characters that are members of a notational (usually linguistic) system.

(state II), typography is now a more restrictive term that covers only states III, IV, and V. We will have more to say about typography in the next chapter.

State IV: quasi-verbal

It's tempting here to leap ahead to the ultimate stage, the terminus represented by the completely legible and verbal state V, so powerfully does it pull at our attention; but to do so would be to neglect an important intermediate step. What happens when someone hands you a hastily written note and you realize the scribbling is unreadable, or you see a newspaper written in a language you do not speak or read? In these situations, you understand that the note or news contains verbal information, but it is information that is unavailable to you, hidden behind the barrier of your ignorance. Although you are quite sure all these characters mean something to people who are familiar with them, who know the coded notation, you are left out of this linguistic loop. Such characters not only allude to language, they actually carry language (to someone else), but you are deprived of its reception. This is a state of quasi-verbal writing. It's much the same state you experienced when you were three or four years old and became aware that your parents could understand words in the patterned graphic lines on a page, but you couldn't yet read. This is quite a different state than the effect of looking at an alphabet (state III). Even though in both cases you cannot receive any verbal information and in both cases you are looking at what you perceive to be linguistic signs, the quasi-verbal shuts you out or perhaps gives you a heightened sense of mystery and intrigue. Curiosity and frustration commingle.

Importantly, because they are not fully verbal, states II, III, and IV have an emphatically enhanced visuality. Lacking a legible verbal text, these are states of writing that one comes to for their visual, physical, and haptic properties. Although they are presumably weak in denotation, they are potentially very high in expression, and possibly all the more so because the denotation is repressed. It is precisely this formal, expressive quality that can be placed in jeopardy as we move on to state V.

State V: the linguistic verbal apex

Finally we come to the fifth state: writing in its fully fledged verbal sense. Once one can read it and understand it linguistically, the entire worlds of poetry and prose are opened to us. Societies place tremendous resources behind the efforts by institutions, parents, and families to help a child learn to read. Yet, in gaining the capacity to read, we become blind to the other states. The shift in perception toward the verbal is so swift, encompassing, and profound that, from the perspective of state V, all previous states—while still lurking as shadowy possibilities—become virtually invisible. It is only with the greatest effort that we can retrain ourselves to see the shapes of the letters we read. Our capacity to see form is in inverse relation to our capacity to read words.

Here lies the source of the tension between word and image, left and right hemispheres, the legible and the illegible. As a professor of typography, the first thing I must do for my students is work against the habit of reading. I try to have my students revert to their three-year-old selves, so they can once more see the alphabet as a set of visents— as visual, not verbal, things.

However, though while reading we lose consciousness of the letterforms as shapes, those shapes are still having a subliminal effect on us. One of the most important roles of graphic design is to compose typography so that the reader has an eloquent and enhanced experience while reading. Even though the reader is generally not cognizant of the feelings she is obtaining from the expression and connotation of the typography, those aspects of the interpretant continue to operate in the background, filling out her experience. The reader is blind to them but still *feels* the effects of the syntactical forms.

During the discussion of state III—the character—I mentioned in passing that typography eventually supersedes calligraphy along the path of the graphic spectrum from mark to word. This occurs at the extreme upper right-hand region of the gamut, the level of the most legible word, the place of the maximum denotative, definite notation. Here, even the most precisely written calligraphy cannot compete in denotative clarity with the carefully wrought typographic word. If these five states were broken down into finer-grained segments (refer back to figure 9.12), you would find the handwritten word ending just short of the apex, which would be occupied by certain well-crafted typographies. While, of course, there are many fonts that are not very legible, and would occupy a level of denotational fuzziness similar to certain handwritings and calligraphies, the epitome of state V is represented by those typefaces that have been carefully wrought to achieve what Beatrice Warde called complete "transparency."[9] No matter how much the calligrapher attempts to make every "t" on a manuscript page the same, he cannot match the perfect and effortless replication of a font. No matter the skill in manipulating the pen to reduce the accidental vagaries produced by the physics of ink, steel, and paper, the scribe can never approach the attention to detail and refinements of each individual glyph afforded the type designer. Having said that, most of the fine type designers of the past century have also been exceptional calligraphers, and in one sense the craft of shaping a well-wrought letter simply slides, almost imperceptibly, from the handwritten to the hand-drawn and finally to the mechanically assisted construction.

Further observations

Before leaving the topic of the five states of writing, let me make a couple of additional observations. First, we seem to be quite good at discerning mechanical and human gestural marks. As with the first two examples of marks in figure 9.15, it seems quite apparent when an abstract mark is made by some gestural human movement, rather than by some mechanical or mindless physical process. We immediately interpret the mechanical mark at top as nongestural. The mark below it, however, even though it is still quite abstract and unlikely to be seen as characters, is read as a human gesture.

Another note is that the five states of writing act as if they are five magnetic centers. They tend to pull the interpretation to a comfortable home within one of the five states, making gradations between them less obvious and difficult to settle on. It is as if our understanding "wants" the visent to settle into the comparative stability of one of these five nodes and feels unsettled when encountering the uncertainty of situations between them. Is it possible to have a character mark that stays right on the cusp of becoming a letter of the alphabet? We seem to see it as either a letter (even a deformed one) or as an abstract gestural mark that is not a letter. If we stare at the mark, we soon decide that its home state is one or the other, and then we tend to stick with that interpretation.

But it is also interesting to notice that these home nodes are not all equal. If we see something as occupying a higher node, it becomes very difficult to see it again at a lesser node. Look back at figure 9.9; once you see the mark as "z-v"—letters of the alphabet—see if you can manage to see it as anything but alphabetical. Once a higher state is arrived at, a mark tends to retain that position. It is difficult to regain the naiveté of seeing only an abstract figure.

Figure 9.15
Moving on the graphic spectrum through the five states of writing. Physical, nongestural marks comprise the first state, which is not writing proper. Calligraphy begins with gesturally made characters, state III when we detect alphabetical characters (here used in a string, but also as individual letters). The fourth state includes writing that you perceive is clearly understandable by others, although still opaque to yourself (if you don't read Latin for instance). State V in this example is only reached by people who understand Latin. Approaching the notational apex of the graphic spectrum, forms become increasingly legible within state V until reaching the maximal level of denotative clarity with carefully designed text typography.

States of Writing

State I		Physical marks
State II		Calligraphy
		Calligraphy
State III		Calligraphy
State IV-V		Calligraphy
		Calligraphy
		Calligraphy
		Typography (Rieven Roman)
		Typography (Garamond)
		Typography (Helvetica)

Conclusion

In this chapter we have looked at what happens when we open up the visual gamut to see how it can provide insights about the way we engage various portions of the map; in this case, the graphic spectrum. We have seen how the graphic spectrum suggests five separate states on the way from pure mark to pure word. The other spectra are perhaps more continuous, not possessing such demonstrative segments. But it is to be expected of the graphic spectrum because it negotiates a transition from complete visual abstraction to a domain that is not visual at all. That is a zone that violently suppresses, indeed strangles, visuality in the process of yielding the verbal word. It is a struggle between realms of expression as great as the gulf between architecture and dancing, and it has an endless fascination for graphic designers. We will look more deeply into it in the next chapter.

10 Typography

We are going ever deeper into just one region of the visual gamut—the graphic spectrum running from mark to word. The preceding chapter showed one way of using the visual gamut as a framework, providing insight into how the continuum from mark to word reveals five states of writing. This chapter turns to just one end of the graphic spectrum, the realm of typography (including very legible hand lettering), so that the focus here will be on the maximally verbal, state V, end of the spectrum.

What is a capital R?

How is it that we recognize those inherited, idealized forms known as letters of the alphabet? They work as part of an alphabetical system; each appearance of a character is a token of that idealized letter as a "master type" in the system. An A must look like an A, a B must look like a B, and so on. But no one was around to draft the identity systems manual for the alphabet. There are all kinds of As and Bs. What happens when a system that requires such exact recognition has no single rulebook for its forms? How much form-departing leeway does a letter have? How is the ideal expressed and maintained through centuries if it is simply by whim of a populace and lacks enforcement by some higher command? Is there any other important social structure that has operated completely informally for so long and so successfully? Can the system evolve, and what kind of impetus provides the agency for that evolution? So many questions; we won't settle them all, but we will begin by asking, What is the most fundamental rule by which one letter can be assigned a shape that distinguishes it from the other letters of the alphabet system?

Hans-Joachim Burgert maintained that each of the letters of the alphabet conforms to the equivalent of a specific set of verbal instructions—for each letter, a "principle."[1] The principle for a capital R, for example, would be something like, "vertical stroke on the left, semicircle attached to the right at top, with diagonal line moving from the bottom junction downward and to the bottom right corner." A character's principle is never actually uttered or written down, but nevertheless operates as a kind of implicit understanding in the background and represents the essence of each character—in this case, an R's "R-ness."

But there is an enormous array of forms that can work as a capital R. Ten rather bizarre ones are shown in figure 10.1. That we can recognize these forms as capital R suggests that if there is something like Burgert's principle at work, such a principle is not one that can be relayed as a simple list of rules. These characters obey no particular rule, nor is there a single verbal description, line of code, or command that is universal across all of them.[2] For instance, the typeface Transistor has no curved lines, while Giddyup has no straight ones. Fette Fraktur has no true diagonal, and Arnold Boecklin has a very complex series of shapes. None of the typefaces share anything that could remotely be described as an "R principle" if the principle gives instructions for stroke direction or kinds of shapes and paths. This suggests that in the case of character identity, something else must be going on.[3]

Fuzzy templates

If you take these ten characters, make them transparent, then overlap them, you have the composite shown in figure 10.2a. Amazingly, from this assemblage of what might

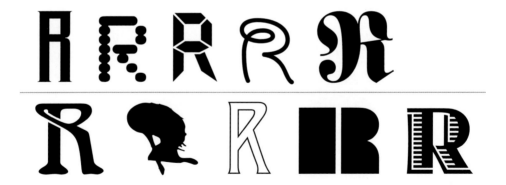

Piston / Synchro / Transistor / Giddyup / Fette Fraktur

Arnold Boecklin / Slawterhouse / Desdemona / Braggadocio / Jazz

Figure 10.1
These ten capital Rs do not have a single feature in common. Whatever it is that causes R-ness must be something other than definite rules about construction.

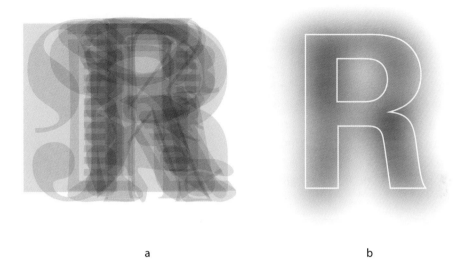

a   b

Figure 10.2
By overlapping the ten capital Rs, a ghost R emerges: the habitually included region of capital Rs.

seem to be random exotic styles, there emerges a darker central area that begins to take the form of a very conservatively styled capital R. This "ghost R" is more visible if you look at the figure from far away or squint. Figure 10.2b shows the composite assemblage blurred, with a Univers 65 capital R superimposed. The Univers cap R captures, in a very good fit, the darkest area—the "most shared" region—of the composite. This tells us that despite extreme diversity in their particular contours, the ten typefaces tend to occupy this R-like region more than any specific area that is outside it. The ghostly capital R acts as a kind of *fuzzy template*. The concept of R-ness may not be a rigidly principled wordlike concept, but a surprisingly resilient visual habit. The fuzzy template points toward typographic truth. Is it possible that we store a kind of fuzzy template of R-ness in our brains, a template that is formed from our having seen a great many kinds of capital R?

If so, typographic fuzzy truth is neither rigid nor permanent. It must allow for tremendous variation in the actual playing out of the structure in any one typeface style, a variation made all the more possible by any single font's consistent redeployment of its unique stylistic tropes in the other characters. In recognizing the letter, we strip away the nonessentials of style in order to recognize, always present beneath the font's exuberant stylistic clothing, the template ghost R within. The template provides the denotative recognition; the style provides the expression and connotation.

If this template is the principle, there is no list of rules, as Burgert suggested, only the character's habituated territory. We can follow some of the implications of this view. First, and perhaps most obvious: if one wishes to construct a very legible typeface, one should conform as closely as possible to the template. I've suggested this in using the Univers R (Univers is known to be highly legible) to show how the ghost R formed an amazingly good fit within the character. But other evidence comes from the fact that the fonts used for maximum legibility tend to be very similar to each other (figure 10.3). To the inexperienced eye, it may even be difficult to tell highly legible fonts apart. Of course, it can only be expected that two fonts, converging on the fuzzy but ideal template, would necessarily begin to resemble each other.[4]

Folio / Helvetica / Univers

AG Old Face / News Gothic / Avenir / Futura

Figure 10.3
The most legible Rs have very similar appearances to each other—and to the fuzzy template of the ghost R.

Do alphabetical templates evolve?

A second implication of fuzzy templates: they might evolve over time. In the case of the capital R, it appears that the template may be in the process of change with respect to the tail. In figure 10.3 we notice two distinct variations, one a curved form and the other straight. This variation is suggested in the ghost template which, as a composite of forms, averages the two variants and so seems to be a hybrid. Will the capital R evolve in such a way that one of the tails becomes dominant, the other anachronistic? If so, it may take a long time to play out, as typefaces tend to endure for many genera-tions, and the template can only change as the averages change. This is a built-in conservative measure. No matter how strange one new capital R is, it cannot sway the average very much. The template can only be altered by repeated, frequent, and habitual practice within the field of capital Rs.

So if alphabet templates do evolve—and there is nothing in any habituated response that completely prevents it—that evolution must work against two powerful constrain-ing influences, one that might be called a self-constraint and the other a systemic constraint.

It is self-constraining because in order to be recognized, each instance of a token R must somewhat conform to the habit of current practice. Therefore through their use, typefaces tend to conserve and reinforce the existing alphabet template. The template, while not itself a typeface, can be thought of as a record of all typefaces' accounting of a character. And since, to be recognized, each typeface must comply, if only roughly, with the template, the result is a stable feedback loop that tends to prevent change in the basic alphabetical form, while permitting variation in stylistic features. The habit of seeing a letterform is nothing but the habit of seeing what has been, and continues to be, *conserved.*

This near tautology of conservation (it conserves because it must be conservative) is joined by a second constraint due to the way the alphabet works as a system. Any template for one character is held in check by the templates of the other characters, from which it must be differentiated. To be successful, R cannot look too much like B or H. If a template is able to overcome the weight of tradition and evolve, its migration as a form bumps into the other twenty-five—characters from which it must be distin-guished—and so for one letter to change the entire alphabet must become destabilized together (highly unlikely without massive social rupture).

Given these constraints to any shift in the system, is it even reasonable to consider that the alphabet template might evolve? If we look at the historical record, there is evidence that this kind of evolution has indeed happened in the migration of writing systems across time and cultures. R evolved from a borrowed Greek letter P, called rho. When the Greek system was carried into lands that spoke different languages with different phonemic needs, adjustments were made. The Etruscans gave rho a very short stub of a tail; the Latin-speaking Romans (whose alphabet we've inherited) extended the tail. The design of the new letter was functional because it provided a sound that was not required in the Greek syllabary, but was needed for the Etruscans and later the Romans. Now with a tail, the new character significantly departed in form from rho and the other letters in the system. R found an open ecological niche.

These modifications happened fairly quickly, then stabilized over a several-hundred-year period, the forms remaining surprisingly fixed considering that the transmission was by handwriting, exemplifying the conservative influence of a template once it is functionally established. Two millennia later, the introduction of the printing press ensured that the template would be reiterated and frozen in typography. Since the fifteenth century, while there have been epochal moments marked by stylistic variants, from Blackletter to Copperplate, the central alphabetical template has remained stable. If the template is to change, the most likely lever to trigger it would be some combination of technological requirements combined with cultural upheaval or assimilation. These were the mechanisms for the arising of the template of the Latin alphabet two millennia ago, and it would likely require a similar combination of causes today.

Do we have "personal templates" and are they replicable?

If there is a narrow band of forms in which the letter is most recognizable (highly denotative), it begs the question: Why are there new fonts?[5] Once legibility is handled to the utmost degree, what is left? Is legibility all there is for a typeface to do? Is denotation always the goal, or is there a place for the connotations of historical allusions, or even the expression of personal whim?

Indeed, while the fuzzy-template capital R is an idealization of all capital Rs, it raises the question of whether particular typeface designers have an internal, "personal template" that is specific to themselves, so that the typefaces they design have a distinctive personal style. This question could stand to be studied more rigorously, but it is easy to find at least superficial evidence that personal preferences do play a part. For instance, figure 10.4 compares a sans serif and a serif capital R by Eric Gill and a sans serif and a serif capital R by Hermann Zapf. If you take the center spine of the letters, which traces the stroke path, there are clear distinguishing characteristics that would indicate that Gill's and Zapf's stylistic preferences diverge in two specific areas. At least when it comes to capital Rs, Gill prefers symmetrical upper bowls with slightly drooping tails,

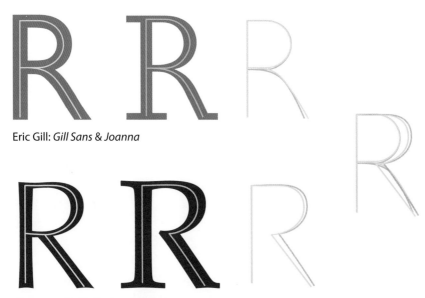

Eric Gill: *Gill Sans & Joanna*

Hermann Zapf: *Optima & Palatino*

Figure 10.4
Eric Gill and Hermann Zapf displayed habitual preferences which indicate personalized versions of fuzzy templates at work.

while Zapf seems to prefer bowls that have a bit of emphasis in the upper portion, with very straight tails.

This can be seen more easily by overlapping the spines of the Gill and Zapf letter pairs. The Gill spines of the letters match very tightly, which indicates that the major difference in these fonts is due to the serifs, weight decisions, and articulations of thicks and thins. The Zapf spines also match fairly closely (although not as tightly as Gill's) especially in their relatively wide proportions. When the Gill and Zapf spines are combined, it is very easy to see the differences between the two pairs. Each designer shows a predilection for departing in characteristic ways from the standard fuzzy-template letterform. This habituated departure becomes the designer's own personalized ghost R—running as a systemic influence in the background as the designer works. The latter template we call "personal taste."

Of course, this speculation is far from a rigorously controlled scientific experiment, and we cannot reach definitive conclusions from a sample size of just two pairs, but it could be that whenever a designer encounters a task governed by a fuzzy cultural template, an individual taste template interacts with the cultural template. If that is the case, and it seems common sense to admit it, then would it be possible to gather enormous metadata sets that would represent cultural templates in the same way that gathering random capital Rs yielded the fuzzy letter template? Would it be feasible to do the same for individual designers to investigate their stylistic habits? Ultimately (if disturbingly), would it not be possible to create a protocol for a silicone Paul Rand? a chip Chip Kidd? a microprocessor Hermann Zapf? Outputting the candidate design solutions might produce forms that would be Rand-like, Kidd-ish, and Zapf-esque, but could they ever get close to the conceptual creativity and innovative moves that typify these and other great designers? These questions will have to be left hanging for the time being.

The sizzle is not transparent

It is to the inverately positive early twentieth-century salesman Elmer Wheeler that we owe the familiar epigram, "Don't sell the steak, sell the sizzle!"[6] People respond to emotion more than they respond to dry facts. Certainly, the play of emotion is an important part of every graphic display, whether it is intended to peddle hamburgers or provide an English translation of Flaubert, but the grinning happy talk of a snappy and suggestive sales pitch (semantic profile XI) is anathema to clear information (profile VI). The conflict between these two areas has interesting ramifications for typography.

In typography, perhaps the opposite of Wheelerism is the view put forward by Beatrice Warde in her argument for the importance of typographic transparency, "The Crystal Goblet."[7] In addition to the analogy of the title of her essay, in which she compares typography holding the author's thoughts to a clear crystal goblet holding a fine wine, Warde draws a second and perhaps stronger metaphor in which the author's words are a garden, the only view of which is through a typographic window. The implication is that any decoration given to the window glass, which would draw attention to itself, can only obscure the view of the garden.

The more stylistic or personal the expression one imparts to a letterform, the more the viewer becomes attracted, and the reader distracted. This tension is always present. If one takes personal expression out of the equation entirely, presenting a text in a completely neutral, normal (and therefore mundane) fashion, a reader will focus solely on the text's verbal content in a complete dominance of the denotative word, but the sizzle, visually at least, has left the steak.[8] On the other hand, the steam from sizzling typography clouds the window.

Calligraphy as fault line

Because it is hand-gestural and immediate, calligraphy always provides an excellent proving ground of fundamental issues surrounding typographic expression, and it provides a fascinating test here. As if straddling two tectonic plates, calligraphy exists between the needs of the eye and hand and the needs of the word; calligraphy is on the fault line. As a hyperexpressive illegible scribble, calligraphy can be the hottest of sizzling steaks, while a carefully controlled classical hand can be (almost) as transparent as Caslon. Acquiring the ability to execute classically legible calligraphy is one of the most difficult of all graphic skills. The calligrapher only goes through that arduous process in order to be able to gain the breadth of expression necessary to extend her reach up the graphic spectrum from the hotly evocative scrawl toward the coolly denotative word.

The latter kind of conservatively restrained and verbal state V calligraphy, although handwritten and therefore inherently personally expressive, is nevertheless intended to be transparent, clear, and legible. It foregrounds the problem of how much personal expression to put into the text. A highly trained and versatile calligrapher has spent many years developing the eye, hand, and memory so that historically derived alphabetical forms can be replicated almost without variation, every "t" and "o" looking identical to every other "t" and "o."[9] This highly technical hand skill permits lengthy texts to be presented as an even texture of writing (from which the word "text" derives). But if you were to become the greatest technical calligrapher in the world, so that every letter looked identical—*exactly* like a printed font—then at that very moment of supreme execution you would cease to be a calligrapher, your craft useless. In such work there would be nothing left of the soul of the writer; you would do better to typeset the characters digitally. The essence of calligraphy lies in the subtle variations of the writer marking the page continually from moment to moment—and also the variations of *this* writer as opposed to *that* writer, for no two writers can write identical hands.[10]

In other words, it is precisely the *imprecision* of the gesture—in the face of the attempt to be perfectly precise—that makes calligraphy worthwhile. It is the struggle for precision, not its acquisition, that is significant. Semiotically, what is happening in calligraphy, aside from whatever historical connotations may be implied by the selection of a certain hand, is that the mannerisms of the handwriting are indexical signs pointing to speed, emotion, and ultimately to the individual writer's personality. The physical process of the ink flowing from the nib or the brush's bristles gives evidence of these things because of the interaction of pressure, paper, and other materials with which it interacts. Moreover, the handwriting also demonstrates the calligrapher's technical mastery, understanding of historical forms, and constancy of resolve. This is why throughout Chinese history, applicants for civil office were often judged worthy on the basis of their handwriting. It wasn't so-called "graphology" that was functioning here,[11] but a deep sense of the writer's ability to enter a zone of "expressive comfort" in which the writing acts as a vehicle for revealing the self as well as his literati scholarship.

In a time when the "authenticity" of visual images is called into question by the ability of digital programs to retouch or emulate them, we are seeing an interest in returning to the handmade. This is reflected in the current popularity of the hand-lettered word and the increasing use of letterpress printing. But in order to make clear to the viewer that the operation is analog, certain features that are unmistakably nondigital are radically exaggerated. In letterpress printing, instead of striving for the technically demanding "kiss impression" (the ideal during the time when letterpress was the dominant technology), now heavy soft paper is used, the typography driven deep into the fibers, casting conspicuous shadows within and across the text. These shadows say "Notice the impression—this is hand-printed." In making clear that hand lettering is authentically made by hand, there is a current fashion for performing the lettering in the most transitory of media—chalk on blackboard.

So what does this talk of calligraphy mean for its brother, typography? Faced with constant tension between expressivity and its connotative, "soft" mechanisms on one hand and the verbal, denotative "hard" demands to be read on the other, every design must walk a path between the two. Adequate research, using semiotic tools such as those provided here, can help the designer decide the relative importance of the objectives. Performing a semantic profile analysis and placing that into the project brief will ensure that the expressive and conceptual objectives are understood beforehand. Finally, it is helpful to remember that every display is doubly polysemous, containing many visents, many graphic elements. If it holds the gaze of the audience, it will be scanned multiple times; there will be more than one semiotic moment, a chance for several interpretive colorations, the striking presence of the display, then another deeper investigation by the viewer into the denotative and connotative semantics. In this way, it may be possible to have one's steak and sizzle too.

Traditional and International Style composition as symbols

In this chapter I am setting up a series of oppositions around the demands for transparency and the demands for expressivity. We see it again in the work of the mid-twentieth-century designer Jan Tschichold, who played an important role in defining the two dominant styles for setting text copy. In his twenties, he wrote *Die Neue Typographie* which outlined the methods of working with Bauhaus and constructivist-inspired modernist settings. Later he rejected his earlier pronouncements and advocated more traditional formats, demonstrated most vividly in his work for Penguin Books.

The general format style I'll call English Traditional is characterized by:

- vertical axial symmetrical text blocks,
- serif fonts,
- generous, vertically symmetrical margins,
- illustrative material embedded within the text (often using runarounds),
- emphasis established mainly by size rather than compositional position,
- main titles centered at the top.

Examples of contemporary settings in English Traditional are shown in figure 10.5a.

Contrasting with English Traditional is the International Style, which uses a grid as a device for structuring the page. International Style compositions are characterized by:

- use of the grid to provide a rational structure for asymmetrical arrangements,
- sans serif fonts,
- asymmetric composition,
- eschewing of regular margins,
- liberal use of white (negative) space on the page,
- frequent use of images or graphic elements distributed among the typography,
- grid position to create hierarchy of emphasis,
- less use of size as an emphasis device.

Examples of International Style compositions are shown in figure 10.5b.

We will have more to say about style in the next chapter. For now realize that, as a classification based on a family resemblance across many displays, style is a systemic class, that is, it is a classification made possible through the repeated similarity of its forms, a similarity that can be generalized as the systematic nonvariant ground of the class. Those class-defining features have been noted above. Because they are systemic, they begin to acquire the status of operating as a symbol, and come to stand, within the respective cultures, for certain cultural values or ways-of-being in the culture. The traditional compositions in the magazine pages of figure 10.5a symbolize traditional values not only because of the content of the photograph, but because compositional decisions reinforce or perhaps invoke them beyond what any photographic content could overturn. The International Style grids of figure 10.5b, despite showing an automobile that dates from approximately the same period as the photograph of the farmer, carry a very different mood by their composition, which is asymmetrically balanced.

Figure 10.5

The so-called English Traditional and International Style layout schemes have become format symbols, in which the arrangement of material on the page or screen communicates expectations of subject matter.

International Style has come to signify a certain urbane modernity which traditional composition tends to suppress.

The lesson is that the arrangement of graphic elements within a well-composed display sends a message of its own well before any words are read or pictures interpreted.

Harper's Monthly Magazine

To illustrate the tensions between competing typographic objectives, we turn to a case study in the most subtle of evolutions: the development of a magazine's title over more than a century of continuous publishing. *Harper's Monthly Magazine* provides an excellent opportunity to study how one institution, in its graphic evolution, attempts to address mutually exclusive goals.

Sometimes typography becomes the primary or even sole conveyor of an identity. This is true of logotypes, of course, and it is also true of the cousin of the logotype: the magazine or newspaper masthead. More than a corporate logotype, a magazine requires a legible title to appear on newsstands. Within the very narrow constraints of legible typography, the designer attempts to convey the attitude of the magazine, while presenting the viewer with a mark of high presence and easy legibility. If there are additional connotations to be had, so much the better (an example of high connotation is the *Rolling Stone* magazine mark). In terms of the conceptual semantic profile groups discussed in chapter 6, magazine title blocks need to be Clear and if possible Emblematic.[12] The subtle changes within the *Harper's Magazine* logotype present an interesting case study as the magazine has delicately balanced these factors for well over a century. (*Harper's* began publication in 1850.)

The title of any magazine sold on newsstands must work both as a declaratory label (identifying itself) and also as a logotype building memory equity in the minds of its readership. As such, it is virtually always necessary that the title be legible and readily readable at a distance, but it must also create some emotional connection through its expression and its ability to appropriately connote the magazine's editorial attitude or stance. Compared to the overwhelming necessity for it to be readable, these other aspects of the semantic profile are often secondary. Yet they account for the fact that most magazine titles today are not straight typography but have been carefully adapted or created by skilled lettering artists, who try to infuse a unique and appropriate character into the title block.

Harper's Monthly Magazine is the second oldest general-readership magazine in the United States. With its younger siblings, *Harper's Weekly* and *Harper's Bazaar*, it was established in the mid-nineteenth century as a vehicle to advertise the novels of serious writers who were published by the New York publishing house of Harper & Brothers.

For its first seventy years, the magazine's cover followed the tradition of the day, a tradition that finds its origin in the early title pages of books: an architectural set piece with the title typography placed inside an appointed space (figure 10.6, left column). A turn-of-the-century illustration by the noted *Harper's* designer Edward Penfield shows a gentleman at a newsstand purchasing a subscription to *Harper's Monthly Magazine*. The cover at this time has not markedly changed from the first issue almost fifty years prior. In 1909 the same tableau set piece is used, although the typography inside has been simplified somewhat. Two years later, in 1911, the set piece was jettisoned and the title, set loose from its entablature, was permitted to gain prominence.

The second column of figure 10.6 shows all of the title logos that *Harper's Magazine* has used from that time to the present. Immediately we notice that the title was soon truncated to simply *Harper's*. Not only does this present the viewer with a more immediate visual and verbal nickname, but the shorter name translates into larger type size and therefore greater presence.

During the twentieth century, *Harper's* became known for two kinds of content: literary fiction and social commentary. The literature was of the highest caliber, as indicated by authors ranging from Mark Twain and Jack London to Ernest Hemingway and Philip Roth. The social commentary was especially sharp, taking a left-of-center progressive position on most issues. Given, in both cases, the need to continue to project the name in a legible manner, there remain the two competing connotations (literary and socially progressive). But these connotations are tonally at odds: a literary stance suggests a gentler, more recessive mood, while the social critic stance suggests a more edgy and forceful treatment. Against the background of these contradictory aims, the *Harper's* logo can be seen to twist over time, oscillating between conflicting directions.

A magazine title can be relatively generic in appearance or it can be unusual and distinctive in form, and it can be presented either loudly or recessively and delicately quiet. A literary approach would suggest a quieter, discretely delicate tone. If we set up these four parameters as the main concerns of the *Harper's* logo (figure 10.7), we have a field of four quadrants: Generic/Delicate, Distinctive/Delicate, Distinctive/Loud, and Generic/Loud. We can make some appraisals of how the logos relate according to this universe. This is a subjective exercise, but basically if the typographic script is doing something out of the ordinary, it ranks higher in distinctiveness and moves away from the generic. If the visent is bold, it is louder than if it is wispy and thin.[13]

January 1894 Poster by Edward Penfield

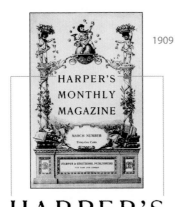

1909

HARPER'S
MONTHLY
MAGAZINE

HARPER'S
MAGAZINE   1911
(Emblematic)

Harpers   1928
(Clear)

Harper's   1947
(Clear)

Harper's   1952
(Clear)

Harper's   1959
(Clear)

Harper's   1965
(Clear)

Harper's   1978
(Emblematic)

HARPER'S   1984
(Emblematic)

Figure 10.6

The *Harper's Magazine* title block provides a case study in subtle graphic evolution over a very long time.

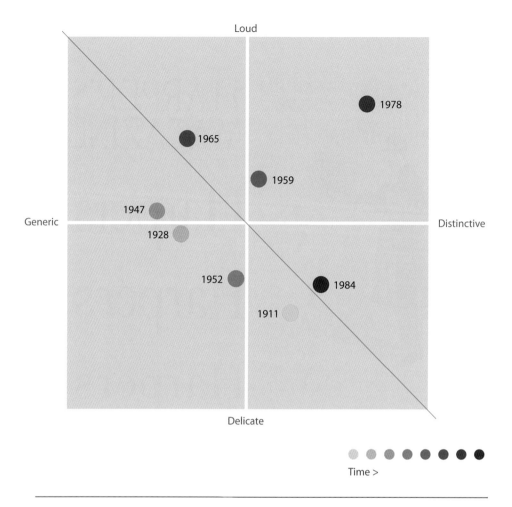

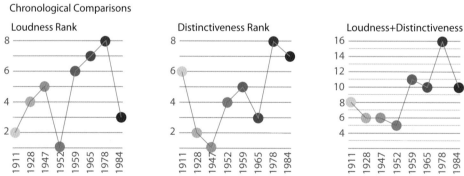

Figure 10.7

Harper's logos compared on two dimensions, Presence (Loudness) and Expression (Distinctiveness). The often subtle changes to the logo reflect attempts, especially since the 1950s, to increase the overall visibility of the marque. The double aim of the magazine makes the job more complex, as literary fiction is coupled with sharp social criticism.

Should the mark be "loud" and be seen in its role as a social voice, or should it relate to its literary heritage and be delicately refined? Should the logo be somewhat a blank canvas so that its generic and denotative abilities help it to be read, or should it be distinctive, unique, and emphasize a more cutting-edge magazine of social criticism?

The logos have been charted against these parameters in figure 10.7. The diagram at the top shows the logos arranged across the four resulting fields. In order to look for chronological relationships, the plotted points are in a gradation of the hue. A marked tendency will begin to show up if dots of similar value are in close proximity.

Discussion of results

At first there does not appear to be a clear pattern in the scatter plot of the results. The dots do not, for example, flow in a linear direction, nor do they cohere in their dates. But a closer look reveals hidden trends. The graph at lower left reveals that over the last century there has been a clear progression toward louder titles with greater presence. Strikingly, however, there have been two interruptions in this progression, and one of these is the logo currently used by the magazine. This current logo is also one of the longest-lived, having been used continuously now for over thirty years. But this 1984 logo is also second most distinctive. It has traded the stridency of social critique for the delicate luster of the literati, but it retains a distinctive look.

Drawing a diagonal line through the fields of the scatter plot, one notices that the four most recent redesigns are all on the top side of this diagonal. The four dots above the diagonal suggest that the magazine, since 1959, has always made the title very distinctive when it has reduced its loudness, or has increased its loudness when it has decreased its distinctiveness. Although the magazine has exhibited some uncertainty about whether to emphasize distinctiveness or how loudly to announce its presence, since the late 1950s *Harper's* has not allowed itself to become both *in*distinctive and *un*loud. Meanwhile, throughout its entire history, the magazine has consistently ping-ponged between emphasizing its literary side with delicacy and refinement in the logo, and then emphasizing its social critic side with a strong, muscular design.

This is confirmed by the graphs at the bottom that rank the eight designs according to loudness, distinctiveness, and loudness plus distinctiveness combined. Here the magazine shows a clear trend toward increasing loudness, with the two years that don't follow the trend—1952 and 1984—both showing concern for distinctiveness (1952 by jumping toward distinctiveness in comparison with 1947 and 1984 by creating one of the two most distinctive logotypes among the set).

Conclusion

We remind the reader that this chapter offers just a few observations of just one side of the visual gamut. The areas that can be opened up by such semiotic analyses are vast. Much of the chapter's discussion has mentioned styles and systems of various kinds, but it remains for us to give a more concise account of what these are, which will bring us out to a larger view of design once again.

11   Motif, Style, Genre

In this final chapter, we return to a somewhat abstract problem, but one that finds its proper place here as a summation of the kinds of semiotic analysis we do, and as a transition as one moves up the theory ladder from semiotics to rhetoric, demographics, marketing, and other human factors—theories that build on semiotic principles. In this chapter we will look at the way our focus oscillates, in analysis and criticism, between the unitary and the plural, and how that back-and-forth process naturally builds from some of the first principles in Peircean semiotics. Looking at the unitary and the plural, in turn, leads us to the broader questions of style and genre that will start the handoff to the social human factors fields.

Real-world analysis: visents and systems

Chapter 4 introduced the full practical system of Peircean sign classification. There we suggested that the last sign class—conclusion—is highly dependent on a receiver's worldview and can therefore be relegated to the pragmatics of human factors research instead of being considered a part of the designed display proper. Now we want to suggest that in an analysis of an *actual* display (as opposed to hypothetical ones), attention can be placed primarily on the sign classes that include visents and systems, reducing the relevant sign classes to the three assertion and the five display types.

To see why this is so, refer back to figure 4.8. There we find that, when considered as a *potential* aspect of a display, features are the first of the ten sign classes. Feature is a potential aspect because when it is considered as an *independent* sign class, it is not yet a part of an actualized visent. It is an abstraction. In practice, however, whether we look at a conceptual sketch or review work postproduction that has already been distributed, the qualitative features that we are paying attention to, such as the tint of a photograph or the particular shape of the typography, no longer exist as abstract possibilities but are actually physically embodied in the visent we see before us. If we accept the premise that, *once in use*, features are *embodied* qualities of the visent-as-display, then for the analysis of actual existing things we can concentrate primarily on the latter two cells of the first trichotomy—the visent and the system—and the resulting sign classes that include them. While red, considered in the abstract, can function as a sign of danger, if we are analyzing something in actual use, we are able to abridge the first trichotomy to simplify analysis, emphasizing visent and system.[1] When we do this, features are not lost, they are simply taken up as a trait possessed by the visent.

The unitary and the plural

So for the analysis of actual physical pieces, we discuss how a display works as a unit (that is, as a visent) or how it works as a set or group of visents, a plurality, held together in a principled way (that is, as a system). Any analysis will continually swing back and forth between whole and parts, visent and system, the unitary and the plural.

A visual system is a "habit group," a principled set, a number of independent visents held together and classified by some trait that determines them to be members of a class. The word "system" refers to the particular principle as well as to members of the class that is held together by that principle. Visent is a unitary concept, conceived as a single whole thing, while system necessarily involves plurality: multiple members and the rule or principle that holds them together as members of the class.

Displays

So is a display a unitary visent or a plural system?

Recall from chapter 4 that a display emerges when we infer that something is a signal, an attempt to communicate. Imagine the following scenario. Suppose you find yourself, on travels to a far-off place, on a hike through a meadow. Periodically, along your walk through the knee-high grass, you encounter large stones that sit on the ground and rise above your head. Your path leads you out of the meadow onto a trail climbing a rather steep hill. Summiting this hill and deciding to take a breather, you turn and look back down upon the meadow you have just traversed below. To your surprise, you now see, clearly spelled out in eight-foot-tall granite letters, the word "MASA." In that instant, you realize the large stones were the sides of the letters. If you are familiar with Spanish, you will understand the word to mean, rather enigmatically given its context, "dough." If you are Malaysian, you will understand it to mean "time." If Japanese, you might make the mental translation to the Kanji characters and think "endure and keep straight forward." If you are confined to English, the word will have no clear denotation at all. But regardless of its verbal content, the fact that you now see the entire meadow as a framing device for this single message unit makes the whole meadow become, for you in that moment, a display.

The meadow, considered as the single whole containing its message of boulder letters, is a unit, but the same meadow, considered as an array of visual parts—grass, boulder letters M, A, S, and A —is a system comprised of many parts. A display combines aspects of both the unitary visent and plural system while adding a third component—the inference by a receiver that it is an intentional message. This last attribute, that it is taken to be an attempt at communication, means that a display has an inherentand inseparable semantic component baked in to the very notion. There is already this ancillary conceptual judgment bound to the notion of display, which visents and systems lack on their own. We will soon see how this gives the display a slightly different semiotic stance, makes the display a somewhat malleable concept, and leads to other connections.

Why unity is important

When we study a work of graphic design, we assume its "signality," the attempt to communicate as a display, and then we find ourselves constantly shifting between the single and plural modes of analysis. Consider how ubiquitous this is in composition. We look at a particular photographic image (unit) and then place it into alignment with a second photograph (the two now plural) on the page (display). The alignment compositionally systematizes the two photos. When we establish this or any other compositional relationship, we are bringing independent units into a connected, plural assemblage. Perhaps we then place typography so that it relates compositionally to these two photographs. We search for a gestalt in which the three (plural) will begin to function as a single holistic cluster in a new complex visent, and if we are successful, the cluster now functions as a single visual unit. This unitary cluster can now be combined with others to create a new, larger system (plural). And this larger-scale plurality can in turn be brought once more into a greater unitary whole. This process can be repeated indefinitely, until an entire display acts as a single gestalt. This ultimate wholeness of an entire display is what artists mean when they say a work has compositional unity.

The reason unity has been valued throughout history is that when a display has been reinforced by a system that is eventually coterminant with it so that there are no "loose parts" left over, the happy result is that the viewer sees them efficiently as a single message signal, a cognition that is true to the display's function. A display that lacks unity has an inherent tension within it: if it is a message unit, why should it look as if it is unresolvedly plural? The eye is accustomed to the work of making sense of the great hubbub of unrelated things, and so the eye is drawn to displays that, while containing subparts, have already done much of the work of reconciling themselves into harmonious whole units. To stand as a message unit, a display must first stand whole.

How to make an ad disappear

We can watch the tension between the fragmented and the whole by looking at vernacular low-price ad pages in a newspaper (figure 11.1). In these spaces, the commercial pressure to be identified better than competitors while delivering persuasive content results in contradictory goals. There is a tendency to do everything as loudly as possible, yet also deliver a great deal of detailed information. But we have seen in chapter 5 with the discussion of battleship camouflage and softball bats that more content often leads to less visibility as edges become less distinct. More content places constraints on the size of the ingredients and at the same time limits the amount of buffering space that can be used to separate the display's content from neighboring displays. The

1948   1978

Figure 11.1
Newspaper pages with movie advertisements. By the 1970s, visual material was being grouped in clusters to provide white space, which acts as visual buffer to help separate adjacent displays. The 1948 movie page tends to become a single texture. The problem in 1948 was also a more difficult one as there were over thirty announcements to fit on this page, compared to just eleven on the page from 1978.

newspaper movie ads from 1948 in New York City sink into a gray, indiscriminate mass. When words or pictures manage to come forward, they do so because of greater size and weight. Of the small ads, "Plaza" and "Paisan" tend to emerge, but the majority of the ads become a texture of approximate sameness. An individual cinema's message, as a unit, is difficult to see. But there is a paradoxical result: the unity of the entire newspaper page. We have difficulty in clearly discriminating each ad as a separate display, but there is a kind of granular, fidgeting energy to the entire surface of the "movie page." Paula Scher, in her work for CBS Records, The Public Theatre, and in her fine art maps, has often intentionally made use of this effect in her design, using the massive clustering for one powerful visual statement that is then unpacked by the viewer to reveal the details.

A movie ad page from thirty years later emphasizes the individual movie titles. Here the individual ad resolves into a gestalt, a unit, each separated from its neighbors. Most of these ads use a centered treatment of the graphic elements to systematize the material through symmetry and white space to create proximity buffers. These devices keep the eye moving within an individual ad's own territory. Meanwhile, the name of the movie theater has been demoted in importance, often being relegated to a list (which also indicates the consolidation of the movie distribution industry that was occurring at this time).

These pages send different metamessages to the reader. The reader in 1948 is aware of "the movies" as a group enterprise with individual shows to be picked through. The reader in 1978 sees each film competing as a separate individual enterprise against the others, striving to corral attention within its own space. The 1948 cinematic culture bespeaks a mass activity, with unity found in the entire movie sector but plurality within the individual ad; thirty years later that activity has been reversed, with unity within each show title but fragmentation in the overall sector.

Harmony: the reconciliation of differences

The newspaper ads suggest what anyone who practices design for long knows: it is difficult to figure out how to work with multiple parts, each carrying significant information, each varying in its importance to the overall message, and ultimately bring them together in a single, whole display.

Using many contrastive parts results in a display that will tend to be seen as multiple visents instead of a single visent—unless wholeness can be reestablished through structure. Strong structural relations, whether centering along an axis or using a grid, bring the parts into a gestalt. Contrast is difference—harmony is the reconciliation of those differences. Across contrastive parts, harmony is produced by the constant employment of some kind of habit, rule, or principle. These systemic influences "tame" the contrastive dissimilarities.

An exercise in the attempt to create harmony from complete chaos is to take every-day snapshots of street scenes with random signs advertising local businesses. These street scenes were never intended to function as an entire, integrated system. The goal of the exercise is to transform the multitude of elements into structured composi-tional wholes. The original street scene in figure 11.2a is much like the movie page in 1948: a swarm of unrelated visual ingredients. Figure 11.2b begins to add some order to the set of parts, a process that figure 11.2c extends by allowing more freedom of decision making. Of course in this exercise, the designer has been granted the happy license to compromise denotative specificity with regard to actual location on the street, and this allows her to pursue arrangements that enhance presence and expres-sion. If pushed to become extremely denotative, one might arrive at a solution such as figure 11.2d.

A Russian doll of visents

The typical graphic design display, then, is a whole that is comprised of parts, those parts are made up of smaller clusters of parts, and so on, like a possibly endless series of Russian dolls. Viewed from any level of compositional plurality, the plural system always contains a set of subparts, and these subparts are considered to be elements of the larger group. Each of these elements in turn can be considered as pluralities, broken into smaller elements, and so on—until the simple visent is reached which can no lon-ger be viewed as a set of smaller units. (All of these elements, including the ultimate simple visent, possess formal qualities[2]—in this way feature as a category is not com-pletely abandoned.)

So it is that in the appraisal of every graphic design piece, the critic is constantly moving back and forth between unities and systemic plural relationships. Each visent is itself a unity, but when the visents are considered as constituent parts, the group of

Figure 11.2
Attempts to provide harmony to a chaotic graphic scene. Starting from the original scene (a), the problem is how to take the information and represent it so that it is visually in greater harmony. How much leeway do we have in changing the graphic forms? Very tight constraints (b) allow only a slight shifting of elements; the typeface, color, and relative size and position must stay constant. Given more freedom (c), the typography and overall color palette are still fixed but posi-tion and size are free. In (d) there are no constraints. While (d) is most harmonious and most effective at delivering the denotative information, it has lost all commercial connotations, any expression of excitement, and pays a price in memorability and delight.

a   Original scene

b   Tight constraints
    (to existing scene's vocabulary)

c   Moderate constraints

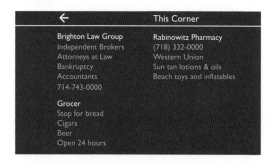

d   Unconstrained
    (by existing scene's vocabulary)

them is a plurality—a system. The parts, if harmoniously and systemically structured, become gestalts, organized bundles that represent (larger-scale) unified wholes. The greater wholes, in turn, can also be broken back down to their constitutive parts, and the process continues back down the chain until the rudimentary graphic element is reached that cannot be broken further (figure 11.3). In much of the best graphic design, this process interlocks up and down these levels, so that the entire display resonates with relation and becomes a unitary gestalt. In its parts there are no loose ends, and the whole gathers up all the parts.

Figure 11.4 shows the discussion so far. The three cells of the Peircean trichotomy have been reduced to two, with features tucked into the visent, acknowledging that

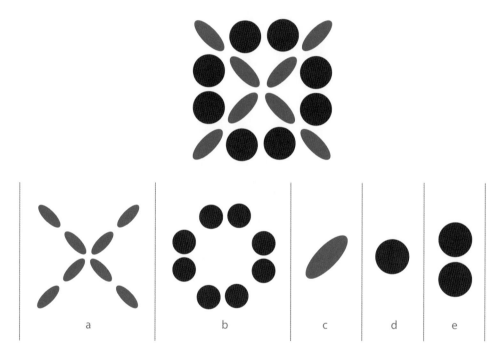

Figure 11.3

Elements and bundles. A graphic element is any discrete visent that is part of the entire display, or part of a complex or compound visent that is itself a part of the display. As a way of illustrating this principle, which is a fundamental one in graphic design, consider that the visent at the top of this figure is a complex visent made up of five different kinds of elements (a–e). Despite the gestalt that serves to bundle them into a single visual object, with concentration each of these elements is also perceivable as a unit. Features, such as blueness or purpleness, roundness or ellipticalness, are not considered graphic elements, although they certainly are traits that the elements possess.

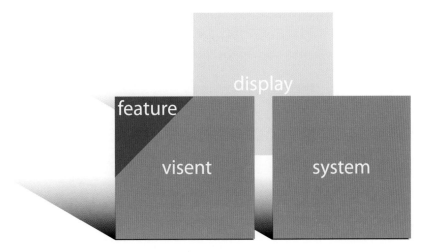

Figure 11.4
Analysis is often fruitfully focused on the visent, the display, and the system. Feature is picked up as an embodied part of the visent. Display stands behind visent and system because it is a hybrid concept involving both a unitary and a plural aspect, and because, unlike visent and system, display already presupposes conceptual judgment.

they will not be treated independently but as aspects of the visent. The display stands in the background, behind visent and system, to indicate that it can be thought of as either unitary *or* plural, and also to suggest that, unlike visent and system, it already carries the semantic content of being interpreted as a signal.

Style, genre, clichés, and lies

We have been discussing the unitary and plural orders of analysis—visents and systems. We have seen how visual features are embodied in the visent. There is a similar embeddedness on the system side. An element (whether it is a simple, compound, or complex visent) that is repeated within a display, is a *motif*. This repetition, which inherently involves positional and structural relationships, is a systemic action, which means it belongs to the plural order of analysis. Just as feature is inherently embodied within the visent, so the element is inherently embedded in the very concept of a motif. A motif is the recurrence of an element, especially the patterned or systemic nature of that recurrence (figure 11.5).

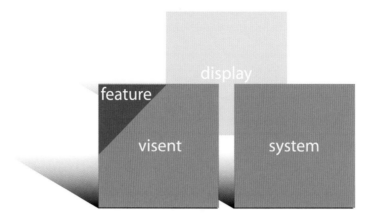

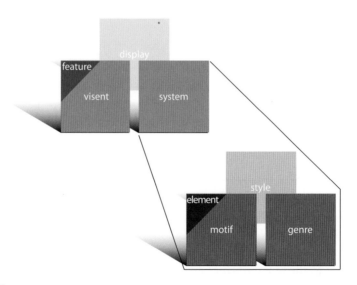

Figure 11.5
Motif, style, and genre repeat the pattern of visent, display, and system, only now they are attributes of the system. A motif is a visent repeated within a given display, a style is a motif repeated with family resemblance across several displays, and a genre is a set of stylistic devices that are habitually employed for certain cultural functions, providing a symbolic link between the stylistic devices within the cultural sector. The cultural functions take the name of the genre, and it is expected that customary styles will be used to reinforce the relation.

Style

Just as a motif is the repetition of a visent within a single display, so the motif, when it is repeated *across several displays*, begins to yield its own characteristic pattern of family resemblances. This repetitive family resemblance of motifs, across different displays, is known as *style*. Unlike the move from element to motif, the move from motif to style need not be a slavish repetition of the same unitary motif, but the recognition that several motifs share certain qualities. The recognition of the shared qualities imparts an iconic semantic component—a conclusion that *this* series of displays *resembles that* series of displays. In the same way that display adds the semantic component of interpreting the visent as a signal, so style is the semantic understanding that various cultural messages are formally, syntactically linked. This linkage is primarily made on the basis of iconic factors (i.e., their likeness) but immediately calls indexical and symbolic connotations into play. Style is never the cold awareness of formal likeness alone. It is imbued, through the interpreter's experience, with the emblematic designations of a culture.

A style's iconicity across displays must not only resemble others so that they (a plural grouping) may be perceived as an integrated (unitary) whole; it must also remain distinct from other patterns of iconicities—those of which it is not a member. Art nouveau is, after all, a different style from art deco. The entire swirling soup of these motivistic groupings of family resemblances eventually constitutes a cultural line of visual thought, distinctive enough to be clearly in this or that stylistic camp. Therefore, style repeats the same hybrid structure as display, being unitary (a single style) or plural (a variety of motifs accorded some systemic relationship of features) depending upon context and the analyst's purpose.

Genre

Finally—to complete for motif-style-genre the mirroring of visent-display-system—if a style is employed within a culture in a way that begins to form a habitual pattern—usually by being employed for a particular kind of message content or subject—then that unifying subject begins to emerge as *genre*.[3] Genre is a systemization of style in such a way that a particular cultural subject matter is associated with a particular style as a class of form. For example, certain melodramatic detective movies share a style marked by darkly lit, rainy urban streets and neon signs, a particular pace of editing, and a first-person narrative with voiced-over action. This is the film noir genre of cinema. The genre consists not merely of the stylistic attributes of rain and dark streets, but of the kind of film content that the style is linked to.

A genre, once established across a culture, will tend to be self-perpetuating, forming a feedback system. Future detective stories that deal with the gritty details of urban life will tend to be filmed with dark lighting and rainy street scenes. The audience expects certain conventions of a film once the film is understood to belong to this genre. The genre "large corporate identity communication" tends to be "businesslike" (a term which already discloses an expressive expectation of a particular visual style and function), with minimal, modernist displays, quiet but authoritative typography, often accompanied by certain kinds of noninvasively pleasant photographs of moderately affluent people.

One might be tempted to conclude that a visual system is comprised entirely of motif-style-genre material, but such is not the case. One can analyze a system in other dimensions than the analysis of element, motif, style, and genre, but the analysis of motif, style, and genre can be expected to yield a great deal of information about how any visual system operates in practice, through its token displays and a display's individual graphic elements.

Five (or six) engines of stylistic evolution

Before graphic design became a subject in the academy after the Second World War, it was transmitted through what was essentially an apprenticeship method. A young person with an artistic bent would obtain employment in a shop "filling glue pots" and would gradually be offered a chance to do creative work. This method of transmission is an indicator of the field's vernacular tradition. The vernacular changes over time through the process of imitating the prevalent styles. Stylistic change therefore, in the vernacular tradition, tends to be slow, incremental, conservative, punctuated by technological evolution more than by desire to change the look of the work on its own terms.

Since graphic design has entered the university as a discipline separate from fine art and advertising, there have been five ways that new styles have spread. The first is through classroom instruction. Design instruction shapes a young designer's choices, and as these younger designers mature, work in the field, and eventually attain professorships, the pattern is repeated, with a slow dissemination of ways of working, seeing, selecting. Such a process, though not as conservative as the vernacular, is usually still quite a conservative influence, tending to retain certain principles and compositional practices that have proved effective. The instruction usually consists of case studies, looking at examples of successful design solutions. In that way, it is learning based on what has proved successful in the past, just as the vernacular is based on doing what has traditionally been done in similar circumstances. Part of this conservatism is necessary as the student's eyes are trained to see more rigorously. But as mentioned in the book's introduction, graphic design is still very close to a folk practice, with a great deal of imitation of the stars.

There is, within academia, one counterinfluence to this conservative principle: graduate schools. Graduate study in graphic design is distinctly different from undergraduate study because its mission is to challenge the profession in many ways, including questioning the traditional formal approaches. The visual designs produced by the students in these graduate programs should be decidedly experimental, and although they may not have immediate practical applications they serve to show new possibilities, paving the way for later changes in style. We have mentioned the edition of *Visible Language* in which students in the graduate program at Cranbrook under the direction of Katherine McCoy designed pages that move from traditional typography to greater freedom until the words are actually broken apart and unreadable. Now, I would not have wanted to have been one of the authors published in that issue, but there is no doubt that the experiment had the effect of prompting other designers to become more adventurous in their use of typography.

A second way that style develops is as a response to new technologies. A new technology sometimes prevents traditional aesthetics from dictating choices. In such situations, the aesthetic itself comes under scrutiny. An example is early digital graphic design, which became possible only in the 1980s. The aesthetic up to that time had always striven for clean, smooth, and highly detailed edges for photographs and letterforms. But given the small memory of computers of the day, any enlargement quickly resulted in loss of resolution and the stair steps of pixelation. April Greiman and others decided to use this pixelation as a given and to design posters that emphasized the gridlike pixel stair steps. That Greiman came from the Basel design tradition that made use of the grid as a structuring device suited this move perfectly. The resulting designs, which used the pixelation as a suggestive assertion of the new digital world, were very influential in making the pixel a "graphic element celebrity" in the 1980s and '90s.

The third way style changes is through a kind of simple fatigue, among designers, with working in a familiar way. Sometimes it is an already successful designer with plenty of work on her hands who takes the plunge into unknown waters, but often it is a young designer with the temerity to go her own way who wins awards, obtains some notoriety, and in the end influences the design masses. An example can be seen in the work of Wolfgang Weingart, who began under the strictures of traditional Swiss typography but soon moved beyond established practice. There was a kind of restless searching for something more, something hidden or maybe just impermissible by the old laws. His massing and texturing of typography seemed very fresh in the 1970s and had an enormous influence on other young designers of the 1980s and '90s. Weingart restored the third dimension and introduced whimsy and irrationality into what had become an excessively objective system.

A fourth way that style changes is through designers being influenced by the work of fine artists. Without the pressures of corporate client expectations, but with the opposite pressure of needing to be individualistically distinctive, fine artists become an ideal petri dish for alert designers. The cross-pollination that happens in these situations can move the design field quickly. One cannot look at Paul Rand's designs of the 1940s and '50s and not be aware of the influence of modernist artists such as Kandinsky, Calder, and Picasso. Of course, the dialogue works the other way too. You cannot consider artists such as Andy Warhol and Barbara Kruger without attending to the design milieu from which they sprang, and which their work continually referenced.

The fifth way style is disseminated among designers is through the rare savant: an untutored but brilliant interloper from the streets. An example is David Carson, who never attended design school but nonetheless possesses a sensitive visual awareness. By running roughshod over the design rules, often through sheer ignorance of them, the savant explodes conventional design practice, rearranging the look of the field seemingly all at once (some would say leaving it a smoking crater). For every David Carson there are a thousand savant would-bes who break the rules and fail to produce anything remarkable at all; nevertheless, design from the street is often more important than design from the boardroom as a catalyst for stylistic change.

A potential sixth force for design innovation is through the direct use of graphic design theory. But this use of theory has not yet been tested, because theory has been largely undeveloped in the field of graphic design. Yet, as the present work hopes to suggest, design theory holds promise for future development.

Genre mixing and appropriation

If styles evolve, albeit slowly, genres present an active constraint on such development. The constraint is informal, de facto, but powerful. It is a stylistic constraint that arises through the habitual repetition or adoption of the very stylistic conventions that are required to announce the genre. A genre only works as kind of metasystem, a habit that links a look to a subject matter. Lose the look and you lose the genre. Therefore, genres are more static than style is; a new genre may require decades to be realized. Once established (and given a name), the genre tends to be fixed and to grow very little. Instead, it becomes a source to tap into in order to pick up connotational cues. Designers either work entirely within the genre (for a given piece, sometimes for a career) or appropriate a portion of the formal vocabulary that the genre represents.[4]

The wink of irony

When one genre's material is appropriated and folded into another genre space, the migration must be accompanied by a device to show insincerity, a knowing wink that cues the receiver that the sender is not authentically from the world of the borrowed genre but is instead lifting it, using it ironically as a commentary or for alien effect. It can be a fine line: fail in the wink and you are left with a message that purports to be from the cultural time and place of the genre. Instead, the wink is a device for semiotically framing the immediate contents with a cultural overlay (carried by the migrated genre), and that overlaying must be seen as a *tactic*, an artificial posturing.

Examples of this abound in postmodern graphic design, in which the designer stands against the (imputed) direct and honest clarity of the modernist message and instead makes the viewer aware of the manipulation of the mediated message. The wink in Rudy VanderLans's *Emigre* design work (figure 11.6), for instance, lies not simply in the appropriation of rococo borders, elaborate script typography, and overtly nineteenth-century mannerisms, but rather specifically in the very *non*-nineteenth-century practice of arranging these elements off-axis; or the mating of these frilly features with brutally robust forms such as bold condensed sans serif type. The pseudo-"rat fink" commercialism of House Industries or the hopelessly corny cuts of C. S. Anderson succeed to the extent that they are able to let us know they are lying; that they are using a certain genre, but are not of the genre. Here the wink comes from the extreme hyperbole, the overabundance of the traits that mark the genre. These two rhetorical moves—ironic genre mixing and hyperbole—are but two of the means of conveying the wink. Winking assumes a public that is culturally and visually aware and astute. Studies of rhetoric (next rung up the theory ladder) continue this line of research.

Genre migration: the Old West, art nouveau, and the Haight

Let's take an example of genre change. Occasionally, taking a broad historical view, it is possible to watch entire genres get lifted and shift completely. One example of this genre migration happened in the 1960s. The episode played out between two historical genres, against the backdrop of two others, and it produced a fifth. A quick overview of the way this happened is enlightening.

NUDGING GRAPHIC DESIGN

No. 66

Armin Vit | Kenneth FitzGerald | Ben Hagon | Mr. Keedy
David Cabianca | Eric Heiman | Kali Nikitas & Louise Sandhaus
Sam Potts | Lorraine Wild

In order to see the graphic development of San Francisco, specifically the Haight-Ashbury district, in the mid-1960s, you have to place it in context. Two graphic genres were prevalent in 1965 San Francisco: the vernacular and modernism. Vernacular graphic design is transmitted orally, from master to apprentice. What this meant for the mid-1960s was a set of stylistic motifs inherited from the commercial art of the 1930s, '40s, and '50s, devoid of any particular conceptual philosophical framework. This genre was directly challenged by minimalist, Bauhaus-derived modernist design, which had been supplanting the vernacular, especially in corporate work, for over a decade by 1965 (figure 11.7).

The artists and musicians who originally found themselves drawn to the Haight were not there because they saw a cultural revolution coming; they were there for the cheap rents. But the movement that developed there found certain visual cues that were in concert with the desire of many of these artists for change.

The Red Dog Saloon in Virginia City, Nevada, provided a place for the new music and a lifestyle that emerged along with it. The owners of the Red Dog were Chandler Laughlin (aka Travus T. Hipp), his wife Lynn Hughes, and Don and Roz Works. The owners decided to build a theme for the saloon: "We had six women in period costume, and the theory of the Red Dog was, when your feet hit the floor in the morning, you were in a B Western movie, and the Red Dog was the saloon at the end of the street where the outlaws hung out, waiting to rustle the cattle of the starving widow lady."[5] Rock groups playing the venue, such as The Charlatans, as well as many of the patrons, began to adopt clothing of the earlier period, originally made possible by buying secondhand consignment clothing. The interest in the late Victorian and Edwardian wardrobes spread to an interest in reflecting the period through the graphic arts promoting events there. What is often thought to be the first "psychedelic" music poster was designed by one of the musicians of The Charlatans in the summer of 1965 (figure 11.8). While the pictured subjects and typography featured the Old West look becoming de rigueur at the Red Dog, the layout was intricate, clearly hand-wrought, and moved the eye through the space in a way that had a closer association to art nouveau than the rigid letterpress displays of the trans-Mississippi west.

Figure 11.6
Irony winks. Rudy VanderLans's *Emigre* journal made use of juxtapositions of conflicting genres. Here the elaborate rococo flourish is wedded to a 1950ish commercial panel and script. That cluster is then centered under a nineteenth-century-styled typeface. A wayward UPC box carefully aligned with the edges of the page but misaligned to the otherwise symmetrical treatment completes the mashup. Cover design by Rudy VanderLans, 2004.

1965 Vernacular   1965 Modernist

Figure 11.7
Vernacular and modernist. In 1965 there were two principal visual languages in the United States. One was the vernacular tradition that can be seen in the signage and graphic displays of the street scene at left (a). The other was modernist design, increasingly adopted by large corporations and typified by the graphics employed by IBM (b). Photos by Herb Greene (a) and Lloyd Hubbard (b).

One speculates that by 1965 there must have already been an influence of the art nouveau genre. The influence of lysergic acid diethylamide (LSD) also played a role in encouraging the growing interest in the swirling lines and interactive organic forms of the old Parisian poster artists. In any case, the art nouveau genre, with its many posters promoting what must have seemed a bohemian demimonde that included absinthe, follies, and theater events, provided an ideal contrast to both the vernacular and the corporate modernist straight societies of the mid-'60s (figure 11.9). Whatever Paris in 1890 was, it was not square.

These two thematic genres, the Old West and art nouveau, were quickly appropriated in opposition to corporate modern and vernacular. The result for the next ten years was two-on-two tag team genre wars, with the genres providing high-relief visual

Figure 11.8

The "seed" poster. The Charlatans played the Red Dog Saloon in the summer of 1965. The Red Dog employed an Old West theme in keeping with Virginia City's desperado silver mining past, but the poster's rugged western typography was combined with swirling art nouveau borders and imaginative hand-drawn lettering. While not refined, the poster conformed to neither vernacular nor modernist standards, and its profligate freedom pointed the way for the adoption of "foreign" styles and genres.

a   b

Figure 11.9

Appropriation and genre migration. The influence of art nouveau on the artists of Haight-Ashbury went beyond imitation to outright theft of elements. The poster for Family Dog by Kelly Mouse (b) shows how these artists were tuned in to people like Alphonse Mucha (a) who were in their prime two generations earlier. The entire genre of art nouveau was transported to a different place and time and combined with other visual influences.

symbols of the underlying cultural conflicts of the American decade of the '60s. In this case, two plus two ended up equaling five, as the graphic designs that arose out of the mix of these four genres became a fifth: psychedelia. Fifty years hence, the use of these motifs is likely to allude to the 1960s, whereas in the 1960s these motifs alluded to the 1890s (figure 11.10).[6]

Styles are localized, like individual streams that issue seemingly at whim from the ground and flow downhill. Genres are the pools that style streams flow into—stable, permanent reservoirs, watering holes of symbolicness. Then the genres are tapped, their waters are used to flow into another pool. So the process continues, a culture's visual habits in a certain area of life coming in time to symbolize that cultural use; then, borrowing those stylistic habits, the cultural use itself is lifted and carried, as connotations, onto new cultural ground.

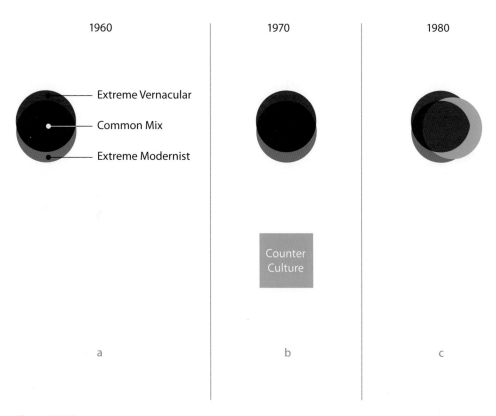

Figure 11.10

Genre wars. Although there were extreme vernacular and extreme modernist outliers, the majority of the visual environment in 1960 was a mix of the two genres. Modernism was being increasingly adopted by corporations, but plenty of vernacular abounded. By the mid-'60s and to the end
of the decade, the counterculture began to adopt styles that were in opposition to both the vernacular and modernism. These styles and genres were imported from other places (as with the
interest in American Indian and Asian motifs) and other times (as with the use of nineteenth-
century Old West themes or art nouveau). By the 1980s, the counterculture had largely been as-
similated into the larger visual culture and became a third stream, providing again a common
mix. It is always at the point of assimilation that the oppositional thrust begins to lose its power
to surprise or shock.

Brands

Given the structure that I've outlined here, what are we to make of brands? Today the word is used as a synonym for what used to be called "corporate image." Actually, a brand is a line of products by one maker or owner: for instance, all the cows that a rancher claims as his, and so marks (a contact mark acting as an assertion by both evidence and appeal) with his "brand." The term has diffused to the point that it now refers not only to the line of his cattle herd but even to the rancher as a person: you should act with integrity so that it enhances *you* as a brand. This is the same kind of reference creep that has occurred with the terms "creative" ("Ann is *a creative*") and "graphic" ("Maybe we should use *a graphic* there"). It's too late to staunch the expansion: these particular verbal cows have left their proper stalls long ago. But if, by brand, we mean the consistency of character an organization maintains to a public, then we can see in what way brand intersects with notions of style and genre.

What style is to genre in the cultural sphere, brand is to marketplace sector in the economic sphere. For example, the use of a grid, absence of ornament, and minimalist aesthetic has become a style that has been linked now to the genre let's call "corporate modern." In that way, a company's visual look, especially if it is a major player, can have the effect of making the marketplace sector that the company is engaged in take on a sense of that look. This is called inflection. Think of Kleenex for facial tissues, International Business Machines (IBM) for computers (once upon a time), McDonald's for fast food, Apple for smartphones. In these cases, the visual look, a style, adopted by a particular company—one that is dominant in its sector—like a giant planet begins to inflect the paths of all the smaller planetoid players in its orbit. The company's visual look is a particular style, but that style can begin to become the visual symbol for the entire market segment. Computer companies begin to use blue, fast food chains yellow and red, smartphones to have rounded corners. These processes lead to court cases that are of enormous interest to those of us interested in the semiotics of identity.

In these cases a company is so dominant that its presence influences the entire sector. But a more common way that brands and logos intersect is when the proper visual expression and tonality are so universally and independently adopted that separate corporate identities find themselves following the same path. An example is found in the automobile industry in which car company logos tend to be bold in weight and sans serif because that expression is somehow suitable for heavy industry and powerful cars.[7]

Indeed, the autos themselves, as visual objects pronouncing themselves as visual symbols, show surprising consistency of style, and when that style changes greatly it often reflects technological or socioeconomic upheaval (figure 11.11). The automobile styling carves out a space in the marketplace so that it becomes a pattern identifying the brand. But this identification by itself is not genre. The consistency of style of a single car does not announce the cultural use of the object, only the identification of the object with the maker—a proper extension of branding in its pure sense. It is the similarity of looks *across* many makes of automobiles that begins to result in a genre: whether American excess, soccer mom (minivan), or eco-lover (hybrids and electrics).

Style as sector identifier

So if brands are rarely able to define a genre singlehandedly, what is the interest of a brand in style? Brands use style in two ways. The first is to associate the brand with the genre that is the market sector in which it competes. This creates a tension. The brand is faced with a Hobson's choice: either conform to the genre that marks the sector (becoming less distinguishable against its competitors in the process) or stand out with great individual presence against the sector's other players, and risk not being seen as a participant in that sector because your look does not align with the expected genre style.

This is the main dilemma facing a designer when beginning a new corporate identity project. The course of action will often be determined by how much marketing budget is on the table, for if the brand is a new player in a sector, and departs from the sector's genre, then it runs the risk of being overlooked entirely. Become a "me-too" follower, however, and the brand runs the risk of invisibility within the field.

Style as identity

The second way brands use style is to establish great internal consistency within an identity program so that the brand is clearly identified. Here the important thing is not so much the connotative linkage with a market sector as genre, but rather simple denotative specificity.[8] If it were sufficient to simply make a logo appear unique, there would be no need for style to come into play (since a single logo is not a repetition of elements across multiple displays), but identity can be formed and strengthened not just in seeing the logo but in seeing family resemblances across displays. This is, as we have seen, the very definition of style. With a unique family resemblance established across displays, seeing any one display references all the others. The system is thereby

1915

1925

1935

1945

1955

1965

1975

1985

1995

2005

2015

strengthened and the style itself not only identifies the brand but deepens the pene-tration of the entire system of identity.

Nonidentical identities

The easiest way to achieve brand identity is the constant repetition of a single unique visent. However, using style to augment or even to establish identity is effective. Figure 11.12 shows an identity system that relies completely on the repetitive employment of a narrow set of color, form, and position relations. Such systems achieve identity through habitual use—the pattern of displays that, while not identical with each other, nevertheless have a principle, similar to the fuzzy template we saw in typography, running in the background. The potential to script such family resemblance patterns offers promise for a kind of metadesign that is partially driven by computer-aided conceptualization.

Cliché

If we step back for a moment and think about system, especially when system becomes genre, we are confronted with the problem of cliché. In order to employ recognition to the genre, we must use the stylistic behaviors that are the symbols of the genre. But in order to do that, we are necessarily working ground that is already well plowed.

What is wrong with using clichés? A cliché is a way of displaying a certain content in a way that is normalized and made routine. The good news is that the very routine means the content will be quickly processed and absorbed. But it does not mean that the display will be noticed or remembered. Nor is it possible with a highly routinized display for it to connote smartness, alertness, creativity, or other positive attributes.

Figure 11.11
Style evolution in a brand. An automobile is part industrial design functional object and part vi-sual design. Looking at the evolution of styles in one brand of auto over a century reveals that change does not occur in even increments (the blue lines show the large breaks in style). This chart shows the lineage of the main, full-sized Ford car from 1915 to 2015. Big Fords changed little in the thirty-year period between 1975 and 2005, becoming more rounded but retaining all of the stylistic motifs of proportion, grill work, headlights, and roofline. Compare that period to the preceding thirty years (1945–1975). Technological developments imperfectly explain the evolu-tion: all these cars except the 2015 model shared body-on-frame, rear wheel drive construction. Socioeconomic factors seem to play a larger part: the postwar boom years account for much of the rapid development, and the Arab oil embargo in 1974 meant that more resources were devoted to developing new smaller cars rather than these fuel-guzzling V-8 models.

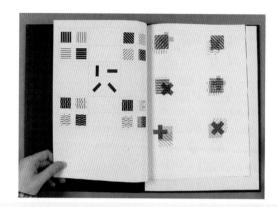

Figure 11.12
Nonidentical identity system. Edouard Pecher's "System of Opposites" established a family relationship system for the Kaai Theatre in 2009. Dividing a square into a matrix, prescribing a narrow
range of colors, providing a series of fundamental elements within the square, and finally establishing a set of relationships between those forms and a logotype resulted in a complex system
that nevertheless retains a family resemblance no matter which one is employed. Here the mutually reinforcing principles produce a habit pattern that makes the identity system successful even
though a viewer may never see the same emblem twice. Courtesy of Edouard Pecher.

The very features that make it most likely to work as a genre symbol render the
cliché impotent to create great presence or expression. This means that the designer
must find a way to twist the genre in some way, to make something that clearly uses
the genre but extends it, plays off it ironically, or otherwise foregrounds the genre itself.
Working genres without being absorbed by them is one of the areas of greatest interest
(and hazard) for a designer. The ability to do this is largely what separates great designers from the norm.

Epilogue

The thesis of this book has been that semiotics forms a vital link on the ladder of theories informing graphic design practice. Semiotics fills the gap between disciplines that answer questions about the nature of seeing and those that explore interpretive preferences of individuals, groups, societies, and cultures.

Semiotics, as it specifically applies to graphic design, has been largely undeveloped, and this project has aimed to address that need. A semiotics that flows from the concepts first put forward by C. S. Peirce is particularly well-suited for the purpose. The discussion here has connected semiotics with the perception sciences at one end of the ladder, and with research in rhetoric and human factors at the other. In the transition to theories of rhetoric and human factors, it must be remembered that semiotics is deeply interwoven into their fabric. You cannot have a complete theory of rhetoric without a notion of signification, while the human factors disciplines are all investigations in pragmatics, Charles Morris's third branch of semiotic research (along with syntactics and semantics).

Our discussion in *FireSigns* has been centered on the insights that may be derived from pure semiotics when applied to graphic design. The story progressed from abstract concepts of the sign to introduce conceptual tools that might prove useful to design analysis and perhaps also to practical, creative work in the studio. Good theory is always useful.[1] Although the exposition here has often been abstract, I hope I have provided enough examples to offer enticing clues to ways the ideas put forward here might be carried into design education and practice.

But this work is only a beginning. Even exploring a single concept, such as the visual gamut, requires more space than a broad survey such as this can offer. In chapters 9 and 10 (investigating the graphic spectrum and typography) I tried to go deeper into a single region of that one conceptual tool to show the kinds of insights it can offer. It is left to the reader to explore other regions of the visual terrain and to make new discoveries there.

In the same way, the discussion of the semantic profiles and valencies was constrained to only a bifactor analysis (high or low valency). There is no reason, other than space, time, and limitations of intellect (human or otherwise), why the valencies cannot be expanded, which would result in a more complexly articulated structure to the specificity shell, the display and assertion models, and implications for the functional matrix.

But in all of this, there is another question—or series of related questions—that has scarcely been addressed. What role has creativity in this semiotic picture? Does such an intellectual analysis assist the creative individual or help the less creative designer to have greater creative muscle? Is it possible that analytical tools such as those offered here actually stymie flights of creative imagination?

I don't know the answers—sorry. I know that semiotic analysis sharpens the eye, gives a proper and precise vocabulary to express in words what we intuitively feel, and helps us to prepare a design brief, dissect a visual problem, and tease out the syntactical and semantic relationships of a complex piece of graphic design. That's a lot. I'm also hopeful that the conceptual tools can be used experimentally in studio to open up new ideas.

But there is, in the creative act, something that is altogether *non*analytical, something that comes from a place that knows nothing of research, philosophy, theories, or even ideas—if by ideas we mean concepts that are available to logic and words. There is also the related making of the expressive mark which is so completely unselfconscious that it comes straight from the center of the maker, unfettered by thought, a direct pipeline to the ineffable integrity of the person. I'm not sure semiotics is an easy on-off button for that kind of direct access to the soul. Perhaps that is too much to ask of any theory, or indeed of teaching. At least it does no harm. Knowing how an automobile engine works may not make you a better driver, but it doesn't make you a worse one—and it may come in handy when the engine overheats. We can still witness a creative act (our own or someone else's) and feel the amazement in it. Semiotic theory may not produce genius, but it can never take that amazement away from us.

Metadesign: designing beyond genre and style

In the end, this has been a book about relationships. Semiotics begins with Peirce's three orders of relation and ends with the relationships between the unitary and plural, the visent and the system—and ultimately the system's mirrored division into motif, style, genre.

In every case, we are working with highly recursive, nested sets of relations. We design a gestalt—a visent composed of visents; we devise a system of systems, extending our reach in the attempt to use and impose style, to borrow from genre, to construct a visual brand. This is metadesign, the design of design.

Today's designer is already doing metadesign. Metadesign will continue to expand as the province of what the designer is asked to do grows. What we do grows from the planning of a single visent, an element in a display, to patterns of visents across several pages, to compositions of virtual and malleable pages on screens on a site, to entire colonies of virtual sites inhabiting large continents of interactive behavior; all of this coordinated according to the prescribed principles of the system's behavior dictated by the metadesign, which, whether specified in an identity manual or simply repeated by force of habit, ultimately becomes a sense of the self. The self of the design agent interacts with the self of the brand, the self of the thematized system.

This process must eventually result in a final relationship issue, the relationship between creator and created selves. Once the goals are well understood, once the human factors data set is collected, and once the semiotic theoretical underpinning suggests the principles and tools to be adopted in the metadesign project of the future, who or what will suggest the creative solutions? Who or what will maintain executive power over design decisions? What will be the relationship between the problem, the human designer, and the solutions that might be suggested by the assisting microprocessor? Will we retain something irreducibly human in the process? Once we have acquired a deep understanding of what we do, how do we deal with the prospect of that body of knowledge (already coalescing and of which this book is a small part) becoming a coded notational script? When we have *Milton*, our digital design assistant, at our side, how do we interact with it and how do we continue to grow that knowledge? We will no longer need to use our hands to practice our craft, we will have left folk practice long behind, and we'd better have a pretty strong idea what sign exchange is all about. Whatever that working relationship turns out to be, I have no doubt that a semiotic theory will be at the heart of the fire signs that result.

Appendix

The four tables that follow give a full taxonomy of the semantics of displays across both affective and conceptual registers. Assuming the analyst makes only the judgment that the display has low or high valencies of presence, expression, denotation, and connotation, and makes an evaluation for both the display and any assertion the display makes, there will be sixty-four possible classes of behaviors. Of course, even this breakdown oversimplifies the complexity of many graphic communications which make many simultaneous (even contradictory) assertions. Nevertheless, by breaking an analysis into fine semiotic moments, complex situations can be prioritized and parsed in layers using this system.

In using these tables, refer to the discussion in chapter 6.

The four tables are arranged by affective register type (presence and expression). Affective register classes are identified according to their relative emphasis on presence and expression. In the tables, a capital letter refers to high valency and a lowercase letter indicates low valency. So an affective register labeled PE is powerful in both presence and expression, while one labeled pE is low in presence but, once noticed, is high in expression.

The conceptual registers are almost identical for each of the tables, differing only in the semantic profiles (since assignment to a semantic profile includes the influence of the affective register). The tables account for the relative influence of denotation and connotation on the conceptual register for each type. Once again, a capital letter stands for high valency and a lowercase letter for low valency. Attributions of high or low valencies in both denotation and connotation are made for both displays and assertions. A marking of dc for a display would indicate that the display was weak in both denotation and connotation—a vague display. That same marking for an assertion would indicate an ambiguous assertion.

The display-assertion strategies are identified both by letter abbreviations and in numerical form. See the discussion in chapter 6 for a fuller explanation. The numerical labels are used to yield the models found in figures 6.9 and 6.10.

Notice that the semantic profile is derived from a combination of the affective register type and the display conceptual register type. The display-assertion strategy, on the other hand, does not involve the affective register, combining instead only the conceptual register's display and assertion functions.

Display-assertion strategy types

ED (Emblematic-Declarative)

EI (Emblematic-Informative)

ES (Emblematic-Suggestive)

EA (Emblematic-Ambiguous)

CD (Clear-Declarative)

CI (Clear-Informative)

CS (Clear-Suggestive)

CA (Clear-Ambiguous)

SD (Stylistic-Declarative)

SI (Stylistic-Informative)

SS (Stylistic-Suggestive)

SA (Stylistic-Ambiguous)

VD (Vague-Declarative)

VI (Vague-Informative)

VS (Vague-Suggestive)

VA (Vague-Ambiguous)

The display-assertion DC valency is an accounting of the power of the visent's denotation and connotation as display and as assertion. It is a total of the high valencies of denotation and the high valencies for connotation. Using the bifactor process discussed in chapter 6, the range for denotation or connotation runs from 0 (weak as both display and assertion) to 2 (high valency as both display and assertion).

Conceptual strength is the total of high valencies in both denotation and connotation across display and assertion domains. The range is from 0 to 4.

The last four columns of each table chart the relative emphasis in terms of denotation, connotation, display, and assertion.

The interplay of these conceptual factors produces the models shown in figures 6.9 and 6.10. If one were to take the affective types into consideration, there would be four pairs of 3D models in all.

P-E Semantic Taxonomy By Affective Register: **Projective Soulfuls: High Presence (P), High Expression (E)**

CONCEPTUAL REGISTER →

AFFECTIVE REGISTER P - E	AS DISPLAY	SEMANTIC PROFILE	AS ASSERTION	DISPLAY-ASSERTION STRATEGY	DISPLAY-ASSERTION D-C VALENCIES	CONCEPTUAL STRENGTH	DENOTATIVE EMPHASIS	CONNOTATIVE EMPHASIS	DISPLAY EMPHASIS	ASSERTION EMPHASIS
PE	DC	I	DC	ED (1-1)	2 - 2	4	0	0	0	0
PE	DC	I	Dc	EI (1-2)	2 - 1	3	1	-1	1	-1
PE	DC	I	dC	ES (1-3)	1 - 2	3	-1	1	1	-1
PE	DC	I	dc	EA (1-4)	1 - 1	2	0	0	2	-2
PE	Dc	II	DC	CD (2-1)	2 - 1	3	1	-1	-1	1
PE	Dc	II	Dc	CI (2-2)	2 - 0	2	2	-2	0	0
PE	Dc	II	dC	CS (2-3)	1 - 1	2	0	0	0	0
PE	Dc	II	dc	CA (2-4)	1 - 0	1	1	-1	1	-1
PE	dC	III	DC	SD (3-1)	1 - 2	3	-1	1	-1	1
PE	dC	III	Dc	SI (3-2)	1 - 1	2	0	0	0	0
PE	dC	III	dC	SS (3-3)	0 - 2	2	-2	2	0	0
PE	dC	III	dc	SA (3-4)	0 - 1	1	-1	1	1	-1
PE	dc	IV	DC	VD (4-1)	1 - 1	2	0	0	-2	2
PE	dc	IV	Dc	VI (4-2)	1 - 0	1	1	-1	-1	1
PE	dc	IV	dC	VS (4-3)	0 - 1	1	-1	1	-1	1
PE	dc	IV	dc	VA (4-4)	0 - 0	0	0	0	0	0

P-e Semantic Taxonomy By Affective Register: **Projective Apathetics: High Presence (P), Low Expression (e)**

CONCEPTUAL REGISTER →

AFFECTIVE REGISTER P - e	AS DISPLAY	SEMANTIC PROFILE	AS ASSERTION	DISPLAY-ASSERTION STRATEGY	DISPLAY-ASSERTION D-C VALENCIES	CONCEPTUAL STRENGTH	DENOTATIVE EMPHASIS	CONNOTATIVE EMPHASIS	DISPLAY EMPHASIS	ASSERTION EMPHASIS
Pe	DC	V	DC	ED (1-1)	2 - 2	4	0	0	0	0
Pe	DC	V	Dc	EI (1-2)	2 - 1	3	1	-1	1	-1
Pe	DC	V	dC	ES (1-3)	1 - 2	3	-1	1	1	-1
Pe	DC	V	dc	EA (1-4)	1 - 1	2	0	0	2	-2
Pe	Dc	VI	DC	CD (2-1)	2 - 1	3	1	-1	-1	1
Pe	Dc	VI	Dc	CI (2-2)	2 - 0	2	2	-2	0	0
Pe	Dc	VI	dC	CS (2-3)	1 - 1	2	0	0	0	0
Pe	Dc	VI	dc	CA (2-4)	1 - 0	1	1	-1	1	-1
Pe	dC	VII	DC	SD (3-1)	1 - 2	3	-1	1	-1	1
Pe	dC	VII	Dc	SI (3-2)	1 - 1	2	0	0	0	0
Pe	dC	VII	dC	SS (3-3)	0 - 2	2	-2	2	0	0
Pe	dC	VII	dc	SA (3-4)	0 - 1	1	-1	1	1	-1
Pe	dc	VIII	DC	VD (4-1)	1 - 1	2	0	0	-2	2
Pe	dc	VIII	Dc	VI (4-2)	1 - 0	1	1	-1	-1	1
Pe	dc	VIII	dC	VS (4-3)	0 - 1	1	-1	1	-1	1
Pe	dc	VIII	dc	VA (4-4)	0 - 0	0	0	0	0	0

p-E   Semantic Taxonomy By Affective Register: **Recessive Soulfuls: Low Presence (e), High Expression (E)**

CONCEPTUAL REGISTER →

AFFECTIVE REGISTER p - E	AS DISPLAY	SEMANTIC PROFILE	AS ASSERTION	DISPLAY-ASSERTION STRATEGY	DISPLAY-ASSERTION D-C VALENCIES	CONCEPTUAL STRENGTH	DENOTATIVE EMPHASIS	CONNOTATIVE EMPHASIS	DISPLAY EMPHASIS	ASSERTION EMPHASIS
pE	DC	IX	DC	ED (1-1)	2 - 2	4	0	0	0	0
pE	DC	IX	Dc	EI (1-2)	2 - 1	3	1	-1	1	-1
pE	DC	IX	dC	ES (1-3)	1 - 2	3	-1	1	1	-1
pE	DC	IX	dc	EA (1-4)	1 - 1	2	0	0	2	-2
pE	Dc	X	DC	CD (2-1)	2 - 1	3	1	-1	-1	1
pE	Dc	X	Dc	CI (2-2)	2 - 0	2	2	-2	0	0
pE	Dc	X	dC	CS (2-3)	1 - 1	2	0	0	0	0
pE	Dc	X	dc	CA (2-4)	1 - 0	1	1	-1	1	-1
pE	dC	XI	DC	SD (3-1)	1 - 2	3	-1	1	-1	1
pE	dC	XI	Dc	SI (3-2)	1 - 1	2	0	0	0	0
pE	dC	XI	dC	SS (3-3)	0 - 2	2	-2	2	0	0
pE	dC	XI	dc	SA (3-4)	0 - 1	1	-1	1	1	-1
pE	dc	XII	DC	VD (4-1)	1 - 1	2	0	0	-2	2
pE	dc	XII	Dc	VI (4-2)	1 - 0	1	1	-1	-1	1
pE	dc	XII	dC	VS (4-3)	0 - 1	1	-1	1	-1	1
pE	dc	XII	dc	VA (4-4)	0 - 0	0	0	0	0	0

Semantic Taxonomy By Affective Register: **Recessive Apathetics: Low Presence (p), Low Expression (e)**

C O N C E P T U A L   R E G I S T E R

AFFECTIVE REGISTER p - e	AS DISPLAY	SEMANTIC PROFILE	AS ASSERTION	DISPLAY-ASSERTION STRATEGY	DISPLAY-ASSERTION D-C VALENCIES	CONCEPTUAL STRENGTH	DENOTATIVE EMPHASIS	CONNOTATIVE EMPHASIS	DISPLAY EMPHASIS	ASSERTION EMPHASIS
pe	DC	XIII	DC	ED (1-1)	2 - 2	4	0	0	0	0
pe	DC	XIII	Dc	EI (1-2)	2 - 1	3	1	-1	1	-1
pe	DC	XIII	dC	ES (1-3)	1 - 2	3	-1	1	1	-1
pe	DC	XIII	dc	EA (1-4)	1 - 1	2	0	0	2	-2
pe	Dc	XIV	DC	CD (2-1)	2 - 1	3	1	-1	-1	1
pe	Dc	XIV	Dc	CI (2-2)	2 - 0	2	2	-2	0	0
pe	Dc	XIV	dC	CS (2-3)	1 - 1	2	0	0	0	0
pe	Dc	XIV	dc	CA (2-4)	1 - 0	1	1	-1	1	-1
pe	dC	XV	DC	SD (3-1)	1 - 2	3	-1	1	-1	1
pe	dC	XV	Dc	SI (3-2)	1 - 1	2	0	0	0	0
pe	dC	XV	dC	SS (3-3)	0 - 2	2	-2	2	0	0
pe	dC	XV	dc	SA (3-4)	0 - 1	1	-1	1	1	-1
pe	dc	XVI	DC	VD (4-1)	1 - 1	2	0	0	-2	2
pe	dc	XVI	Dc	VI (4-2)	1 - 0	1	1	-1	-1	1
pe	dc	XVI	dC	VS (4-3)	0 - 1	1	-1	1	-1	1
pe	dc	XVI	dc	VA (4-4)	0 - 0	0	0	0	0	0

Notes

Introduction

1. Steven Heller, "W. A. Dwiggins: Master of the Book," *Step-by-Step Graphics*, January-February 1991, 108.

2. David Jury, *Graphic Design before Graphic Designers* (London: Thames and Hudson, 2012).

3. For more on the debates about fashion and style, and how an "authentic" style could be developed, see Frederic Schwartz's *The Werkbund*. The Deutsche Werkbund was a predecessor of and greatly influenced the philosophy of the Bauhaus. Frederic J. Schwartz, *The Werkbund* (New Haven: Yale University Press, 1996).

4. Derrida's *On Grammatology* and other writings provided the main inspiration for deconstruction and the experiments of the decon designers. Jacques Derrida, *Of Grammatology*, trans. Gayatri Chakravorty Spivak (Baltimore: Johns Hopkins University Press, 1976).

5. Roland Barthes, *Image, Music, Text* (New York: Hill and Wang, 1977).

6. Ellen Lupton and J. Abbott Miller, "Deconstruction and Graphic Design: History Meets Theory," *Visible Language* 28, no. 4 (1994), 346.

7. Raphael Satter (Associated Press), *Louisville Courier-Journal*, reported March 8, 2013.

8. Steven Skaggs, "Good Theory Is Useful Theory," *AIGA Journal* 15, no. 2 (1997), 7.

Chapter 1

1. Jessie J. Peissig and Michael J. Tarr, "Visual Object Recognition: Do We Know More Now Than We Did 20 Years Ago?," *Annual Review of Psychology* 58 (2007), 75.

2.

Nor over-marvellous must this be deemed
In these affairs that, though the films which strike
Upon the eyes cannot be singly seen,
The things themselves may be perceived.

Lucretius (Titus Lucretius Carus), *De rerum natura*, trans. William Ellery Leonard, Gutenberg Project eBook #785, http://www.gutenberg.org/files/785/785-h/785-h.htm#link2H_4_0021, release date July 31, 2008; updated February 4, 2013; accessed April 4, 2015.

3. David L. Gosling, *Science and the Indian Tradition: When Einstein Met Tagore* (New York: Routledge, 2007), 8–9.

4. Tagore refers here to the notion that what is apparently "solid" is in fact made up of atoms which, from *their* perspective, would be as far apart from each other as the planets of the solar system—therefore what is solid is really mostly space.

5. Paul Coates, *The Metaphysics of Perception* (New York: Routledge, 2007), 57–60.

6. Irving Biederman, "Recognizing Depth-Rotated Objects: A Review of Recent Research and Theory," *Spatial Vision* 13 (2000), 241–253.

7. To be fair to Tagore's subtle position here, he only says it makes no sense to speak of Truth or Reality that is separate from, not the individual's mind, but rather a supposed "universal mind," i.e., what would be perceived by a "super-personal" human mind. The qualia therefore become idealized and generalized factors, not the particular sensations of the individual.

8. J. K. O'Regan, "Solving the 'Real' Mysteries of Visual Perception: The World as an Outside Memory," *Canadian Journal of Psychology* 46, no. 3 (1992), 461–488.

9. This situation has changed somewhat with the current interest in so-called "blind sight."

10. Christoph M. Michel, Margitta Seeck, and Micah M. Murray, "The Speed of Visual Cognition," *Supplements to Clinical Neurophysiology* 57 (2004), 617–627.

11. Martin J. Tovée, "Neuronal Processing: How Fast Is the Speed of Thought?," *Current Biology* 4, no. 12 (1994), 1125–1127.

Chapter 2

1. I'm using the words visual "entity" instead of visual "object" because all too often the word "object" is thought to refer only to physical objects like cups and balls. I want to allow for a much broader range of reference.

2. Other words that designers often use that are somewhat equivalent to "visent" are "design," "graphic," "display," "figure," "piece," "visual thing," "element," and "text." Each of these other terms (all are meant here as nouns) often try to get to the notion of a single thing to be the focus of some discussion or analysis. These other terms are also confusing and problematic, which is why the broad neutral term "visual entity" has been adopted here. I will assign more proper and narrow references for some of these other terms during the course of this book.

3. By differential I simply mean a difference in the field of photons—the "light field" or "light map"—that will reach the eye.

4. This might seem remarkably facile, but it's important that we keep in mind that graphic design is the planning of visents in such a way that they will operate within a particular circumstance. The visent is not the circumstance itself, nor is it an actually perceived thing if it is never gazed upon.

5. Jacob Feldman, "What Is a Visual Object?," *Trends in Cognitive Science* 7, no. 6 (2003), 256.

6. This collapse is not the instantaneous wave collapse that physicists speak of in quantum theory. Rather there is a quick funneling, or limiting, of possibilities leading up to the actual experience. Going back to the playing card analogy, if you turn over an ace of clubs, then the possible information set of the next card lying face down has been reduced from fifty-two to fifty-one. Perhaps it will be possible some day to define better this "limiting progression" of possibilities.

7. A path that begins at a particular point, goes all the way around the figure, and ends at the same point to produce a closed shape. A ready example is any fillable closed path in a vector drawing program.

8. For instance, the counter of an "e" or an "a" can make those letters complex visents within the compounded visents of the sentence, paragraph, or text block.

Chapter 3

1. In citing Peirce, I will be employing the standard practice in Peirce scholarship of abbreviating his *Collected Papers* as CP and then providing volume and paragraph numbers: CP 2.168 is Charles Sanders Peirce, *Collected Papers*, ed. Charles Hartshorne, Paul Weiss, and A. W. Burkes, 8 vols. (Cambridge: Belknap Press of Harvard University Press, 1958–1966), vol. 2, paragraph 168.

2. Semioticians will note that in referring to these as first-order, second-order, and third-order relations, I depart from Peirce's more abstract terminology of Firstness, Secondness, and Thirdness.

3. Peirce showed that all apparent relational orders above three can be reduced to these three. For his argument for the nonexpansion and nonreducibility of the triadic set of relations, see CP 4.530–572 and CP 3.456–552.

4. Floyd Merrell, *Signs Grow: Semiosis and Life Processes* (Toronto: University of Toronto Press, 1996).

5. The interpretant generally becomes, in its turn, a sign for additional interpretation, thereby establishing the chain reaction of signification that gives the sense of flow to experience and to thought. This chain of sign action is called *semiosis*. See CP 5.484–489.

6. We are adopting a Peircean view of the sign. In Saussurian semiology, a sign is the uniting of a signifier and a signified. The two perspectives resist translation from one to the other.

"Interpretant" is used instead of "interpretation" in order to distinguish it from the verb form of the latter word; it carries roughly the same meaning as "interpretation" when used as a noun.

7. Peirce, in a famous 1908 letter to Lady Victoria Welby, calls the interpretant the sign's "effect upon a person"—then immediately calls that framing a "sop to Cerberus" by admitting that the limiting condition "upon a person" was included only because "I despair of making my own broader conception understood" (*The Essential Peirce: Selected Philosophical Writings*, vol. 2, ed. Peirce Edition Project [Bloomington: Indiana University Press, 1998], 478). If we recognize that when we speak of interpersonal visual communication, we are working a particular subset within Peirce's "broader conception" of the interpretant, we can usefully think of the interpretant as the effect a sign has upon one's interpreting of it, the manifestation of that interpretive effort—in other words, an understanding. This comes with one proviso: that we must include within the notion of "understanding" not just the denotata, but also all the feelings, expressions, associations, and nuances that occur when we observe a thing.

8. We owe to Charles W. Morris in his *Signs, Language and Behavior* (New York: Braziller, 1946) this threefold division of semantics, syntactics, and pragmatics.

9. A similar analogy with a design project: the referent can be considered to be the targeted meaning or purpose of the communication as stated in the project brief; the sign is the design itself—the visent or system of visents deployed; and the interpretant is the actual effect that the project has on its audience when it is seen. One usually hopes in this case that the referent and the interpretant are very close.

10. For this reason, the Peircean system has the Derridean concepts of play, bricolage, and deference already built into it. For a Peircean, there is nothing revolutionary in reading poststructuralist semiology.

11. In order to be reminded of this externality, listen to how we speak. When we point to a visual object and speak about what "it" is, or the qualities "it" has, we are always subtly suggesting with the pronoun "it" this primal perspective outside of, and yet so fundamental to, our particular instance of experiencing it. But because a visent has perception "baked in" to its very core as possibilities of *experience*, we find it impossible to completely separate the "waving yellowness" that we are experiencing from the visent that is collapsing from a set of possibilities to this one subject of attention. Even as our consequent perception of it is the product of a long string of fallible decisions made within neural networks both within and outside the visual cortex, involving our experience living in the world, our immediate expectations, and in many cases our idiosyncratic hopes and desires, our visual experience flies over this gap of process and we simply "see it." We are, in every perceived experience of sight, implicated fully in the world—and the world fully implicated in us.

12. When employed as signs, Peirce called such actual things or events "sinsigns" (i.e., single signs).

13. The other two kinds of things that can act as signs are qualities and habits (principled regularities), which we will get to in the next chapter.

14. Signs, referents, and interpretants do not actually have precise verbal translations such as I have used here. Verbal translations are, of course, other signs, and they are always trying to pin down referents that are squirmingly impossible to completely localize. Words translating other

words is an impossibility, as any translator will submit, so words translating nonverbal entities is even more of a fool's errand. But we fools have no other device (except pictures and diagrams, which bring their own logic and hazards).

15. Notice that by separating referent and interpretant, a designer is continually asked to compare the desired reference with what a public in the end understands the reference to be. This continuous feedback is indispensable in the design process and is one of the features of Peircean semiotics that fits neatly into design practice.

16. Roland Barthes, "The Rhetoric of the Image," in *Image, Music, Text*, trans. Stephen Heath (New York: Hill and Wang, 1977), 32–51.

17. In semiotic analysis, the first principle is to state what it is that you are taking to be the subject of your investigation; if you do that at every turn, you will be defining each successive semiotic moment of the analysis, ultimately the moment that includes the entirety of the subject, and you will keep the discussion clear.

Chapter 4

1. A word about terminology. Words are used carefully in this book. Even so, as Whitehead warned, words are imperfect, especially when we are asking them to make the kind of fine, recursive distinctions we have in play here. Rarely I will introduce a term (such as "visent" or "interpretant") that may be new to the reader, and in that case the problem is one of expanding a vocabulary. More often, I want to restrict a quite common term to a specific technical usage. This is in some sense a more delicate situation, because the common usage of the word will mask or interfere with the narrow use I am intending. So when I use common words in technical, narrow ways, I will try to provide common synonyms to the technical term to clarify the intended usage, and I will sometimes make the case for why my preferred term is more suitable. We are about to encounter some of these terms in the upcoming discussion.

2. We could call this kind of experienced sign a work, a graphic (as a noun—a locution I dislike), a design, a piece, or any number of other descriptive labels, but the word "display" is especially apt. It is suitably general, not restrictive conceptually. It suggests by its own connotations (etymology: to scatter, disperse, unfold) that it is meant for an outward reach, to call to other minds. It also has an excellent pedigree, having been adopted since the 1980s by Edward Tufte.

3. This reading of a display as involving the inference of intentionality is related to the definition of "a work" in art. See Steven Skaggs and Carl R. Hausman, "Toward a New Elitism," *Journal of Aesthetic Education* 46, no. 3 (2012), 83–106.

4. Indeed, such disjunctions happen all the time. They can be a source of important problems, from personal relations to foreign affairs: cases in which one party's accidental actions are taken by another party to be an act of deliberate signaling.

5. For those wishing to follow Peirce's thinking directly, see CP 2.219–442, especially CP 2.254–265.

6. As we are interested in restricting our framework to a functioning theory for graphic design, I have translated Peirce's terminology into a specifically visual lexicon which applies to our visual concerns. The original technical terms for the nine cells are: Qualisign, Sinsign, Legisign; Icon, Index, Symbol; Rheme, Dicisign, Argument.

7. The "icons" on a computer screen are often likenesses of the physical objects that perform the same or similar purpose in the analog world.

8. An Internet search of the significance of yellow ribbons will turn up over two dozen referents in fifteen countries. It would make an interesting study to show, for any one country, the importance of divergent contextual placement of the yellow ribbon; this would be necessary in order to distinguish the otherwise overlapping message content.

9. Priscila Borges has further broken these ten into subclasses, resulting in an analysis of some sixty-six classes of sign. Borges, "Experience and Cognition in Peirce's Semiotics," *American Journal of Semiotics* 30, nos. 1–2 (2014), 1–26.

10. The numbers associated with the sign classes refer to the relational orders of each class component. So, for example, a feature is first-order in all three trichotomies (1.1.1).

11. The word "display" is used effectively by Edward Tufte. It is a far better term than "text," which Barthes uses and which is doubly burdened by a linguistically centered point of view and unfortunate confusion of the word with typography.

12. Merriam-Webster online dictionary, referenced May 28, 2014.

13. Hans-Joachim Burgert, "If One Only Knew What Calligraphy Is!," *Letter Arts Review* 12, no. 4 (2002). Also Steven Skaggs, "La semiotica della tipografia come immagine," *Progetto Grafico* 4, no. 7 (2007), 30–37.

14. The problem with these marketing practices rarely has to do with the efficacy of the test itself, but rather with the fact that the three tested designs are often based on little more than trends and custom. As a result they are unlikely to utterly fail, but neither are they likely to turn heads. Choosing among such packages is often a selection among the mundane.

15. Steven Skaggs, "Do Designers Ever Construct an Argument?," *Chinese Semiotic Studies* 4, no. 2 (2010), 301–308.

16. Martin Krampen, "Signs and Symbols in Graphic Communication," *Design Quarterly* 62 (1965), 5.

17. Wilhelm Wundt, the first modern experimental psychologist, called the store of such life experiences the "apperceptive mass," a term that may be returning to favor.

Chapter 5

1. Richard Poulin, *The Language of Graphic Design: An Illustrated Handbook for Understanding Fundamental Design Principles* (Beverly, MA: Rockport Publishers, 2011).

2. Alex W. White, *The Elements of Graphic Design* (New York: Allworth Press, 2011).

3. Floyd Merrell is an important exception. See *Peirce, Signs, and Meaning* (Toronto: University of Toronto Press, 1997) and *Signs Grow: Semiosis and Life Processes* (Toronto: University of Toronto Press, 1996).

4. There are exceptions to the desirability of "high presence," some of which will be noted in the next chapter.

5. Animals use a third strategy, which is to pose as something else, causing the viewer to mistake the kind of animal it is. But this technique does not rely on hiding, and indeed sometimes exaggerates the deceptive animal's presence.

6. John Graham Kerr, 1914 letter to Winston Churchill, quoted in Hugh Murphy and Martin Bellamy, "The Dazzling Zoologist: John Graham Kerr and the Early Development of Ship Camouflage," *Northern Mariner* 19, no. 2 (April 2009), 177.

7. Hannah M. Rowland, "Abbott Thayer to the Present Day: What Have We Learned about the Function of Countershading?," *Philosophical Transactions of the Royal Society B* 364 (2009), 519–527.

8. Expressive qualities are inherently difficult to capture with language. While some have adjectival names, these are usually poor at getting at the nuances of the feelings they excite, and most expressions remain ineffable. Part of the reason for having critiques in design classes at the university is to develop ways to recognize and speak about the expressiveness of displays.

9. This is a major point in the semiology of Jacques Derrida and other poststructuralists. See, for example, the initiation of this idea in his lecture "Structure, Sign and Play" in *Writing and Difference* (1967; London: Routledge, 1978) or the later *Of Grammatology* (1974; Baltimore: Johns Hopkins University Press, 1976). But the point as developed here comes through the Peircean tradition, which, a half century prior to Derrida, also stressed the indeterminacy of meaning. Comparing Derrida and Peirce on matters of play and fallibility is a worthwhile enterprise. Derrida seemingly goes beyond Peirce's claims when he argues that the very concepts—which one wishes to communicate through the very imprecise medium of language—cannot themselves be localized, so that any imputed precision is doubly compromised. However, Peirce makes the distinction between the immediate and dynamic objects (referents), which introduces a similar "play" in that for which the sign (linguistic or graphic) acts as a surrogate.

10. CP 1.171 (1897).

11. This idea of indeterminacy is a current running clear through the twentieth century and into our own, in all sorts of disciplines. Peirce developed his "fallibilism" between 1897 and 1903. During the 1920s, in physics, Heisenberg advanced his uncertainty principle, which noted a limit to the precision with which a particle's momentum and position can simultaneously be known; in the 1930s, in mathematics, Gödel's incompleteness theorems demonstrated limitations in all axiomatic systems; Shannon and Weaver's influential model of physical communication, first put forward in the late 1940s, includes, as a necessary component, noise, which always corrupts the "purity" of a sent message; the poststructuralism of Derrida includes *différance* and "play" in

any code system, implying that the signifier and the signified are never so tightly bonded as Saussure postulated. Indeed, in Derrida's scheme, the "transcendental signified"—a signified/signifier unit that is definite and specific—is a concept that is notable for being forever absent (even if we must behave as if it exists).

12. Now realize that it's not simply a matter of your *feeling* of complete confidence or strong belief in your understanding, but the actual (as judged by some imagined third, all-knowing party) impossibility of being in error or misinterpreting the information. The Absolute goes beyond your sensing or belief, to the actual, which is why it must always remain an ideal limit, approachable but never attainable.

13. Steven Skaggs and Gary Shank, "Codification, Inference, and Specificity in Visual Communication Design," *Zed* 4 (1997), 54–69.

14. Peirce referred to this unachievable ideal as the "Final Interpretant."

15. This is not to say that a house number will have no additional meaning other than its index as a street location, but simply that one of its bundle of interpretants—in particular its denotation as a claim to be a location along a given street—will tend to remain constant. Denotations, unlike connotations, are more easily subjected to validity tests to determine whether they are right or wrong. Consider the house number that seems to be out of sequence and therefore raises questions about whether it is being read correctly or whether it is simply the wrong house number for a particular house, or the driver's license photo being compared to the check casher's face before a bank teller cashes a check.

16. *The Notebooks of Leonardo da Vinci*, trans. Edward MacCurdy (New York: Braziller, 1955).

17. This distinction was raised in *Image, Music, Text*. Although Barthes's terminology is problematic and I have not adopted it, putting it here in quotation marks, I agree with his larger point.

18. This dichotomy was explored by McCoy's graduate students at Cranbrook in their infamous design for the journal *Visible Language* ("French Currents of the Letter," *Visible Language* 12, no. 3 [Summer 1978]), in which each successive article was rendered increasingly illegible by departures from typographic custom and orthography. While the verbal content became clouded, the visuality of the page became increasingly exciting—the reader experienced becoming viewer.

Chapter 6

1. It's important to keep two points in mind here. First, although high valency refers to the functional power or influence of a display, and that is often a virtue one strives for, a high valency is not, in every case, better than a low valency. You can only determine which is better in a given case when you have a sense of how a display or display element must work within the context of an entire project and for a particular ideal receiver. Determining those functions becomes a large part of every designer/client brief. Of course, an understanding of the possible semantic class profiles that will be introduced below provides an important framework for the research and thinking that goes into that brief.

2. The full range of sixty-four interactions is given in the appendix.

3. In the discussion here, I will generally be speaking of a visent as a display, although what I have to say can also be applied to visents that are subelements within a display.

4. This implicit assertion may be weakening with time. The ubiquity of virtual reality systems and Photoshop techniques means that today a photograph loses some of its documentary overtones.

5. The symbols were so standardized that a reference work known as an "emblem book" was available as a handy guide for artists and patrons alike.

6. Compare the color scheme to that of a Duracell battery!

7. The display level includes the denotations and connotations that are within the subject matter of the display itself, whereas the assertion level looks at statements about the world beyond. We might be tempted to say that we interpret the display to be a portrait of Queen Elizabeth only because the display *asserts itself* to be a portrait of Queen Elizabeth, but "assertion" in this sense is merely the same as having subject matter. This kind of "assertion of identity"—that what something appears to be is, in fact, what it is—does not move us away from the display but rather simply establishes the subject matter of the display. Assertions, as I use the term in the profiles, refer to claims a display makes *about the world outside of itself*.

8. The eye motif was reprised by Jimi Hendrix on his cover photograph for his 1967 *Are You Experienced* album.

Chapter 7

1. Every professor of graphic design runs into this split when a student tries to convey in words an idea she has. The student wants the professor to say whether it is going to be a good design, but the professor can never do that because so much of the success has to do with the form and connotations, which cannot be spoken.

2. H.K.M., "The Unseen World," *New Republic*, February 9, 1918, 63–64. The first sentence of this quotation is thought to be the original source for the Martin Mull version, "Writing about music is like dancing about architecture" (Garson O'Toole, quoteinvestigator.com/2010/11/08/writing-about-music/ accessed July 3, 2014).

3. It's important to note here that by recognition, I am not referring to a logo's ability to stand for its ultimate referent—the host institution. Indeed it turns out that virtually any logo can, through education of the public, come to be understood as the signifying device of any host—it is simply a matter of repeated frequent exposures. What is meant here, rather, is that if you are showing an apple it should be recognized as an apple and not a pear; if you are including the letter Q it should not be misread as a D, and so on. In other words, the recognition is recognition within the display, not a recognition of the logo in the world.

Chapter 8

1. As will be explained shortly in the text, "word" is shorthand for the more proper term—"notational script"—which covers nonlinguistic as well as linguistic symbolic code systems.

2. In the following discussion, it may be better to think of a visual element rather than a display. Displays usually are complex, composed of combinations of many visual elements, and so while the individual elements may adhere strictly to given locations on the map, the display as a whole is less easily confined to a narrow position.

3. The physical proximity of the typography to the photo, or to the signature, also acts indexically to make the identifying claim. It is the equivalent of saying: "The person represented in this photograph, and the person whose signature appears here, is the person so named by the typescript."

4. Although our alphabet descended from pictographic glyphs, it is no longer a pictographic system.

5. Actually, to the contrary, designers often desire to have the possible interpretations converge toward a highly specific denotation.

6. Of course one ought not put too fine a point on this: there are many exceptions, for example collage that includes words, or the image/word matings of an Anselm Kiefer or Barbara Kruger. But in a general way I believe the general point holds true—that graphic design almost always has many informational components, while a fine art display tends to have one.

7. For examples, see Roland Barthes, Marshall McLuhan, and many other commentators.

8. See Roland Barthes, *Image, Music, Text* (New York: Hill and Wang, 1977).

9. For a detailed semiotic account of the image, see Goran Sonneson, *Pictorial Concepts* (Lund: Lund University Press, 1989), or Group μ, *Traité du signe visuel* (Paris: Seuil, 1992).

10. The earliest reference I could find for this long-used term was a lecture given by Melville J. Herskovits, given before the University of Pittsburgh's Chapter of the Society of Sigma Xi in 1933. In 2015, it could be found here: http://www.jstor.org/stable/27824494?seq=1#page_scan_tab _contents

11. See Umberto Eco, *A Theory of Semiotics* (Bloomington: Indiana University Press, 1978), for this extension of Roman Jakobson's concept of the aesthetic sign.

Chapter 9

1. Salvatore M. Aglioti, Paola Cesari, Michela Romani, and Cosimo Urgesi, "Action Anticipation and Motor Resonance in Elite Basketball Players," *Nature Neuroscience* 11 (2008), 1109–1116.

2. Just as we take a visent to be a visual entity that is perceptible by human eyesight, we will assume that the gesture is a human being's gesture. I leave open the question of whether the gesture, and therefore writing, can be made by other beings or other things.

3. In order to better make the distinction, which is otherwise ambiguous in English, between writing as a strictly verbal enterprise and the graphical form that that this sentence alludes to, I will refer to the writing of character marks as handwriting.

4. The word comes from the Greek *kalli* (beautiful) + *graphia* (writing).

5. Historically, many linguistic notational systems were pictographic, the Mayan system and Egyptian hieroglyphs being two noteworthy examples. The Phoenician/Greek alphabet was also adapted from pictographs. Current scripts are character mark abstractions that still harbor vestigial traces of their pictographic progenitors.

6. Indeed, the great mid-twentieth century calligrapher Ray DaBoll claimed that the essence of calligraphy is "disciplined freedom."

7. H. Halliday Sparling, *The Kelmscott Press and William Morris Master Craftsman* (London: Macmillan, 1924), 14.

8. In *A Thief among the Angels* (documentary film), Kessler Brothers, 2000 (broadcast PBS, 2001).

9. Beatrice Warde, "The Crystal Goblet, or Why Printing Should Be Invisible," in Warde, *The Crystal Goblet: Sixteen Essays on Typography* (Cleveland: World Publishing, 1956), 11–17. This famous text, which sees ideal typography ("the transparent page") as holding the author's precious thoughts the way a clear wine glass holds fine wine, was first given as a speech entitled "Printing Should Be Invisible" delivered to the British Typographers Guild, St. Bride Institute, London, October 7, 1930. It has been reprinted many times in the intervening years.

Chapter 10

1. Hans-Joachim Burgert, "If One Only Knew What Calligraphy Is!," *Letter Arts Review* 12, no. 4 (2002).

2. This problem, from a digital programming perspective, is taken up in Douglas Hofstadter's *Metamagical Themas* (New York: Basic Books, 1985). Similar problems persist in other artificial intelligence attempts to replicate human recognition.

3. Steven Skaggs, "La semiotica della tipografia come immagine," *Progetto Grafico* 4, no. 7 (2007), 32.

4. What is truly surprising is that, as shown in figure 10.2, even fonts that are wildly dissimilar also suggest the same template in their composite.

5. Peter Bil'ak of type foundry Typotheque put the number of commercially downloadable fonts at 150,000 in 2012 (https://www.typotheque.com/articles/we_dont_need_new_fonts, retrieved March 2015).

6. John McNulty, "The Sizzle," *New Yorker*, April 16, 1938.

7. Beatrice Warde, "The Crystal Goblet, or Why Printing Should Be Invisible," in Warde, *The Crystal Goblet: Sixteen Essays on Typography* (Cleveland: World Publishing, 1956), 11–17.

8. How often is one called upon to set completely generic text? Usually the problem becomes how to impart some subtle and subconscious expression without that expression overbrimming into the focus of conscious attention. Fortunately, there is a large space for compromise here in which small tweaks to the body copy can provide the suitable subtle notes of expression without overwhelming the verbal content of the message.

9. Visiting the George Salter collection at Chicago's Newberry Library, I saw correspondence in which a university was approaching Salter to teach calligraphy. He replied that he would do so only if he were given seven years to develop the student's abilities, because that is how long is needed to develop the requisite mind and body skills.

10. I have, however, seen examples by the calligrapher John Stevens that look so much like his mentor Hermann Zapf that it took close inspection, and ultimately paying attention to other compositional decisions, to tell the difference. If a calligrapher can master another calligrapher's hand to that level, then I think it may be possible for him to duplicate a typeface. Almost.

11. In this pseudoscientific practice, "graphologists" find a one-to-one fixed correspondence between specified graphic features in a sample of handwriting and imputed personality traits that these features indicate. The kind of linkage between handwriting and character I am referring to in this section is much more subtle and global in its effect. It has to do with the individualistic expression that any highly skilled and practiced movement suggests. See Mihaly Csikszentmihalyi, *Flow: The Psychology of Optimal Experience* (New York: Harper and Row, 1990).

12. To be precise, magazine title mastheads usually need to be type I (Emblematic-Declarative), type II (Emblematic-Informative), type V (Clear-Declarative), or type VI (Clear-Informative). Occasionally they can belong to the Stylistic group (if devoted to fashion, for example), but such a magazine would need a great deal of marketing support behind it to become established. Few magazine mastheads are members of the Vague group.

13. We are looking at three of the four semantic profiles here. Generic logotypes would be those semantic types that are low in both expression and connotation; Distinctive logotypes would tend to be higher in expression and connotations; Loud logotypes would be high in presence; Delicate logotypes would be low in presence. Given that all the logotypes must be very legible, denotation is held constant (high) in the exercise.

Chapter 11

1. This conceptual abridgment is acceptable as long as you keep in mind that it works simply because the analysis is of something already existing in the world. Feature is restored as a fully independent factor when you wonder what color to choose for a hazard message, and the color red comes to mind because it is able to signify danger: in all *imagined* creative acts, you are considering features independently, restoring the first cell of the first trichotomy.

2. Notice how, in the fact that elements have formal qualities, the first sign class of Peirce's trichotomy, features, is restored—now embodied in the graphic element.

3. Note that genre goes beyond style. It is not so much a style viewed independently as a form, but a set of forms associated with a cultural subject (or use for which the style tends to be employed), that results in the emergence of a genre.

4. This approach is almost definitional of work called postmodern.

5. Chandler Laughlin, as reported by Karen Woodmansee, *Virginia City News*, May 19, 2012.

6. Psychedelia would remain a powerful graphic force until it was supplanted in the 1970s by what Patrick Cramsie (*The Story of Graphic Design*) calls the "Homespun" genre of the blue-collar worker, the country, simple rural life, in which—to choose just one example—the increasing use of typefaces like Goudy Old harked back to the early twentieth century. This represented a truce in the culture wars of the 1960s by finding heroism in the smith, the craftsperson, the personal integrity of an earlier time that perhaps was unassailable by either side.

7. Exceptions apply, especially if the company was started in the early twentieth century by a single individual after which it is named, as in the case of Ford, in which case they often use some variation of the founder's signature.

8. Of course these two goals are not mutually exclusive, and in a corporate identity campaign the designer is always striving for the second use of style being discussed in this paragraph, while also attempting to achieve one of the two objectives relating to the market's sector.

Epilogue

1. Steven Skaggs, "Good Theory Is Useful Theory," *AIGA Journal* 15, no. 2 (1997), 7.

Glossary

Absolute specified   An idealized (unattainable) point at which the matching of referent and interpretant is completely and infallibly certain. The point of no possibility of error in interpretation.

Affective register   One of the two semantic registers; the affective register relates to the emotional, *pre*conceptual feelings that are engendered upon seeing a display. (*See also* Conceptual register; Expression; Presence.)

Alphabet   A notational script whose code connects a graphic symbol to a phonemic speech sound.

Ambiguous   Low in both denotation and connotation (of an assertion).

Analytical   A characteristic of the semiotic moment, acknowledging that it is a mechanism for rendering judgments.

Antagonist pair   In the functional matrix, a given attribute and the attribute that is not contiguous to it.

Apathetic   Having a low degree of expression (of a display).

Appeal   An assertion made through symbolic means, such as through words.

Assertion   A claim or proposition about the world.

Baseline spectrum   On the visual gamut, the continuum opposite an apex.

Brand   A line of products offered by a maker, requiring careful systemization of the visual system of relations.

Calligraphy   "Beautiful handwriting," the writing of character marks that are unselfconsciously coherent in form and expression.

Character marks   Simple gestural marks with discrete structures having individual identities, including, but not limited to, letters of the alphabet.

Clear   High in denotation and low in connotation (of a display).

Clone   To produce an exact replica by digital or mechanical means.

Code   A prescribed (scripted) set of symbolic, unmotivated relations between a set of visents and referents.

Complex visent   A gestalt of two or more discrete visents that, as a whole, appear as a larger visent.

Compound visent   A visent that has one continuous surface but appears to create more than one visent. An example is a donut in which the hole appears as a second visent.

Conceptual metaclasses   In the conceptual register, the four combinations of denotation and connotation valencies which become a determining factor in semantic profiles.

Conceptual register   One of the two semantic registers; the conceptual register has to do with the conceptual understandings that are engendered on seeing a display. (*See also* Affective register; Connotation; Denotation.)

Conclusion   A judgment made by a receiver upon considering an assertion.

Concrete   In the functional matrix, a semantically hard attribute, concerning a visent's denotative and explicit function.

Connotation   In the semantic conceptual register, the associative and allusive referents.

Content   A less precise term than "semantics," referring in a general way to the interpretant, the overall meaning of a message.

Contexts of the moment   The set of possibles that are available to perform the role of sign, referent, or interpretant within a semiotic moment.

Convergence   An influent tendency in denotation toward a settled belief, confidence, or satisfaction in an interpretation, which yields a sense of knowing, cutting off further inquiry. (*See also* Divergence.)

Declarative   An assertion that is high in both denotation and connotation.

Demonstration   An assertion by trying out or modeling.

Denotation   In the semantic conceptual register, the direct—often coded—convergent referent.

Denotative spectrum   On the visual gamut, the baseline spectrum opposite the mark apex. The denotative spectrum runs from image to word (notational scripts) and is characterized by highly specific visents.

Diagram   A visual portrayal of process or of systematic relationships.

Display   Any visent interpreted to be a communication unit, a signal. Examples: a page, a work, a piece, a poster, etc.

Divergence   An effluent tendency in connotation which seemingly generates additional possible associations. (*See also* Convergence.)

Edge   A discontinuity of surface, important in the perception of visents.

Element   (1) A visent that is a part of a display. (2) A submember of a compound or complex visent.

Emblem   A display that is high in both denotation and connotation.

Evidence   Assertion by means of implications due to physical contact or environmental contiguity.

Expression   In the affective semantic register, the particular quality of feeling or emotion due to the syntax of the display.

Flow   The current that develops through the transactions of semiotic moments.

Form   (1) The physical shape or geometrical attributes of a visent syntax. (2) In the functional matrix, a syntactically hard attribute, concerning a visent's expression.

Format   A scheme for controlling compositional consistency and the order of visents in a display or across display systems.

Fraternal clusters   In the functional matrix, the two related attributes contiguous to a given attribute.

Functional matrix   A conceptual tool that aligns syntactical and semantic features by hard and soft attributes.

Fuzzy template   A form habituated so that it tends to be replicated without a defined script prescribing its principles.

Genre   A style linked to subject matter within a culture.

Genre migration   The lifting of entire genre-related styles from one time or place to another.

Genre mixing   The appropriation of elements from one genre and application of them to a second genre. (*See also* Ironic wink.)

Gestalt   A visual figure composed of sub-visents that is seen as a unitary whole visent.

Graphic design   The planning of visents to act as displays.

Graphic spectrum   On the visual gamut, the baseline spectrum opposite the image apex. The graphic spectrum runs from marks to notational scripts (words) and is characterized by nonpictorial visents.

Ground   The localized context of the semiotic moment. The way or particular light in which a sign relation is considered. (*See also* Synthetic.)

Hard attributes   With regard to the functional matrix: immediacy, directness, practical effects. (*See also* Soft attributes.)

Harmony   The visual consolidation of plural visents into a unitary whole.

Human factors   The receiver's influence on the reception and interpretation of a message. The context of the interpretant.

Iconic   Of a relationship between a sign and its referent that is based on resemblance.

Ideogram   A graphic device used symbolically to represent an idea.

Image   (1) A visent that is a visual likeness of another visent, the latter being its subject. (2) The iconic apex of the visual gamut characterized by pictorial realism.

Indexic   Of a relationship between a sign and its referent that is based on proximal or physical contact.

Information   A change in a state of understanding.

Informative   Of a display that is high in denotation and low in connotation.

Interpretant   The effect a sign has on a receiver; an understanding.

Ironic wink   A rhetorical device, such as hyperbole, used to inform the viewer that the methods being used in genre mixing are not naive.

Lettering   The drawing, as opposed to gestural writing, of scripts.

Logo   A visual device that functions as, or in place of, a proper name.

Logotype   A unique graphically formed word used symbolically and emblematically, often as a logo.

Look (noun)   The syntactical characteristics of a visent, especially concerning its replicability as style.

Mark   The indexic apex of the visual gamut characterized by an inherent, causal or necessary relationship between the visent and the physical environment.

Meaning   *See* Semantics.

Message   A general term referring to the intended contents of a signal.

Motif   The repetition of a visual element within a display.

Motivation   A nonarbitrary (and therefore nonsymbolic) relation between a sign and a referent.

Nesting   A recursive transaction in which a set or series of semiotic moments becomes an element in another semiotic moment.

Notational script   The symbolic apex of the visual gamut characterized by arbitrary coded relations between a symbolic visent and its referent. The most common notational script is the visual word.

Persuasion   The changing of an attitude or disposition.

Photography   The making of visents through a process of mechanically transcribing light energy onto a material.

Pictogram (pictograph) A graphic device used iconically to represent something it visually resembles.

Picture A visual likeness retaining gradations in tonality and value.

Piece (noun) *See* Display.

Plural analysis Analysis that emphasizes a group of visents, especially the structural relationships between them.

Pragmatics The characteristics of an audience of receivers and the effect a message is likely to have on them. (*See also* Human factors.)

Praxis In the functional matrix, a syntactically hard attribute, involving the visent's functional relation to its environment.

Presence In the affective semantic register, the impact a display has as a visent in the environment. The ability to attract the eye before the concept is absorbed.

Projective Of a display that stands out starkly against a background so that it is easily noticed.

Quality The first cell of Peirce's first trichotomy—a (visual) attribute, considered independently of its embodiment in anything.

Quasi-verbal The fourth state of writing, in which a visent is understood to be verbal, but is unreadable by the viewer.

Recessive Of a display that blends into a background so that it is easily overlooked.

Recursion A process repeated in a similar way at a different scale.

Referent That for which the sign stands.

Script (1) A prescribed, coded system of symbolic relations. (2) Historical styles of handwriting.

Semantic profile The categorization of kinds of semantic behavior according to the display's blend of affective- and conceptual-register valencies.

Semantics Pertaining to the relationship between a sign and its referent. More generally, meaning.

Semiology The study of signs from a structuralist or poststructuralist (Saussurean) perspective.

Semiosis Signification through the continuous flow of sign action.

Semiotic moment The three-part relation between a sign, its referent, and an interpretant.

Semiotics The study of signs and signification, especially from a Peircean perspective. (*See also* Semiology.)

Sign Something that stands for something else to someone's understanding.

Signal A sign interpreted by the receiver as a communication attempt.

Signification   A sign's relationship to referent and interpretant.

Simple visent   A visent that is irreducible to sub-visents.

Soft attributes   With regard to the functional matrix, indirect, associative, compositional effects. (*See also* Hard attributes.)

Soulful   Of a display that has a high level of expression.

Specificity   The degree of precision or proximity of the referent to the interpretant.

Specificity shell   The specficity surface extended to include connotations as well as denotation.

Specificity surface   The range of possible specificity for an interpretant's relation to a referent.

States of writing   Five divisions of the graphic spectrum—marks, character marks, alphabet, quasi-verbal, and fully verbal—which delineate distinct semiotic functions of visual writing.

Stimulus   Anything that excites the visual apparatus.

Style   A family resemblance of motifs across multiple displays.

Stylistic   Of a display that is low in denotation and high in connotation.

Stylize, stylization   The manipulative smoothing of a photographic image or gestural mark.

Suggestive   Of an assertion that is low in denotation and high in connotation.

Symbolic   Of a relationship between a sign and its referent that is unmotivated and based on consensual agreement.

Syntax, syntactics   The materiality of the sign; the form and composition of visents.

Synthetic   A characteristic of a semiotic moment that recognizes it as a cut into the continuum of experience for the purpose of analysis. Any particular semiotic moment is said to be synthetic because the cut is a decision that could have been made otherwise.

System   Multiple displays maintaining a principled, habitual, or rule-based coherence.

Threshold of resolution   In praxis, the limit of distance or reduction possible while still retaining all the features of a graphic device.

Threshold of semiosis   The place where the match between a referent and an interpretant is so vague that an infinite number of referents is possible. Here, triadicity fails and gives way to dyadic, presemiotic relations.

Tone   In the functional matrix, a semantically soft attribute, involving a visent's attitudinal and associative functions.

Transparency (typography)   Completely denotative words in which the reader takes no conscious notice of form.

Typography   Graphic elements of a writing system in which characters (glyphs) are clones and deployed by mechanical means.

Unitary analysis   An analysis that emphasizes the whole and its features.

Vague   Of a display that is low in both denotation and connotation.

Valency   The relative power, forcefulness, or emphasis of a factor in semantic analysis.

Viewing situation   The nexus of light, eye (organs of sight), and visent.

Visent   Visual entity. Something perceptible by eyesight, having an individual, independent character.

Visual gamut   The map of all the possible kinds visual entities. It is defined by the triangular region between the three apexes: image, mark, and word (notational scripts).

Visualistic spectrum   On the visual gamut, the baseline spectrum opposite the word (notational script) apex. The visualistic spectrum runs from marks to image and is characterized by visents that do not function through codes.

Word   A meaningful speech unit of a verbal language. (*See also* Notational script.)

Work (noun)   Any artifact, visual or otherwise, taken as a nonaccidental whole object intended for attention.

Writing   Gestural character marks.

Bibliography

Aglioti, Salvatore M., Paola Cesari, Michela Romani, and Cosimo Urgesi. "Action Anticipation and Motor Resonance in Elite Basketball Players." *Nature Neuroscience* 11 (2008): 1109–1116.

Arnheim, Rudolf. *Art and Visual Perception*. Berkeley: University of California Press, 1974.

Arnheim, Rudolf. *Visual Thinking*. Berkeley: University of California Press, 1974.

Barthes, Roland. *Image, Music, Text*. Trans. Stephen Heath. New York: Hill and Wang, 1977.

Barthes, Roland. *Mythologies*. Trans. Annette Lavers. New York: Hill and Wang, 1987.

Berger, John. *Ways of Seeing*. London: Penguin Books, 1977.

Biederman, Irving. "Recognizing Depth-Rotated Objects: A Review of Recent Research and Theory." *Spatial Vision* 13 (2000): 241–253.

Blonsky, M., ed. *On Signs*. Baltimore: Johns Hopkins University Press, 1985.

Borges, Priscila. "Experience and Cognition in Peirce's Semiotics." *American Journal of Semiotics* 30 (1–2) (2014): 1–26.

Buchanan, Richard. "Wicked Problems in Design Thinking." *Design Issues* 8 (2) (1992): 5–21.

Buchanan, Richard, and Victor Margolin. *Discovering Design: Explorations in Design Studies*. Chicago: University of Chicago Press, 1995.

Burgert, Hans-Joachim. "If One Only Knew What Calligraphy Is!" *Letter Arts Review* 12 (4) (2002).

Coates, Paul. *The Metaphysics of Perception*. New York: Routledge, 2007.

Cramsie, Patrick. *The Story of Graphic Design: From the Invention of Writing to the Birth of Digital Design*. New York: Abrams, 2010.

Crow, David. *Visible Signs*. Lausanne: AVA Publishing, 2003.

Csikszentmihalyi, Mihaly. *Flow: The Psychology of Optimal Experience*. New York: Harper and Row, 1990.

Davis, Meredith. *Graphic Design Theory*. London: Thames and Hudson, 2012.

Derrida, Jacques. *Of Grammatology*. Trans. Gayatri Chakravorty Spivak. Baltimore: Johns Hopkins University Press, 1976.

Derrida, Jacques. *Writing and Difference*. London: Routledge, 1978. (1967).

Drucker, Johanna. "Artists' Books and the Cultural Status of the Book." *Journal of Communication* 44 (1994): 12–42.

Eco, Umberto. *A Theory of Semiotics*. Bloomington: Indiana University Press, 1978.

Ehses, Hanno. *Design Papers 1: Semiotic Foundation of Typography*. Halifax: Nova Scotia College of Art and Design, 1976.

Ehses, Hanno. *Design Papers 4: Design and Rhetoric—An Analysis of Theatre Posters*. Halifax: Nova Scotia College of Art and Design, 1986.

Ehses, Hanno. *Design Papers 6: Design on a Rhetorical Footing*. Halifax: Nova Scotia College of Art and Design, 2008.

Ehses, Hanno, and Ellen Lupton. *Design Papers 5: Rhetorical Handbook*. Halifax: Nova Scotia College of Art and Design, 1988.

Feldman, Jacob. "What Is a Visual Object?" *Trends in Cognitive Sciences* 7 (6) (June 2003): 252–256.

Floridi, Luciano. *The Philosophy of Information*. Oxford: Oxford University Press, 2011.<bok[REMOVED IF= FIELD]></bok>

Fodor, J., and Z. Pylyshyn. "How Direct Is Visual Perception? Some Reflections on Gibson's 'Ecological Approach'." *Cognition* 9 (1981): 139–196.

Frascara, Jorge. *Communication Design: Principles, Methods and Practice*. New York: Allworth, 2004.<bok[REMOVED IF= FIELD]></bok>

Gibson, James J. *The Ecological Approach to Visual Perception*. Hillsdale, NJ: Lawrence Erlbaum, 1986.

Gombrich, E. H. *The Image and the Eye*. Ithaca, NY: Cornell University Press, 1982.

Gombrich, E. H. *Julian Hochberg, and M. Black. Art, Perception and Reality*. Baltimore: Johns Hopkins University Press, 1972.

Goodale, Melvyn A., and A. David Milner. "Separate Visual Pathways for Perception and Action." *Trends in Neurosciences* 15 (1) (1992): 20–25.

Goodman, Nelson. *Languages of Art: An Approach to the Theory of Symbols*. Indianapolis: Hackett Publishing, 1976.

Gosling, David L. *Science and the Indian Tradition: When Einstein Met Tagore*. New York: Routledge, 2007.

Gregory, Richard L. *Eye and Brain: The Psychology of Seeing*. 4th ed. Princeton, NJ: Princeton University Press, 1990.

Gregory, Richard L. *The Intelligent Eye*. New York: McGraw-Hill, 1970.

Group μ (Francis Edeline, Jean-Marie Klinkenberg, Philippe Minguet). *Traité du signe visuel: pour une rhétorique de l'image*. Paris: Seuil, 1992.

H.K.M. "The Unseen World." *New Republic*, February 9, 1918, 63–64.

Heller, Steven. "W. A. Dwiggins: Master of the Book." *Step-by-Step Graphics,* January-February 1991, 108–113.

Hofstadter, Douglas. *Metamagical Themas*. New York: Basic Books, 1985.

Jury, David. *Graphic Design before Graphic Designers*. London: Thames and Hudson, 2012.

Katz, Joel. *Designing Information: Human Factors and Common Sense in Information Design*. New York: Wiley, 2012.<bok[REMOVED IF= FIELD]></bok>

Kepes, Gyorgy, ed. *Education of Vision*. New York: George Braziller, 1965.

Kepes, Gyorgy. *Module, Proportion, Symmetry, Rhythm*. New York: George Braziller, 1966.

Kepes, Gyorgy, ed. *Sign Image Symbol*. New York: George Braziller, 1980.

Krampen, Martin. *Meaning in the Urban Environment*. London: Routledge, 2007. (1979).

Krampen, Martin. "Signs and Symbols in Graphic Communication." *Design Quarterly* 62 (1965): 5.

LeFloch, Albert, and Guy Ropars, et al. "The Sixteenth Century Alderney Crystal: A Calcite as an Efficient Reference Optical Compass?" *Proceedings of the Royal Society of London* 6 (March) (2013). doi:10.1098/rspa.2012.0651.

da Vinci, Leonardo. *The Notebooks of Leonardo da Vinci*. Trans. E. MacCurdy. New York: Braziller, 1955.

Lucretius (Titus Lucretius Carus). *De rerum natura*. Trans. William Ellery Leonard. Gutenberg Project eBook #785. 2008.

Lupton, Ellen, and J. Abbott Miller. 1994. "Deconstruction and Graphic Design: History Meets Theory." *Visible Language* 28 (4) (1994): 346–366; also, an earlier version, Lupton: www.typotheque.com/articles/deconstruction_and_graphic_design_history_meets_theory (accessed June 7, 2016).

Margolin, Victor. *Design Discourse: History, Theory, Criticism*. Chicago: University of Chicago Press, 1989.

Margolin, V. "The Visual Rhetoric of Propaganda." *Information Design Journal* 1 (1979): 107–122.

Merrell, Floyd. *Peirce, Signs and Meaning*. Toronto: University of Toronto Press, 1997.

Merrell, Floyd. *Signs Grow: Semiosis and Life Processes*. Toronto: University of Toronto Press, 1996.

Michel, Christoph M., Margitta Seeck, and Micah M. Murray. "The Speed of Visual Cognition." *Supplements to Clinical Neurophysiology* 57 (2004): 617–627.

Morris, Charles W. *Signs, Language and Behavior*. New York: Braziller, 1946.

Murphy, Hugh, and Martin Bellamy. "The Dazzling Zoologist: John Graham Kerr and the Early Development of Ship Camouflage." *Northern Mariner* 19 (2) (April 2009).

Nadin, Mihai, and Richard D. Zakia. *Creating Effective Advertising Using Semiotics*. New York: Consultant Press, 1994.

O'Regan, J. K. "Solving the 'Real' Mysteries of Visual Perception: The World as an Outside Memory." *Canadian Journal of Psychology* 46 (3) (1992): 461–488.

Peirce, Charles Sanders. *Collected Papers*. Vols. 1–6, ed. Charles Hartshorne and Paul Weiss; vols. 7–8, ed. A. W. Burkes. Cambridge: Belknap Press of Harvard University Press, 1958–1966.

Peirce, Charles Sanders. *The Essential Peirce: Selected Philosophical Writings*. Vol 2. Ed. Peirce Edition Project. Bloomington: Indiana University Press. 1998.

Peissig, Jessie J., and Michael J. Tarr. "Visual Object Recognition: Do We Know More Now Than We Did 20 Years Ago?" *Annual Review of Psychology* 58 (2007): 75–96.

Poggenpohl, Sharon H., and Dietmar R. Winkler. "Diagrams as Tools for Worldmaking." *Visible Language* 26 (3/4) (1992): 252–269.

Poulin, Richard. *The Language of Graphic Design : An Illustrated Handbook for Understanding Fundamental Design Principles*. Beverly, MA: Rockport Publishers, 2011.

Rowland, Hannah M. "Abbott Thayer to the Present Day: What Have We Learned about the Function of Countershading?" *Philosophical Transactions of the Royal Society of London. Series B, Biological Sciences* 364 (2009): 519–527.

Saint-Martin, Fernande. *Semiotics of Visual Language*. Bloomington: Indiana University Press, 1990.

Satter, Raphael (Associated Press). *Louisville Courier-Journal*, reported March 10, 2013.

Schwartz, Frederic J. *The Werkbund*. New Haven: Yale University Press, 1996.

Skaggs, Steven. "Do Designers Ever Construct an Argument?" *Chinese Semiotic Studies* 4 (2) (2010): 301–308.

Skaggs, Steven. "Good Theory Is Useful Theory." *AIGA Journal* 15 (2) (1997): 7.

Skaggs, Steven. *Logos: The Development of Visual Symbols*. Menlo Park: Crisp (Thompson), 1994.

Skaggs, Steven. "La semiotica della tipografia come immagine." *Progetto Grafico* 4 (7) (2007): 30–37.

Skaggs, Steven. "A Transactional Model of Peircean Semiotic." *Cognitio* 7 (1) (2006): 133–149.

Skaggs, Steven, and Carl R. Hausman. "Toward a New Elitism." *Journal of Aesthetic Education* 46 (3) (2012): 83–106.

Skaggs, Steven, and Gary Shank. "Codification, Inference, and Specificity in Visual Communication Design." *Zed* 4 (1997): 54–69.

Sonnesson, Goran. *Pictorial Concepts*. Lund: Lund University Press, 1989.

Sparling, H. Halliday. *The Kelmscott Press and William Morris Master Craftsman*. London: Macmillan, 1924.

Tovée, Martin J. "Neuronal Processing: How Fast Is the Speed of Thought?" *Current Biology* 12 (4) (1994): 1125–1127.

Tufte, Edward R. *Envisioning Information*. Cheshire, CT: Graphics Press, 1990.

Tufte, Edward R. *The Visual Display of Quantitative Information*. Cheshire, CT: Graphics Press, 1983.

Warde, Beatrice. "The Crystal Goblet, or Why Printing Should Be Invisible." In Warde, *The Crystal Goblet: Sixteen Essays on Typography*. Cleveland: World Publishing, 1956.

White, Alex W. *The Elements of Graphic Design*. New York: Allworth Press, 2011.

Index